Final Séance

Final Séance

The Strange Friendship Between

Houdini

and

Conan Doyle

Massimo Polidoro

Prometheus Books

59 John Glenn Drive
Amherst, New York 14228-2197

Published 2001 by Prometheus Books

Inquiries should be addressed to
Prometheus Books
59 John Glenn Drive
Amherst, New York 14228–2197
VOICE: 716–691–0133, ext. 207
FAX: 716–564–2711
WWW.PROMETHEUSBOOKS.COM

05 04 03 02 01   5 4 3 2 1

Library of Congress Cataloging-in-Publication Data

Polidoro, Massimo.
    Final séance : the strange friendship between Houdini and Conan Doyle / Massimo Polidoro.
        p. cm.
    Includes biobliographical references and index.
    ISBN 1–57392–896–8 (cloth : alk. paper)
    1. Houdini, Harry, 1874–1926—Friends and associates. 2. Magicians—United States—Biography. 3. Doyle, Arthur Conan, Sir, 1859–1930—Friends and associates. 4. Doyle, Arthur Conan, Sir, 1859–1930—Knowledge—Occultism. 5. Authors, Scottish—20th century—Biography. 6. Occultists—Great Britain—Biography. 7. Spiritualism. I. Title.

GV1545.H8 P65 2001
793.8″092—dc21
[B]   00–051830

Printed in Canada on acid-free paper

This book is dedicated to my mother, Enrica,
and to the memory of my father, Rolando

CONTENTS

7. A MAGICIAN AMONG THE SPIRITS 163

8. THE FINAL YEARS 207

ACKNOWLEDGMENTS

I WOULD NOT HAVE WRITTEN this book had I not seen, when I was five years old, the Houdini movie with Tony Curtis and Janet Leigh. What I saw fascinated me and I was even more enthralled when soon after that I found out that Houdini had really lived and was an even more fascinating person than the character portrayed so well by Curtis. Later in my youth I discovered the Sherlock Holmes stories and was completely captured by their ingeniousness. Another surprise, however, was waiting for me when I learned that Harry Houdini and Arthur Conan Doyle, the author of the Sherlock Holmes stories, had been friends!

I wanted to know all about these two amazing personalities who had made my youth richer and who had fueled so much my imagination. For years I collected books, newspaper clippings, letters, and anything that pertained to these two great men, until I had so much material that I could write a book on them: the one you are holding now.

I have been extremely lucky, however, in having had so many friends around the world helping me in my research. First of all, I wish to thank James Randi, whom I consider as a second father. I have had the great fortune of studying and working daily with him for over a year. I followed closely his investigations, and if now I understand a little about proper scientific testing of psychic claims I owe it first of all to him. I will always be grateful to him for having been so generous and helpful, and for having shared with me his sensible and rational approach to life: an approach that, I hope, I have been able to make mine. Thank you, Randi, a million times.

Thanks to Arthur E. Moses, Tom Boldt, and Leslie Price, who have kindly read the manuscript in various stages of its preparation and have passed along useful comments, corrections, and notes: any mistake that might have slipped by is my fault only.

Thanks to Linda Safarli for her painstaking help in locating long-lost articles and newspaper clippings: her help, kindness, and hospitality are greatly appreciated.

Thanks to Luigi Garlaschelli who, as always, has been a precious friend and a helpful supporter of this project.

Thanks to José Alvarez who, apart from being a splendid friend, has once again proved to be someone on whom one can always count.

For having helped me through the years with information, ideas, notes, details, and comments I would like to thank: Jerry Andrus; Piero Angela; Joseph Anuff; Eugene Burger; Christopher Clark; Michael H. Coleman; Patrick Culliton; Sergio Della Sala; Chip Denman; Jeanine De Noma; Sergio De Santis; Hilary Evans; Marino Franzosi; Kendrick Frazier; Francesca Guizzo; Michael Hutchinson; Ray Hyman; Lewis Jones; Barry Karr; Paul Kurtz; Kimberly Louagie, curator of the Houdini Historical Center; Tully McCarroll; Martin Mahner; Riccardo Mancini; Kit Moser; Chiara Montali; Lorenzo Montali; Marco Morocutti; Joe Nickell; Franco Ramaccini; Silvio Ravaldini; Tullio Regge; Gian Marco Rinaldi; Laura Rossetti; Ian Rowland; Ranjit Sandhu; Tiziano and Cristina Sclavi; Silvan; Ray Spagenburg; the late Gordon Stein; Jamy Ian Swiss; Marcello Truzzi; James Underdown; and Richard Wiseman.

A big thank-you to all those people who have conducted previous research in both Houdini's and Doyle's histories and who have made my life easier in the preparation of this book, in particular: Milbourne Christopher (*Houdini: The Untold Story*, and his other works), Bernard M. L. Ernst and Hereward Carrington (*Houdini and Conan Doyle*), James Randi and B. R. Sugar (*Houdini: His Life and Art*), Kenneth Silverman (*Houdini!!!*, undoubtedly the greatest Houdini biography), Daniel Stashower (*Teller of Tales*), and Thomas R. Tietze (*Margery*).

Thanks to P.P.G. for . . . the little socks!

Thanks to Elena for the joy, the enthusiasm, and the inspiration that she gives me every day: I hope I can make her as happy as I am.

Thanks to my mother, Enrica, and to my sister, Elisa, for the strong encouragement and support that they always give me.

Thanks to my father, Rolando, for having been a powerful role model in my upbringing and, above all, a caring and loving father: I miss you, Dad.

And, finally, the biggest thank-you goes to Harry Houdini and Sir Arthur Conan Doyle, without whom . . .

HOUDINI AND CONAN DOYLE

1

Two Amazing Personalities

THE INTREPID AMERICAN

Ladies and gentlemen, in introducing my original invention the Water Torture cell. . . . Although there is nothing supernatural about it, I am willing to forfeit the sum of $1,000 to anyone who can know that it is possible to obtain air inside of the Torture Cell when I am locked up in it in the regulation manner after it has been filled with water. I will first thoroughly explain the apparatus, and then I will invite a committee to step upon the stage to examine everything to see that things are just as I represent. The cover is made to fit into the steel frame which prevents it from being opened even if it were not locked. The steel grill acts for the doublefold purpose of condensing the space inside the Torture Cell which at the same time prevents my turning around even were I capable of throwing both of my feet through the cover. In front, a plate of glass for self-protection. Should anything go wrong when I am locked up, as it's absolutely impossible to obtain air, one of my assistants watches through the curtains, ready in case of emergency, with an axe, to rush in, demolishing the glass, allowing the water to flow out, in order to save my life. I honestly and positively do not expect any accident to happen, but we all know accidents will happen and when least expected. The bands of steel form an impromptu cage held together with padlocks that enclose the same. I would like to invite eight, ten, or twelve gentlemen to kindly step up on the stage. I assure you I have no confederates, and any gentleman is perfectly welcome. A staircase at your service on this side of the stage, and now is your opportunity. I thank you for your attention.[1]

AS HIS ASSISTANTS POUR 100 gallons of warm water into what looks like an infernal telephone booth, the man who is going to be sealed in it leaves the stage and returns wearing a black one-piece bathing suit. He then lies on the floor and the stocks are fitted around his ankles. Finally, the apparatus is raised into the air and the man imprisoned in it is slowly lowered headfirst into the water-filled cell. He is padlocked in, and every-

Houdini and the Water Torture Cell stunt ca. 1913. (McManus-Young Collection, Library of Congress, Rare Books and Special Collections Division, LC-USZ62-112434)

body is able to see him through the glass until a curtain is dropped over the entire cell. The orchestra starts playing "Asleep in the Deep" and the assistants take their places on the sides of the cell, fire axes in hand. One minute, two minutes: the tension grows tangibly. Has something gone wrong? The assistants become more and more impatient and start to raise their axes but, right at that moment, the curtains part and the man, wet and exhausted but smiling, emerges to the erupting roar of the audience. Behind him, the cell is still filled with water and its padlocks are still intact!

The name of this intrepid man was Harry Houdini and when he introduced the Chinese Water Torture Cell act into his show in 1912, he had already become famous as the greatest escape artist the world had ever seen.

Born Erik Weisz (later Americanized to Ehrich Weiss) on March 24, 1874, in Budapest, Hungary, he immigrated to the United States with his family when he was four years old. His father, Rabbi Mayer Samuel Weiss, had departed Europe in 1876 to look for a job in America. When two years later he finally announced he had located a rabbinical post in the Midwest, his wife, Cecilia, and his children reached him after a fifteen-day voyage on board the steamer *Frisia*.

Still a child, Ehrich became fascinated by the apparent miracles performed by the occasional wandering magician and started studying, first with a friend and then with his brother Theo—whom he called "Dash," an Americanization of his Hungarian middle name, Deszo—the rudiments of magic. He was mesmerized by the adventures described in the book *Memoirs of Robert-Houdin, Ambassador, Author, and Conjuror*, the autobiography of the great French conjurer Jean Eugène Robert-Houdin (1805–1871), considered to be the founder of modern magic. It was only natural that, when he was about sixteen years of age, Ehrich decided to change his name to "Houdini," to resemble that of his hero. The "i" ending was used because Ehrich thought that it meant "like" in French, and also because there was a long tradition among magicians of using an "i" at the end of

Bess and Harry Houdini in 1899. (McManus-Young Collection, Library of Congress, Rare Books and Special Collections Division, LC-USZ6-2100)

their names to invoke the name of a famous Italian conjurer, Cavalier Pinetti (1750–1800?). He also changed his name Ehrich to the more American "Harry." Thus, Harry Houdini was born.

For years he struggled as a magician in beer halls and dime museums, along with his wife, Beatrice Rahner, or "Bess" as he called her, a vaudeville singer whom he had turned into his partner-assistant. Life was quite grim during those early years, but Harry never gave up hope of becoming a great magician.

His act, meanwhile, took a new turn compared to the traditional magicians' acts of the time. He did perform card tricks (he even had posters printed in which he billed himself as "The King of Cards") and other conventional magical stunts, but he became more and more proficient in the art of self-liberation from bonds of any kind: ropes, chains, and handcuffs.

He had discovered that if he allowed himself to be chained and locked up, and then appeared to struggle to get free, the audience paid much more attention to him than when he made his escapes seem too easy. He soon started inviting the local police to lock him up, using their cuffs and restraints, and this greatly increased the drama of the act.

However, he would have soon become old hat had he not hit upon his first great publicity stunt. In 1899 he challenged the Chicago police to lock him up in one of their jails. When he escaped, however, the journalists didn't seem too impressed; they suspected he had used some hidden keys or tools. Typically, he reacted with a new challenge: "Suppose you strip me and search me before you lock me up!" The newsmen jumped at the opportunity and, just to be on the safe side, locked his clothes in another jail. Within ten minutes Houdini entered by the street door of the police station fully dressed. The next day he made the front page!

From that moment on, Houdini understood how powerful the tool of publicity could be if one could only learn how to use it, and it was only a matter of time before he became the greatest self-publicizer the world had ever seen.

In little more than one year Houdini's popularity skyrocketed and, under the management of vaudeville tycoon Martin Beck, owner of the Orpheum theatre circuit, he quickly became one of the biggest names in American entertainment. He toured America with an act in which his classic magic tricks left room for his more amazing escapes. Besides handcuffs, he brought on stage a new sensation: the straitjacket escape. He got the idea for the stunt after visiting an insane asylum and watching the strenuous efforts of a patient in a vain attempt to free himself from his canvas restraint. Houdini practiced for a week and then he tried the escape in front of the public: first behind a screen, then in full view, and finally suspended head down by the ankles, usually from some high building. "All my public escapes from a straitjacket," he later explained, "have been made by me high in the air for two reasons: first the sensationalism of the feat, to be sure; but secondly and more important, for the reason that, being so far up, with the crowd below me rather than on a level with me . . . it is impossible for the people to follow the movements employed by me to effect the 'escape.' "

Meanwhile, his fame spread so far that he decided to try his luck on the Continent. With only enough money for one month abroad and no bookings, but strongly confident of his success, Houdini sailed with Bess from New York on May 30, 1900. When he arrived in London he failed to impress local agents with his book of clippings and certificates from police chiefs. Finally, the manager of the Alhambra Theatre liked the idea of the escape challenge but was dubious about Houdini's ability to accomplish it: "If you escape from handcuffs at Scotland Yard," he said, "I'll sign you up."

Houdini challenged the manager on the spot to go with him directly to the Yard. Once there, one of the officers stretched Houdini's arms around a pillar, placed a pair of English cuffs on his wrists, and remarked: "Here's how we fasten Yankee criminals who come over and get into trouble." Then he turned and invited the manager to join him in the office; but before they had reached the door, they heard a clatter and turned to see an unmanacled Houdini standing away from the pillar shouting: "Here's how Yankees open the handcuffs!"

And so Houdini's name quickly became synonymous with "escape," first throughout England and then all over Europe. He astounded audiences in Germany, France, and even Russia, and when he returned to the United States he was able to outdo himself by rising to incredible challenges. He seemed to be able to escape from any confinement that man could invent and, along the way, he also introduced some new challenges that thrilled audiences, as well as the newspapers. He would have himself handcuffed and chained on top of a bridge and then would jump in the water under it, performing this stunt during summer as well as winter. Later, he even let himself be nailed inside a packing box that was roped and chained and thrown into the sea. Always, Houdini emerged free and smiling from the waters. Other impossible-looking escapes were the "Milk Can Escape," in which Houdini was locked inside an oversized milk can filled with water, and the "Water Torture Cell" described at the beginning of this chapter.

Besides escapes, Houdini had been fascinated all his life by the history of magic and anything related to it. He had amassed an enormous amount of books, prints, posters, handbills, letters, and memorabilia, the majority of which now resides at the Library of Congress in Washington, D.C. His magical collection was undoubtedly the greatest in the world. He also collected material on Spiritualism and the occult: he had scores of spiritualistic magazines, such as the *Spiritualist, Medium and Daybreak,* and *Light,* among others. He had gathered hundreds of pamphlets and books, and newspaper clippings by the thousands. He even possessed complete collections of personal letters and documents relating to Cagliostro[2] and to famous mediums like the Davenport Brothers and D. D. Home. He must have spent enormous amounts of money to acquire these treasures, and had a network of friends and informants who kept him updated on anything related to his interests that he should own. There was probably no one else who had the means and the interest in putting together such a collection. All this, teamed with his unparalleled knowledge of illusions and trickery, would soon transform him into the foremost critical investigator of Spiritualism.

THE KNIGHT OF THE SPIRITS

Arthur Conan Doyle was born in Edinburgh, Scotland, on May 22, 1859, into a Roman Catholic family. He was sent to Catholic schools, first at Hodder, then at Stonyhurst. At age seventeen he began the study of medicine at Edinburgh University, finally taking a Doctor of Medicine. While at Edinburgh University he decided that he no longer subscribed to the Catholic point of view. "I remember," he wrote in his autobiography *Memories and Adventures*, "that when, as a grown lad, I heard Father Murphy, a great fierce Irish priest, declare that there was sure damnation for everyone outside the church, I looked upon him with horror, and to that moment I trace the first rift which has grown into such a chasm between me and those who were my guides."

After a while, he not only abandoned Catholicism in particular but Christianity in general, becoming virtually a materialist and an agnostic. "Never," he declared, "will I accept anything which cannot be proved to me. The evils of religion have all come from accepting things which cannot be proved." Later in life, however, he would change his mind, substituting his own opinion for proof.

In 1882 he joined a medical practice in Plymouth, but after quarreling with his partner, he opened his own practice in Southsea. For many years he remained a struggling young doctor, and to pass time he began writing short articles and stories, and later novels. His first important work was *A Study in Scarlet* (1887), the novel in which Sherlock Holmes made his first appearance. Then came his other books, *Micah Clarke*, *The Sign of Four*, *The White Company*, and *The Doings of Raffles Haw*. With the huge success of the Sherlock Holmes stories he decided to give up his medical practice, devoting his time entirely to his literary interests.

Thanks to the success of Holmes, he was able to conduct a remarkably varied life. He married twice: first, in the mid-1880s, to Louisa Hawkins, the sister of one of his patients. After her death in 1906, he married Jean Leckie in 1907. He was involved in two wars, first as a correspondent in Egypt during the Sudan War between British troops and the local dervishes, and later running a hospital in South Africa during the Boer War. A popular pamphlet he wrote in support of the Boer War led to his being knighted in 1902. After his second marriage he settled in Crowborough, Sussex, but was ready to return to the front when the First World War broke out in 1914. This time he helped organize a local volunteer force, covered the war as a correspondent, and later wrote a six-volume history, *The British Campaign in France and Flanders*.

Conan Doyle's strongest interest, however, was Spiritualism. When he was a student he had been skeptical about it: "I had read of mediums being convicted of fraud, I had heard of phenomena which were opposed to every known scientific law, and I had deplored the simplicity and credulity which could deceive good, earnest people into believing that such bogus happenings were signs of intelligence outside our own existence." Soon after his marriage, he also had some experience of the séance room, participating with a group of friends in a "table-tipping" session: "It seemed to me," he wrote, "that we were collectively pushing the table, and that our own wills were concerned in bringing down the leg at the right moment. I was interested but very skeptical."

At this time, Major General Alfred Drayson, who had a strong interest in Spiritualism, entered upon the scene. Conan Doyle started discussing the subject with him and explained his unhappy experience with it. Drayson's theory was that "every spirit in the flesh passes over to the next world exactly as it is, with no change whatever. This world is full of weak or foolish people. So is the next."

Doyle continued to attend table-turning séances and also had a chance to sit with an "actual" medium, Hostead by name. "On sitting," Conan Doyle reported, "our medium came quickly under control, and delivered a trance address, containing much interesting and elevating matter. He then became clairvoyant, describing one or two scenes which we had no opportunity of testing. So far, the meeting had been very interesting, but not above the possibility of deception. We then proposed writing. The medium took up a pencil, and after a few convulsive movements, he wrote a message to each of us. Mine ran: 'This gentleman is a healer. Tell him from me not to read Leight Hunt's book.'"

In those days Conan Doyle had actually been thinking of buying a book by Hunt; Hostead's mention of it was the definitive proof he was looking for. He even wrote a letter, on July 2, 1887, to *Light*, the spiritualist journal, describing the episode, which he defined as an "incident which, after many months of inquiry, showed me at last that it was absolutely certain that intelligence could exist apart from the body."

The Hunt incident and his readings had been enough for him to publicly declare: "After weighing the evidence, I could no more doubt the existence of the phenomena than I could doubt the existence of lions in Africa, though I have been to that continent and have never chanced to see one."

He started corresponding with members of the Society for Psychical Research (SPR), including one of its founders, F. W. H. Myers, and finally he joined the society in 1893.

Conan Doyle's practical interest in Spiritualism, in the ensuing years, however, limited itself to a visit to a home in Dorset that, according to its owner, was disturbed by eerie noises at night. Conan Doyle accompanied two well-known members of the SPR, Sydney Scott and Frank Podmore. During the first night nothing happened. On the second night a loud noise broke the silence of the house. It was not possible to determine what had caused it, but on leaving the place the next day, Conan Doyle could not rule out the possibility that he and his friends had been the victims of some practical joke by the owners of the house. During the following years, however, this episode would be amplified and retold many times by Conan Doyle as an example of his long experience in psychic investigation. Actually, this was probably his only direct experience of what may be called a psychic investigation.

The occasion that would convert Conan Doyle to Spiritualism was World War I, a tragedy in which his family lost heavily, his beloved son Kingsley being among the casualties. At a meeting of the London Spiritualist Alliance on October 25, 1917, in the presence of his good friend Sir Oliver Lodge (1851–1940)—a pioneer of radio telegraphy who had announced in 1909, in his book *The Survival of Man*, that he believed in human survival after death and in the possibility of communicating with the dead—he declared himself publicly a dedicated spiritualist:

> The subject of psychical research is one upon which I have thought more, and been slower to form my opinion about, than upon any other subject whatever. . . . There is a column in that excellent little paper, *Light*, which is devoted to what occurred on the corresponding date a generation—that is, thirty years—ago. As I read over this column recently I had quite a start as I saw my own name, and read the reprint of a letter which I had written in 1887, detailing some interesting spiritual experience which had occurred to me in a séance. This will confirm my statement that my interest in the subject is one of some standing, and I may fairly claim since it is only within the last year or so that I have finally announced that I was satisfied with the evidence, that I have not been hasty in forming my opinion.
>
> . . . When an inquirer has convinced himself of the truth of the phenomena, there is no real need to pursue the matter further. The real object of investigation is to give us assurance in the future and spiritual strength in the present, to give us a clear perception of the fleeting nature of matter and reveal the eternal values beyond all the shows of time and sense—the things which are indeed lasting, going on and ever on through the ages in a glorious and majestic progression.[3]

From then on, his time would be spent in the promotion of Spiritualism. "When the war came," he wrote in his *The New Revelation*, "it brought earnestness into all our souls and made us look more closely at our own beliefs and reassess their values. . . . I seemed suddenly to see that this subject with which I had so long dallied was not merely a study of a force outside the rules of science, but that it was really something tremendous, a breaking down of the walls between two worlds, a direct undeniable message from beyond, a call of hope and of guidance to the human race at the time of its deepest affliction."

The scientific side of Spiritualism immediately lost its interest for Conan Doyle, who had once declared that he would not believe in something that could not be proven. "The objective side of it," he wrote, "ceased to interest, for having made up one's mind that it was true there was an end of the matter. The religious side of it was clearly of infinitely greater importance." Such an attitude explains his tendency to be fooled over and over again by unscrupulous mediums. Although he would describe himself to Houdini as a "cool observer" who doesn't "make mistakes," his real attitude toward belief and deception is better expressed through the voice of Stark Munro in Conan Doyle's autobiographical novel *The Stark Munro Letters*: "I am, I think, one of the most unsuspicious men upon earth, and through a certain easy-going indolence of disposition I never even think of the possibility of those with whom I am brought into contact trying to deceive me. It does not occur to me."

CONAN DOYLE DESCRIBES HOUDINI

It is interesting at this stage to read Sir Arthur Conan Doyle's estimate of Houdini's character, written in 1930, well after the end of their friendship and four years after Houdini's death, and collected in his book *The Edge of the Unknown*:

> Let me say, in the first instance, that in a long life which has touched every side of humanity, Houdini is far and away the most curious and intriguing character whom I have ever encountered. I have met better men, and I have certainly met very many worse ones, but I have never met a man who had such strange contrasts in his nature, and whose actions and motives it was more difficult to foresee or to reconcile.
>
> . . . He had the essential masculine quality of courage to supreme degree. Nobody has ever done, and nobody in all human probability will ever do, such reckless feats of daring. His whole life was one long succession of them, and when I say that amongst them was the leaping from one aeroplane to another, with handcuffed hands at the height of three thousand feet, one can form an idea of the extraordinary lengths that he would go.[4]
>
> . . . Apart from his amazing courage, he was remarkable for his cheery urbanity in every-day life. One could not wish a better companion so long as one was with him, though he might do and say the most unexpected things when one was absent. He was, like most Jews, estimable in his family relationships. His love for his dead mother seemed to be the ruling passion of his life, which he expressed on all sorts of public occasions in a way which was, I am sure, sincere, but is strange to our colder Western blood. There were many things in Houdini which were as Oriental as there were in our own Disraeli. He was devoted also to his wife, and with good

reason, for she was as devoted to him, but again his intimacy showed itself in unconventional ways. When in his examination before the Senatorial Committee he was hard-pressed by some defender of Spiritualism who impugned his motives in his violent and vindictive campaign against mediums, his answer was to turn to his wife and to say, "I have always been a good boy, have I not?"

. . . Another favourable side of his character was his charity. I have heard, and am quite prepared to believe, that he was the last refuge of the down-and-outer, especially if he belonged to his own profession of showman. This charity extended even beyond the grave, and if he heard of any old magician whose tombstone needed repair he took it upon himself at once to set the matter right.

. . . A prevailing feature of his character was a vanity which was so obvious and childish that it became more amusing than offensive. I can remember, for example, that when he introduced his brother to me, he did it by saying, "This is the brother of the great Houdini." This without any twinkle of humour and in a perfectly natural manner.

This enormous vanity was combined with a passion for publicity which knew no bounds, and which must at all costs be gratified. There was no consideration of any sort which would restrain him if he saw his way to an advertisement. Even when he laid flowers upon the graves of the dead it was in the prearranged presence of the local photographers.

It was this desire to play a constant public part which had a great deal to do with his furious campaign against Spiritualism. He knew that the public took a keen interest in the matter, and that there was unlimited publicity to be had from it. He perpetually offered large sums to any medium who would do this or that, knowing well that even in the unlikely event of the thing being done he could always raise some objection and get out of it. Sometimes his tactics were too obvious to be artistic.

In passing, it is curious to note that the charge of personal vanity might be directed to Sir Arthur as well, though in a lesser degree. Conan Doyle felt that his word must be final upon the settlement of any question; he considered himself immune to trickery as well as the greatest investigator of Spiritualism. "With all modesty," he wrote, "I am inclined to ask, is there any man on this globe who is doing as much psychic research as I?" Also, he liked to show pictures of himself with various celebrities: in his book *Our Second American Adventure* there are frequent examples of this fact.

HOUDINI DESCRIBES CONAN DOYLE

Let's now consider Houdini's opinion of Conan Doyle, expressed in his book *A Magician Among the Spirits*, published in 1924, when their friendship was ending:

His name comes automatically to the mind of the average human being to-day at the mention of Spiritualism. No statistician could fathom the influence he has exerted through his lectures and his writings or number the endless chain he guides into a belief in communication with the Realm Beyond. His faith and belief and confidence in the movement have been one of the greatest assets of present-day believers and whatever one's views on the subject, it is impossible not to respect the belief of this great author who has wholeheartedly and unflinchingly thrown his life and soul into the conversion of unbelievers. Sir Arthur *believes*. In his great mind there is *no* doubt.

He is a brilliant man, a deep thinker, well versed in every respect, and comes of a gifted family. . . . His home life is beautiful and Lady Doyle has told me on numerous occasions that he never loses his temper and that his nature is at all times sunshiny and sweet. . . . He is a great reader who absorbs what he reads but he believes what he sees in print *only* if it is favorable to Spiritualism.

. . . Our viewpoints differ; we do not believe the same thing. I know that he treats Spiritualism as a religion. He believes that it is possible and that he can communicate with the dead. According to his marvelous analytical brain he has had proof positive of this. There is no doubt that Sir Arthur is sincere in his belief and it is this sincerity which has been one of the fundamentals of our friendship. I have respected everything he has said and *I have always been unbiased*, because at no time have I refused to follow the subject with an open mind. I cannot say the same for him for he has refused to discuss the matter in any other voice except that of Spiritualism and in all our talks quoted only those who favored it in every way, and if one does not follow him sheep-like during his investigations then he is blotted out forever so far as Sir Arthur is concerned.

. . . There is no doubt in my mind, Sir Arthur believes implicitly in the mediums with whom he has convened and he knows positively, in his own mind, they are all genuine. Even if they are caught cheating he always has some sort of an alibi which excuses the medium and the deed.

. . . To Sir Arthur it is a matter of most sacred moment. It is his religion, and he would invariably tell me what a cool observer he was and how hard it would be to fool him, or in any way deceive him [ALL Spiritualists say that].

"HOUDINI AND DOYLE: I KNEW THEM WELL"

Walter Franklin Prince (1853–1934), was a minister and pastor of numerous churches and Principal Research Officer for the American Society for Psychical Research. He was one of the members of the *Scientific American* committee for the investigation of psychic claims, of which Houdini was another member. He thus had many opportunities of working—and clashing—with Houdini. "He was a remarkable man," wrote Prince in his book *The Enchanted Boundary* (1930), "one of the most dynamic of personalities. I knew him well, and the world seemed poorer when his big heart and eager brain were stilled. He always remained something of a boy, enthusiastic, boisterous, vain, apt to think that he only had preserved from scrapes and blunders any group to which he belonged, but in the genial sunshine of his presence one hardly minded these little peculiarities."

As for Sir Arthur Conan Doyle, Prince considered him "big-hearted, zealous, sincere, and 'an earnest godly man,' but these qualities, admirable as they are, do not define an astute psychic researcher. And however excellent the cases may have been which first brought about his conviction, as the years went on he surely showed himself lacking in the power or will to analyze calmly and dispassionately, and to discriminate between the certainly or probably authentic and the certainly or probably spurious, without fear or favor, solely from the evidence. The persistency and ingenuity with which he argued in favor of some of the most suspicious mediums of our day or the most discredited ones of an earlier day has conferred no benefit upon the sober business of psychic research."

Prince felt that Conan Doyle and Houdini, "who seemed personally to like, even though they belabored, each other, resembled one another in several respects. With each, propaganda in relation to Spiritualism partook of a religious nature, and perhaps with each it was a substitute for the religion of his youth. . . . Each felt that his personal work was vastly important to mankind. If Houdini showed plainly that he felt no one else understood the subjects so well as himself, or could test claims as well as himself, if he felt that no old-time faker was quite exposed until *he* administered a finishing stroke, so also Doyle felt entitled to say: 'With all modesty I am inclined to ask, is there any man on this globe who is doing as much psychic research as I?' . . . Certainly Houdini was biased in one direction, and Doyle was equally biased in the other. Houdini's bias shows itself by his paying attention almost exclusively to physical mediums, some of whom he paints blacker than the evidence really warrants, and by the impression which he conveys to the reader that he has, nevertheless, sounded the depths of all purported psychical phenomena and found all wanting. . . . Doyle's bias shows itself particularly by the ingenuity of the devices through which he persuades himself that mediums of extremely doubtful character are or were genuine."

"The more I reflect on what I knew of Houdini and what I have heard of Doyle," concludes Prince, "the more it seems that the two men resembled each other. Each was a fascinating companion, each big-hearted and generous, yet each was capable of bitter and emotional denunciation, each was devoted to his home and family, each felt himself an apostle of good to men, the one to rid them of certain beliefs, the other to inculcate in them those beliefs; and each urged his views as a lawyer or preacher might, but not in the manner of a dispassionate judge or a painstaking historian."

BOTH RIGHT AND BOTH WRONG?

Bernard M. L. Ernst, who was Houdini's lawyer, and Hereward Carrington, a famed psychic researcher who participated with Houdini on the *Scientific American* committee, and who had frequent quarrels with him, were both friends of Conan Doyle. They even published a book about the correspondence between the two men. "There are many," they write in their book,

> who believe that both Sir Arthur Conan Doyle and Houdini were right in their attitudes toward psychic phenomena—and that both of them were also wrong! That Sir Arthur was right in his acceptance of the reality of certain psychic manifestations, and that Houdini was right in his exposures of fraudulent mediums; that Sir Arthur was wrong in his wholesale acceptance of Spiritualism, and that Houdini was wrong in his wholesale rejection of it. Personalities, prejudice, emotionalism and vituperation should be rigidly excluded from investigations such as these,—which require the most calm, judicial, levelheaded and impartial analysis. This and this alone will ultimately arrive at the truth—whatever that may prove to be— as in all other scientific inquiry, and extreme partisan pleading will probably only serve to hinder, rather than to help, the ultimate attainment of this truth.
>
> All this, however, it must be admitted is an ideal; and both Conan Doyle and Houdini were human beings, with strong feelings and convictions. They therefore presented their utterly divergent viewpoints as forcibly as possible. Both men, perhaps, were at times somewhat unduly overconfident and dogmatic. Both were certain that they were right. Both were special pleaders for their Cause. . . . Under these circumstances, it was hardly possible that they could ever have arrived at any mutual understanding or similarity of viewpoint. Their paths were bound to become more and more divergent as they proceeded.
>
> It is all the more remarkable, therefore, in view of these facts, that their mutual respect, admiration and almost affection for one another should have continued for so long under these circumstances; that Conan Doyle and Houdini should have corresponded as they did, and that their relationship should have continued so cordial for so long a time. . . . It was assuredly one of the most remarkable friendships in history—uniting two manly, courageous, vital souls into a warm, personal relationship, despite the diametrically opposed characters of their minds and their radically different viewpoints. . . . It was one of the strangest friendships of which we have any record, and the story of it will serve to illumine the thoughts and lives of these two strong, strange men: Conan Doyle and Houdini.

It is with these inviting words, then, that we begin to tell this fascinating story.

Notes

1. James Randi and Bert Randolph Sugar, *Houdini: His Life and Art* (New York: Grosset & Dunlap, 1976).

2. Conte Alessandro Cagliostro (real name Giuseppe Balsamo, 1743?–1795) was a fabulous character: magician, alchemist, fake count, and "quack." Born in Palermo, Italy, he toured Europe with his fanciful claims and was involved, in 1785, in Paris, in the famous Affair of the Diamond Necklace, a scandalous event that is thought by some historians to have been an important element in precipitating the French Revolution. His adventurous life was described in, among others, Alexander Dumas' *Joseph Balsamo, Mémoires d'un médecin*, Goethe's *Grand Cophta*, and Gregory Ratoff's movie *Black Magic* (1949), notable only because Cagliostro is played by a larger-than-life Orson Welles.

3. Oliver Lodge, *Survival of Man: A Study in Unrecognized Human Faculty* (London: Methuen & Co., 1909).

4. The stunt described by Conan Doyle took place only in fiction, being a scene from Houdini's movie *The Grim Game*. In reality, the passage from one plane to the other in midair (but without handcuffs) was performed by a stunt double: Houdini had volunteered to act the scene, despite an arm sling, but the director refused the offer, for fear of aborting the movie because of the star's death.

A Mutual Interest 2

The Davenports

I T IS NOT CLEAR EXACTLY how Houdini and Conan Doyle met, but it had to happen sooner or later, and it was an interest they shared—Spiritualism—that made this possible in 1920. Spiritualism, however, was hardly the only thing they had in common. They were both worldwide celebrities, and while their career paths were quite different, they shared an energy and a virility that few could match. Houdini's athletic feats were obviously central to his act; as for Conan Doyle he was an avid sportsman and adventurer. Physically they could not have been more different: Conan Doyle was a large man, tall, with drooping moustaches that made him look like a sympathetic walrus. Houdini, on the contrary, was short, stocky, and muscular, with penetrating blue eyes and a broad smile.

It appears that Houdini had sent Sir Arthur one of his books, probably *The Unmasking of Robert-Houdin*, in which reference is made to the Davenport Brothers, two American medium-magicians who became very famous in various parts of the world during the middle of the nineteenth century. Their specialty was the presentation of the "Spirit cabinet," a wooden cabinet in which they sat and were securely tied with rope. No sooner had the cabinet doors been closed than rappings would be heard, a bell and a tambourine would play, and hands would appear at the openings of the doors. Examination of the mediums at the conclusion of the séance, or at any time during its progress, revealed the mediums tied as before.

Were they genuine mediums or clever magicians who somehow managed to free themselves from their bonds and produce the manifestations themselves? Houdini had had a chance in 1910 to speak at length with Ira Davenport, the only surviving brother, and felt privileged to learn directly from him the clever secret of their act. Houdini later wrote that Ira "said that he recognized in me a past master of the craft and therefore spoke openly and did not hesitate to tell me the secrets of his feats ... [H]e

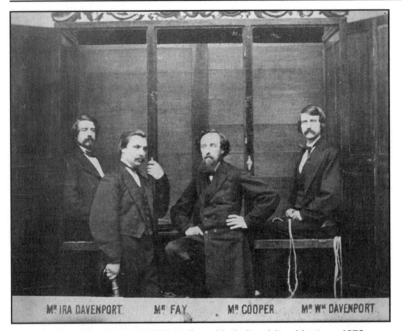

MᴿⁱRA DAVENPORT   Mᴿ FAY   Mᴿ COOPER   Mᴿ Wᴹ DAVENPORT

The Davenport Brothers and William Fay with their spirit cabinet ca. 1870.
From left to right: Ira Davenport, William Fay, Mr. Cooper, and William Davenport.
(McManus-Young Collection, Library of Congress, Rare Books and Special Collections
Division, LC-USZ62-112384)

frankly admitted that the work of the Davenport Brothers was accomplished by perfectly natural means and belonged to that class of feats
commonly credited to 'physical dexterity.' "[1]

They were forerunners of the escape act that later made Houdini famous,
and Ira admitted to him that they had always used trickery; however, for publicity reasons, they let their audiences decide for themselves as to the true
source of their sensational demonstrations.

Conan Doyle was convinced of the genuinity of their mediumship and
naturally defended them in the first surviving letter that he wrote to Houdini, on March 15, 1920:

Dear Mr. Houdini:

I thank you for your book and I am much interested for it treats with
authority some points upon which I want information. I have always wondered whether the Davenports, for example, were ever really exposed. As
to Spiritualist "Confessions," they are all nonsense. Every famous medium
is said to have "confessed," and it is an old trick of the opposition. The
Davenports gave their first performance when they were little more than

children, so it cannot have been elaborate art. I can only learn, so far as "exposure" goes, that there were occasions when they could not undo the knots, but as there are intermittent periods in all real mediumship, that is not against them. It is the man who could always guarantee spirit action whom I should suspect most.[2]

And he added in a postscript: "Some of our people think that you have yourself some psychic power, but I feel it is art and practise." As we shall see, Sir Arthur would radically change his opinion on this matter.

As for the Davenport Brothers, in a later letter he stated: "I value your testimony about the Daven-

Houdini (right) with Ira Davenport ca. 1910. (McManus-Young Collection, Library of Congress, Rare Books and Special Collections Division, LC-USZ62-66398)

ports greatly. Many of those early exposures were really exposures of the ignorance of the investigators. . . . I've been reading the Davenport book you gave me. How people could imagine those men were conjurers is beyond me. The want of power of appreciating evidence is very great in the world."

Houdini, on his part, anxious to cultivate a friendship with Conan Doyle, replied somewhat ambiguously:

Dear Sir Arthur Conan Doyle,

Pleased to hear from you and that you were interested about some of the points in my book.

Regarding the Davenport Brothers: it will interest you to know that I was an intimate friend of Ira Erastus Davenport, and was the last man outside his family circle to visit him in Maysville, Chautauqua County, New York. In fact he was waiting for me and had passed away the morning I was leaving to pay him my annual visit.

I can make the positive assertion that the Davenport Brothers never were exposed. Their first trouble at the Salle Herz, in Paris, came about through the fact that one of the legs of the cabinet was dislodged, and the cabinet tripped over, and this happened only a short time after the arrival of the brothers in Paris.

The trouble they had in Leeds and Liverpool did not arise from the fact that they were exposed. Mr. Ira Davenport told me they were bound so inhumanly that Dr. Fergusson cut the rope before the séance started (in Liverpool).

I know for a positive fact that it was not essential for them to release these bonds in order to obtain manifestations.

Here Houdini actually means to say that it was not necessary for the Davenports *always* to free their hands, in order to produce manifestations, many of which could be produced with their hands still tied or with their feet. The letter then continued:

> The reason why Mr. Ira Davenport became so friendly with me was that, during my tour round the world I visited the cemetery where his brother William Henry Harrison was buried,—near Melbourne, Australia. His grave had not been visited for many years and I had it put in order.
>
> I have all the Davenport Brothers' scrapbooks, and intend, some time in the future, to write a biography about their career from a different "angle" than any which has hitherto appeared.
>
> I trust you will not think I am egotistical in making this statement; that I know more about the Davenport Brothers than anyone living. The widow is still alive and there are two sons and a daughter in this "vale of tears."
>
> I remember distinctly, in talking to Mr. Davenport, that he was astonished at my knowledge of their tours, and he remarked, "Houdini, you know more about myself than I do!"

In closing his letter, Houdini states: "Regarding my own work, I never claim spiritualistic or supernatural aid, always informing the public that it is accomplished by natural means, or as you suggest by 'art and practice.' "

In a postscript, continuing in an ambiguous tone, he also writes that: "My escapes from prison and police cells, under test conditions, have never been solved. Am sending you an old book of mine, in which you will find a number of certificates from Chiefs of Police, and I pledge you my word of honour that I was never given any assistance of any kind whatever, nor was I in collusion with anyone; and that everything was accomplished through my own 'art and practice.' "

After receiving this letter, and after reading with more attention Houdini's book, Sir Arthur wrote him on March 18:

> I think your book, which I have now fully read, is very remarkable, for you really have got to the bottom of things in a way that is rare. These old forgotten worthies must rejoice in your vindication.
>
> I feel the same about early Spiritualists, who asserted with much bravery things which I now know to have been true, and who are still vilified even in their graves. Davenports are a case in point for our enemies continually allude to their "exposure," their "confession," and so on. Unless I hear to the contrary, I will take it that I may use your authoritative statement as the occasion serves.

To this letter Houdini replied as follows on March 23:

Thanks for your letter, and I hasten to reply, so that you will know your letters to me are digested.

When I wrote my book I had not met Mr. Davenport, and the letter, or portion I published, was one received before our actual meeting.

His first letter was written to me Jan. 1909, and I met him 1909, July.[3]

He had been living quietly and rarely saw visitors.

It required over twenty years for the book to be finished, and, not knowing Davenport while writing it, there can be no doubt as to the sincerity of my convictions.

Am rushing this letter through to you, and, if it appears a bit disconnected, attribute it to my haste.

P.S. I have letters from Ira Davenport in which he expresses his ambition to return to Liverpool even at his age, and perform what is termed in America as a "Come Back."

Conan Doyle felt that Houdini's reply was too ambiguous and so he got directly to the point in a subsequent letter dated March 26:

I am sending you two little books of my own on psychic matters, though I fancy in your busy life you have little time for reading. I had meant to ask you, in my last, and I will do so now, whether you, with your unique experience, consider that the Davenport phenomena were clever physical tricks, or whether their claim to occult power was a true one. Their first manifestations seem to have begun when they were quite boys. Of course both alternatives might be true, for when psychic force has failed it might be imitated by skill. Your word on the matter, knowing as you do both the man and the possibilities of the art, would be final.

Again, Houdini refused to commit himself to a "final" word and his only comment on the matter, in his next letter, was: "Regarding the Davenport Brothers, I am afraid that I cannot say that all their work was accomplished by the spirits."

DISCUSSIONS IN SPIRITUALISM

In the first two weeks, Houdini and Conan Doyle exchanged about ten letters, discussing various aspects of Spiritualism. Aware of Conan Doyle's standing in the world of Spiritualists, and possibly thinking that this might be of help in nurturing their friendship, Houdini presented himself as a possible disciple: "You will note that I am still a sceptic, but a seeker after the Truth. I am willing to believe, if I can find a Medium who, as you suggest, will not resort to 'manipulation' when the Power does not 'arrive.' . . ."

He also presented himself as a sort of expert on the field: "I have gone out of my way for years to unearth mediums, so that I could really find a truthful representative—and regret to say that, so far, I have never witnessed a séance which had the ring of sincerity." This attitude can also be gathered from the following letter written on March 30, 1920, in reply to Doyle's letter of the twenty-sixth:

> Your two books arrived yesterday, and I wanted to read them both before replying to your welcome letter.
>
> I am very, very busy, but I managed to take the time, and read your books through *twice*.
>
> I digested all the material, and when you say there are ninety-six volumes on your desk, it may interest you to know that I travel with a bookcase containing over one hundred volumes, and recently, in Leeds, I bought two libraries on Spiritualism. I found an exceptionally fine collection of pamphlets, and expect to go over them when I get a few days to myself.
>
> It may interest you to know that Dr. Funk—of Funk and Wagnalls Company—left a letter behind, sealed, which, up to the present time, has not been read; but Dr. Frank Vizetelly, the Editor-in-Chief of the *Standard Dictionary*, had a dream or vision, in which he spoke to Dr. Funk, who told him that he had left instructions to bring out, in special volumes, Victor Hugo's works.
>
> During my tour in Australia, I met a man who was supposed to have laid low Mrs. Piper; I was in Berlin, Germany, at the trial of Miss Rothe, the flower medium; I know the methods of the Bangs Sisters, the famous Chicago mediums; I was in court when Anna O'Delia Diss De Bar, who was mixed up with the lawyer Luther Marsh, was sentenced. Carl Hertz, the magician, showed the Court some of her Hocus Pocus. By the way, Miss DeBar claimed to have been the daughter of that once beautiful Lola Montez, who made two thrones totter. I visited her grave two years ago, in Brooklyn, and there she lies, alone and forgotten.
>
> Did you ever read *Behind the Scenes with the Mediums*, written by a friend of mine—David P. Abbott? If not, I shall be pleased to send you a copy, as I know where I can lay my hands on one.

Conan Doyle did not appear to be much impressed by Houdini's knowledge of Spiritualism: "I see that you know a great deal about the negative side of Spiritualism—I hope more on the positive side will come your way. But it wants to be approached not in the spirit of a detective approaching a suspect, but in that of a humble, religious soul, yearning for help and comfort. This need not preclude all common sense in judging results."

He also tried to clear up a few points raised by Houdini in this letter dated April 2:

My dear Houdini:

There are points in your letter that I am not very clear about. I don't want
to involve you in a correspondence, so I just note them for your consideration, but not necessarily for your answer. . . .

I know a good deal about Crookes's life and experiments. I know
there were only a few mediums whom he trusted. Home, Mrs. Jencken
(Kate Fox), Mrs. Corner (Miss Cook), and Hope, the Crewe photographer.
None of them ever played him false. I should like to know who it was that
did so, for it was no one whom he ever quoted. . . .

Fräulein Rothe, the flower medium, I know little of, but I notice that
von Schrenck-Notzing, the German scientist, holds that her case was one
of "transfiguration," and that there was an error of judgment. I think this
error is often made by ignorance of the laws. . . .

Excuse this rigmarole—caused by my taking the subject very seriously.

Anna Rothe, whom Houdini and Conan Doyle refer to in their letters,
was a German medium who had specialized in the materialization of
flowers and fruits. French astronomer Camille Flammarion (1842–1925),
who had sat with her in May 1901, had suspected fraud on her part and was
confirmed in his doubts by a colleague of his who saw the medium
"adroitly slip one hand beneath her skirt and draw out branches which she
tossed into the air." Shortly after that episode, in 1902, detectives posing as
inquirers found 150 flowers and several oranges and apples in a series of
baglike folds of her petticoat. She was thus brought to court and sentenced
to eighteen months imprisonment for fraud.

Houdini didn't appear to be bothered at all by Conan Doyle's attempts
at clearing up a few points and did so himself, by writing the following day
a long letter detailing a few cases of fraud he personally handled or knew
about:

Dear Sir Arthur Conan Doyle:

Am only too delighted to correspond with you, and if there is anything in
my little Kingdom of Knowledge that you wish to know, will only be too
pleased to give you any information that I may possess.

For I am seeking truth, and it is only by knowing that Analytical
Minds are going in for it, that I am treating this matter seriously.

As a rule, I have found that the greater brain a man has, and the better
he is educated, the easier it has been to mystify him.

A man in New York, named, or calling himself—Dr. Reese, is, without
doubt, the cleverest reader of Messages that ever lived.

He has deceived the great minds of Germany—in the Courts—win-
ning a lawsuit, and in America, I know he has made children of our
brainiest men.

Edison actually believes in him, and when charged with fortune-telling in Judge Rosalsky's Court, he gave a test for that shrewd man of the world, and convinced him that he was genuine; and was discharged.

Reese knew who I was, when I called for a sitting, and I will say that, of all the clever sleight-of-hand man, he is the brainiest I have ever come across.

He performs the Pellet Test in such a marvelous manner that, if you ever come to America, I want you to have a séance with him, and wonder if you could "fathom" his work.

I was amazed at his skill, and if I had not been extremely familiar with all sleights, and all moves of Mediums, who resort to the Pellet Test, I would have been completely fooled.

Why, he allows you to hold the Pellets in your hands, place them in your pocket and asks you which one he will read and answer first—you open them yourself,—and, sure enough, it has been properly read!

He failed to answer one peculiar question I put in writing: "What am I building, and for whom?"

Rather a strange question, but it happened that I was having constructed an Exedra for my Beloved Mother, and naturally he could not "guess," though, from the other questions he answered, he is a gifted reader of character and judges human beings perfectly.

I caught him red-handed, and he acknowledged it was the first time in his life that anyone had ever "recognized his Powers." And I'll put it in writing that he was the slickest I have ever seen. . . .

The trick to which Houdini refers in the letter consisted in the substitution, by swift manipulation, of the paper containing the question with an identical blank paper. Houdini had been able to discover the maneuver by purposely bending the papers in peculiar ways, difficult to duplicate on the spot by Reese.

As for Anna Rothe, Houdini did not wish to let his doubts on her pass untold, and so he wrote in the continuation of his letter:

Fräulein Rothe, I have every reason to believe, was actually detected, and there is not even the slightest doubt that she was a poor, deluded quasi-"wishing to entertain" medium.

In fact, it was not even mysterious. Have you ever seen the two cowboys who did that as a Vaudeville turn a few years ago? Why, they were placed on the top of a step-ladder, after being searched, and produced hundreds of flowers.

I, at one time, made exhaustive notes on all these items, but when I became too busy to witness the various demonstrations—why, I let it go.

When I was in Australia, in 1910, I met Driver and Hoskins. Driver was instrumental in exposing one Baily; and Hoskins gave me the inside information regarding Mrs. Piper, and a good many others. [*In the original letter, here is an interlineation in Sir Arthur Conan Doyle's handwriting:* Mrs. Piper's record was never impugned.]

Hoskins has since passed away, but Driver is very much alive. I did not bother about their work—perhaps I had run across too many fake demonstrations.

I have read M. Sage's work *Mrs. Piper and the Society for Psychical Research*; the manner of watching the medium is uncertain. It explains how Dr. Hodgson had Mrs. Piper watched. A school-boy would probably do it that way. If there was any trickery, the poorest medium in the world could have circumnavigated this watching.

The successful Mediums I have come across (none of any reputation), fail at their first or second test; and, when the sitter arrives at the next sitting,—All's well!

They have a system of having the sitters watched. [*Interlineation in Sir Arthur Conan Doyle's handwriting:* My experience has been the exact opposite.]

In St. Joe, Mo., I had a unique experience about 22 years ago.

The Medium held his sittings near the Public Library, and "WE" would leave the place, after he had managed to get all our names.

He had a local citizen, who "cued" him as to the proper persons, walk over to the Library, get out old City Directories, and, in his séance, would mention addresses where their grand-fathers and grand-mothers had lived.

For, by questioning, he could easily find out if they had lived in certain neighborhoods.

This St. Joe Medium, "Baynes," —I was supposed to expose, but, the year before that, when I did try to expose a certain "Pettibone," for taking money from the poorer class of people, they tried to kill my performances,—hiring hooligans; but my show went on.

The following year, they tried to engage me to expose their "Star Medium."

I said I would, but the man threw himself on my mercy and I did not do so.

He eventually exposed himself, having taken someone into his confidence, and he had to leave the town.

Unfortunately, I have never seen Mrs. Piper, and will admit that I never went out of my way to get a sitting, being under the impression all the time that it was the usual "accomplishment."

And I am still in the dark regarding the same.

In my early days, I actually discovered a murderer in Wilmington, Delaware, during my search for news; and that was one of the reasons that I gave things up.

I was then engaged to expose Baldwin, who has now retired, and who was prognosticating terrible things for the town; and the people were terror-stricken.

In confidence, I wish to tell you that I have since become well acquainted with S. S. Baldwin, and there is no such thing in his life as "real mediumship" watched. [*Interlineation in Sir Arthur Conan Doyle's handwriting:* Never heard of him.]

He is living in San Francisco, and made a number of world tours, exploiting the "Katie King Séance." . . .[4]

Mrs. Leonora E. Piper (1859–1950), of Boston, Massachusetts, was possibly the most revered "mental medium," that is, she did not perform physical manifestations like most of her colleagues, but she appeared to be able to disclose personal details about her sitters' lives by apparently supernatural means. She was "discovered" in 1885 by Professor William James (1842–1910) of Harvard University, who worked with her for some twenty-five years. He was initially impressed by the private details she was able to disclose about himself, although he may not have known that a maid in his household was friendly with a maid in Mrs. Piper's.

Conan Doyle felt that the experimental work done with Mrs. Piper stood "beyond challenge"; consequently, he could not easily digest Houdini's innuendos about her possible cheatings. In particular, he endeavored to enlighten Houdini as to the facts in the case concerning Richard Hodgson (1855–1905), who had been one of the most active members of the SPR:

> Dr. Hodgson was judged to be the greatest of all psychic detectives by those who knew his work. It was he who exposed Madame Blavatsky, and he also, at Cambridge, who first showed that Eusapia Palladino occasionally cheated, when her psychic force failed. You may be sure, therefore, that he really checked Mrs. Piper in all possible ways. I know that Myers did so in this country, when she was a complete stranger. He even controlled all her correspondence, and a detective was put on to watch her. There is no possible doubt that her powers were genuine, tho' she has her off-days, as every medium has.
>
> Hereward Carrington was a renowned exposer, as you have clearly been, but he has now publicly admitted his conversion, so perhaps some day the evidence may come to you. . . .
>
> I won't worry you any more on the subject. If you ever index your psychic library I should like to see the list. I have 200 now—and have read them too!

Finally, when the occasion arose, they met. Very early in their correspondence, Conan Doyle had stated that he hoped they might meet "when our busy orbits happen to intersect." During the first part of 1920 Houdini was touring the provinces of postwar England and was enjoying enormous success, fueled by his first cinematographic series, *The Master Mystery*. When Conan Doyle heard that Houdini was performing close to his Sussex estate, called Windlesham, in the town of Crowborough, he wrote to him: "Why not run up and see me? I would come down, but this is my one resting week, amid many lectures, and my wife holds me to it. . . . We lunch at one, but you can't come too early—any day."

Houdini promptly replied the very next day: "(I) will avail myself of the opportunity of calling on you Wednesday morning. . . . Mrs. Houdini is with me, but will not be able to come along at the present time, and wishes to thank you for your kind invitation."

And so, on April 14, Houdini had lunch with Conan Doyle; his wife, Jean Leckie; and their three children. He amazed them with his tricks and listened, fascinated, to Doyle's personal stories on Spiritualism: "Six times I have spoken face to face with my son, twice with my brother, once with my nephew." The meeting went well and Houdini considered Doyle "just as nice and sweet as any mortal I have ever been near." Later that day, he noted in his diary: "Visited Sir A. Conan Doyle at Crowborough. Met Lady Doyle and the three children. Had lunch with them. They believe implicitly in Spiritualism. Sir Arthur told me he had spoken six times to his son. No possible chance for trickery. Lady Doyle also believes and has had tests that are beyond belief. Told them all to me."

VISITING MEDIUMS

Not wanting to spoil a nice friendship at the outset, Houdini kept his skepticism to himself and remarked that he really wanted to believe but had never found a convincing medium: could Conan Doyle be of help?

"I will do what I can that you may have practical experience," was Conan Doyle's reply. "The great physical mediums are all in the provinces." Anyway, he warned him: "Something must come your way if you really persevere and get it out of your mind that you should follow it as a terrier follows a rat."

Houdini assured him of his open-mindedness: "I am very, very anxious to have a séance with any medium with whom you could gain me an audience. I promise to go there with my mind absolutely clear, and willing to believe. I will put no obstruction of any nature whatsoever in the medium's way, and will assist in all ways in my power to obtain results. I give you my tour for the next four weeks, and if you can arrange for a séance for any Sunday I could come to Town. I am asking this of you, as I believe that you are one of the most serious men I know, on the positive side of this Question, and trust implicitly in your endeavors."

Conan Doyle suggested Houdini contact some psychics that he believed to be the best in the country, and also presented a few guidelines on visiting mediums:

> These clairvoyants, whose names I have given you, are passive agents in themselves and powerless. If left to themselves they guess and muddle— as they sometimes do. When the true connection is formed, all is clear. That connection depends on the forces beyond, which are repelled by frivolity or curiosity, but act under impulse of sympathy. Thus if you think of your lost friend before going, and breathe a prayer that you may be

allowed to get in touch, you will have a chance—otherwise none. Most investigators have ruined their investigation before it began. It really does depend upon psychic or mental vibrations and harmonies. To disregard this is folly.

I fear there is much fraud among American mediums, where Spiritualism seems to have deservedly fallen into disrepute. Even when genuine, it is used for Stock Exchange and other base, worldly purposes. No wonder it has sunk low in the very land that was honored by the first spiritual manifestation of this series.

Here I think it is reasonably pure, tho' occasionally we catch a rogue. Most of our great mediums at present are unpaid amateurs, inaccessible to any but spiritualists. I have sampled nearly all of them, and they are beyond suspicion. When we get a trickster we publish his name in the Spiritual papers, and that is the end of him—or her. We did it lately with a materialization medium called Chambers, whom we caught in muslin, doing impersonation. . . .

One of the first mediums that Houdini met was Mrs. Annie Brittain, whom Conan Doyle considered "his favorite." "Mrs. Brittain is the best," he wrote to Houdini, "In a series of 72 clients whom I sent her, she got through 60 times, 5 failures and the rest half and half. When my son came back to me, my friend Cyholm had a journalist pal talking directly to him at the same moment that my son was talking to me. Four other sitters testified to the facts, as they overheard it. What could be more final?"

"I met . . . Mrs. Anna [sic] Brittain," wrote Houdini to Doyle afterward, "who claims she has five 'Controls.' She was also very interesting to me, and that is all I can say about this medium."

In his diary, however, Houdini could say a little more; this is the entry for April 25, 1920: "Clairvoyant medium, Mrs. Anna [sic] Brittain, 3 o'clock. Bess and Julia along. Held at home of W. H. Robinson. . . . Robinson's daughter admitted that she did not believe in the Past she used to 'see.' Confessed it was not true. Fooled her parents. . . . Mrs. Brittain not convincing. Simply kept talking in general. 'Saw' things she heard about. One spirit was to bring me flowers on the stage. All this is ridiculous stuff."

In a later letter to Houdini Conan Doyle wrote: "Mrs. Brittain, who has been giving birth to a little medium, is now back at work. . . . I have an idea that your wife would get better results than you. Why not send her first? You follow in a day or two." Houdini didn't follow his advice.

Next, Conan Doyle directed Houdini to Mrs. Wriedt, a Detroit medium who specialized in "direct voice" phenomena and who often visited England: "Mrs. Wriedt is to be heard of now at 59 Holland Park. She is good but varies."

Direct voices were those obtained by mediums, during dark séances, by using trumpets: it was supposed that these objects could help the sitters hear better the faint voices of the spirits.

Mrs. Wriedt knew Houdini from Detroit and during her séance with him failed to obtain any voice. "Sat over an hour," wrote Houdini in his diary. "My belief—she was afraid of me." He wrote so to Conan Doyle who replied: "So sorry you got nothing with Mrs. Wriedt. I hope she will come down here for two days and I will have a try. She is either splendid, or an utter failure, which is as it should be."

Eventually, Mrs. Wriedt went to visit Conan Doyle, who immediately wrote to Houdini: "I had a sitting with Mrs. Wriedt the other day. Only my wife, self and Major Wood present. We sang, and while I could quite clearly hear Mrs. W's voice on my right, and the other two as well, a fourth voice joined powerfully in. Now, is not that quite final? It was in the children's nursery here. What possible loophole is there in that for deception?"

During her visit, Mrs. Wriedt had evidently intimated to Sir Arthur that Houdini was, in her opinion, out "to make trouble." He communicated this to Houdini who wrote: "Re Mrs. Wriedt; she is mistaken. I never look for trouble, and regret that she weighed me up in that light."

In a final word regarding this medium, Sir Arthur writes: "I am sorry you and Mrs. Wriedt don't hit it. She seems to think that you are out to make trouble. I assured her it was not so. She sat in our nursery with my wife and me, and Major Wood. We sang together. As we sang, and as I clearly heard all four voices, a fifth very beautiful one rose up in our midst. That is surely occult beyond doubt."

Another direct-voice medium met by Houdini during this period was Mrs. Roberts Johnson, of Stockton-on-Tees, who claimed that her "control" was David Duguid, a dead trance-painting medium. "She is rather more flippant that I like," wrote Conan Doyle about her, "but she is genuine. But, as I have said before, it is intermittent and can't be controlled. 'It bloweth as it listeth!' " Nothing of interest, however, seems to have happened during Houdini's visit.

THE EVA C. INVESTIGATION

It was in May 1920 that Houdini finally had a chance to witness something interesting, when he sat with one of the most famous and controversial mediums of the time, Eva C. Her real name was Marthe Béraud (1886–?), and it was with this name that, fifteen years earlier, she had started her career as a materializing medium in Algiers. Here she had been studied and verified by none other than Prof. Charles Richet (1850–1935), physiologist and Nobel Prize winner. Her most famous materialized ghost was "Bien Boa," an Indian brahmin. The surviving pictures of such a ghost show its unequivocal fakelike nature: it is Marthe herself, wearing a robe with a hood, a shiny helmet of some sort, and a fake beard.

Richet's opinion on the manifestation was clear, Bien Boa had to be one of two things: "either a phantom having the attributes of life; or . . . a living person playing the part of a phantom." However, there was no doubt as to what he chose to believe: "To suppose that Marthe, the daughter of an officer, and the fiancée of the General's son, should concert with a negress and a palmist to practise an odious deception . . . for twelve months, is absurd." His opinion notwithstanding, in 1908 the trick was revealed: an accomplice, the house coachman, confessed how he had helped Marthe put on the play; first it was meant only to entertain and mystify their houseguests, but then it took over. The scandal forced Marthe to leave Algiers for Paris and change her name into that of Eva Carrière, or Eva C. as she was going to be known among Spiritualists.

In Paris she went to live with her friend Juliette Bisson, the wife of the well-known French playwright André Bisson, who was interested in the phenomenon of materialization. Helped by Bisson, and studied by a German physician, the Freiherr von Schrenck-Notzing, Eva began producing a new phenomenon: the materialization of "ectoplasm," a formless substance which, it was claimed, emerged from the medium's orifices and could take the shape of human limbs and faces. On the basis of his experiments with her, Schrenck-Notzing published a book, *Materialisations-phänomene* (1914), filled with pictures of Eva and her ectoplasm.

Conan Doyle, who had heard much about her but still hadn't sat with her (he would meet her a few months later in France), considered Eva C. a wonderful medium and Schrenck-Notzing's tests "the most notable of any investigation which has ever been recorded."

Houdini had attended a lecture by Eva and Mme. Bisson and, during that occasion, had heard the latter resenting the attack of a French magician and explaining in unmistakable tones her antagonism toward prestidigitators. Dining with Everard Feilding (Francis Henry Everard Feilding, 1867–1936), past secretary of the Society for Psychical Research, he asked for help on how to get close to her.

"Mr. Feilding assured me I was correct about her antipathy towards magicians," writes Houdini in his book *A Magician Among the Spirits*, "and suggested that the only way I could ever hope to attend one of her séances was to convince the medium that I was not one of the biased prestidigitator class, and proposed as a means to attain this end a theatre party to see my performance and thus enable Mme. Bisson and Mlle. Eva to judge for themselves."

The plot worked and Houdini received the following letter from Mme. Bisson, dated May 19, 1920:

Dear Mr. Houdini,

We, Mlle. Eva and I, shall be charmed to see you at the performance of which you have spoken to me, on next Wednesday. Since you have had the great kindness to offer us several tickets, it gives me great pleasure to accept, and if you wish, you may send us four, as we expect to join in the applause with Mr. and Mrs. Feilding.

I also wish to tell you something else!

You know that we give séances here, showing the phenomena of materialization. These are not spirit studies. They are scientific.

It would interest Mr. Feilding and ourselves to have at our séances a master in the art of prestidigitation, but I have always refused to admit to my house, an ordinary prestidigitator, or even one of better rank. Our work is serious and real, and the gift of Mlle. Eva might disappear forever, if some awkward individual insists on thinking there is fraud involved, instead of real and interesting facts, which especially interest the scientific.

For you this does not hold! You are above all this. You are a magnificent actor, who can not call himself a prestidigitator, a title beneath a man of your talent.

I shall therefore, (rather we shall) be proud to see you attend our séances and hear you tell us all, after you have been thoroughly convinced yourself, that their merit is far beneath your own, for these manifestations depend merely upon allowing the forces of nature to act, and lie simply in truth of fact. Whereas with you, it is your merit, your talent, and your personal valor that have enabled you to attain the place of King in your art.

With kind and esteemed regards to Mme. Houdini and yourself.[5]

This was exactly what Houdini needed to be admitted to the series of séances that Eva was going to present at the offices of the Society for Psychical Research.

Houdini attended eight séances, which took place on June evenings. The other usual sitters included Everard Feilding, W. W. Baggally, both of the SPR, E. E. Fournier D'Albe, Sir William Crookes's biographer, and Eric J. Dingwall (1895–1986), a bright SPR investigator who Houdini found particularly valuable: "Dingwall and I understand each other," he noted, "not to let ourselves be hoodwinked."[6]

"At these séances," wrote Houdini later, "my word was pledged to give full and sacred thoughts and I tried to control my thoughts so that my whole attention could be given to the medium. There was no scoffing and there was the will to believe. I felt that if anything was manifested by the Spirits my conscience would be clear. However I sat with my eyes open, taking in even the most minute details and keeping on my guard against any trickery."[7]

The procedure followed at these séances was always the same. After Eva had been stripped and searched in an adjoining room by the lady members of the committee, she returned dressed in tights. Mme. Bisson then put her into a "mesmeric sleep" and the séance began. Houdini usually sat at the medium's left, while Dingwall sat on her right. For about three hours the sitters were periodically invited by Mme. Bisson to intone the word "donnez" (give) to induce Eva to bring forth ectoplasm.

Nothing of interest happened during the first séance. This, in fact, is Houdini's sparse entry in his diary for June 18, 1920: "Séance at 20 Hanover Square. Present Mr. and Mrs. E. Feilding, Baggally, Dingwall and myself. 7.30 to 11. Nothing happened. A nail in chair discommoded Eva. After the séance I went to 5 John Street with the Feildings. Had a cup of coffee."

Houdini, however, was hopeful. "Baggally and Dingwall," he wrote to Doyle, "inform me that she has really mystified them, with her manifestations, and I am rather keen to be present, and am going again Monday night."

Something notable happened during the séance of June 22. Here is how Houdini described the events in a letter to Conan Doyle:

> Well, we had success at the séance last night, as far as productions were concerned, but I am not prepared to say that they were supernormal.
>
> I assure you I did not control the medium, so the suggestions were not mine. They made Mlle. Eva drink a cup of coffee and eat some cake (I presume to fill her up with some food stuff),[8] and after she had been sewn into the tights, and a net over her face, she "manifested,"
>
> 1st. Some froth-like substance, inside of net. It was about 5 inches long; she said it was "elevating," but none of us four watchers saw it "elevate."
>
> Committee, Messrs. Feilding, Baggally, Dingwall and myself.
>
> 2nd. A white plaster-looking affair over her right eye.
>
> 3rd. Something that looked like a small face, say 4 inches in circumference. Was terra-cotta colored, and Dingwall, who held her hands, had the best look at the "object."
>
> 4th. Some substance, froth-like, "exuding from her nose." Baggally and Feilding say it protruded from her nose, but Dingwall and I are positive that it was inside of net and was not extending from her nose; I had the best view from two different places. I deliberately took advantage to see just what it was.
>
> It was a surprise effect indeed!
>
> 5th. Medium asked permission to remove something in her mouth; showed her hands empty, and took out what appeared to be a rubberish substance, which she disengaged and showed us plainly; we held the electric torch, all saw it plainly, when presto! It vanished.
>
> The séance started at 7.30 and lasted till past midnight.
>
> We went over the notes, Mr. Feilding did, and no doubt you will get a full report. I found it highly interesting.

On June 23, again, nothing happened, but regarding the séance of the twenty-fourth Houdini noted: "Bisson very angry with Feilding. Thinks he is against her, which is not the case. Nothing happened." The following day,

Houdini reported another phenomenon: "After a few hours the veil was cut off by Madame Bisson. Eva produced a membrane-like substance."

At the end of the series, Houdini wrote to Doyle: "I have had a wonderful lot of interesting sittings during my stay over here, and thoroughly enjoyed them." He also wrote about the séances to a psychic researcher, William J. Crawford, stating: "It certainly is a wonderful affair and there is no telling how far all this may lead to."

Houdini's enthusiasm can be explained by the fact that he probably wanted to keep good relations with the leading researchers of the time, in the hope of being introduced to séances with their best mediums. Privately, in fact, his opinion on the incidents of the séances with Eva was quite different: "I was not in any way convinced by the demonstrations. I believe that Eva's feats are accomplished by regurgitation." The ectoplasm "appeared to be inflated rubber" and the disappearing "rubberish substance" he thought had been obtained by slipping "it into her mouth while pretending to have it between her fingers." This appeared to Houdini to be the same kind of manipulation that he himself used when presenting the "needle-swallowing trick": "I know positively that the move she made is almost identical with the manner in which I manipulate my experiment."[9]

His conclusion was quite clear: "I regret that I do not believe Mme. Bisson entitled to a clean bill of health. During the séances which I attended she kept up a quasi hypnotic work full of gestures and suggestions as to what could be seen, putting into the minds of those present 'shadows and faces'. In my estimation she is a subtle and gifted assistant to Eva whom I do not believe to be honest. On the contrary, I have no hesitation in saying that I think the two simply took advantage of the credulity and good nature of the various men with whom they had to deal."

Many years later, Eric J. Dingwall confirmed the magician's opinion: "Houdini gave a very fair account of the sitting. He and I both came to the same conclusion about the substance being inside the net. It was a pretty effect indeed."[10]

Conan Doyle did not show much interest in Houdini's description of the "successful" séance with Eva C.: "This is very interesting. I am glad you got some results," he wrote. "It is certainly on the lowest and most mechanical plane of the spiritual world, or borderline world, but at least it is beyond our present knowledge." More important than similar demonstrations was, in fact, to him, vital message of Spiritualism: that life does not end with death. However, he was conscious of the importance of physical manifestations as a form of "convincing-tool" from the other side. "I believe," he wrote in fact in his introduction to Sydney A. Mosley's *An Amazing Séance and an Exposure*, "that we are dealing with a thoroughly material generation, with limited and self-satisfied religious and scientific lines of thought, which can only be broken up and finally rearranged by the shock of encountering physical phenomena which are outside their philosophies. The whole campaign is, I believe, engineered from the other side, and one can continually catch glimpses of wisdom and purpose beyond that of the world. The levitation of the tambourine or the moving of furniture may seem humble and even ludicrous phenomena, but the more thoughtful mind understands that the nature of the object is immaterial, and that the real question has to do with the force that moves it."

Conan Doyle also appeared intrigued by Houdini's collaboration with the SPR: "I am amused by your investigating with the S.P.R. Do they never think of investigating *you*?"

Here again, Conan Doyle gave voice to a suspicion he had already mentioned in one of the very first letters he wrote to Houdini: "Some of our people think that you have yourself some psychic power, but I feel it is art and practise." A few days later Houdini wrote: "Herewith you will find enclosed the *Hull Morning News*, and although I never, in any way, try to make believe that I have occult aid, nevertheless, paragraphs on the style of the enclosed frequently appear." To which Sir Arthur replied: "I don't wonder they put you down as an occultist. As I read the accounts, I can't conceive how you do it. You must be a very brave man as well as extraordinarily dexterous."

More and more, however, Conan Doyle was becoming convinced that Houdini could not perform his wonderful stunts by mere "art and practice" or just "bravery and dexterity." He reasoned that Houdini was in the same league of the Davenports, possessing a "dematerializing and reconstructing force" that could momentarily separate "the molecules of that solid object towards which it is directed."

"Yes," he wrote in a later letter, "you have driven me to the occult! I heard of your remarkable feat in Bristol. My dear chap, why go around the world seeking a demonstration of the occult when you are giving one all the time? Mrs. Guppy [a well-known medium] could dematerialize, and so could many folk in Holy Writ, and I do honestly believe that you can also—in which case I again ask you why do you want demonstrations of the occult? My reason tells me that you have this wonderful power, for there is no alternative, tho' I have no doubt that, up to a point, your strength and skill avail you. . . ."

Again, when he heard of a seemingly impossible escape from a packing-case prepared by a local firm, Conan Doyle sent Houdini a long telegram urging him, for his own good, to acknowledge his "wonderful occult power": "You should get your proofs soon, unless all proofs and all higher personal development are cut off from you because you are not playing the game with that which has been given to you already. This is a point of view to consider. Such a gift is not given to one man in a hundred million that he should amuse the multitude or amass a fortune. Excuse my frank talking, but you know this is all very vital to me."

The Goligher Circle

During his stay in England, Houdini became interested in the strange case of a group of mediums known as the "Goligher Circle." Doyle had written to him: "Mr. Crawford sent me four photos to show that he has photographed the same stuff (ectoplasm) pouring from Miss Goligher. This is the *third* separate medium from whom it has been photographed. Incredulity seems to me to be a sort of insanity under these circumstances. The Goligher photos are most curious. The stuff seems to come from the womb."

Houdini was sufficiently impressed by Conan Doyle's description to start a correspondence with William J. Crawford (1865–1920), a lecturer on mechanical engineering at the Belfast Technical Institute, who had been studying the Goligher case. "As promised," he had written shortly after the Eva C. séances, "am writing to let you know that I have witnessed Mlle. Eva, in a successful sitting. She manifested the other night, after a few blank sittings, but your medium must be a great deal more powerful, according to your report. Sir Arthur tells me he thinks that the power comes from the womb, it certainly is a wonderful affair and there is no telling how far all this may lead to."

One day, while dining at Everard Feilding's home in London, Houdini finally met Crawford. "Met Dr. Crawford who has an ectoplasmic girl in Belfast," noted Houdini in his diary under the date of May 23.[11] The phenomena he had been studying did take place in the presence of the Golighers, a family of mediums consisting of a father, four daughters, a son, and a son-in-law. Of the seven the most successful appeared to be one of the daughters, Kathleen.

In his book *The Reality of Psychic Phenomena* (1918), Crawford had described how, in the presence of Kathleen, tables would be lifted from the floor, raps would resound, and a number of so-called physical phenomena occurred. Being an engineer, Crawford reasoned: "If a table is lifted or 'levitated,' *something* must move it, and we ought to be able to find out what that 'something' is." By experimenting with different kinds of technical apparatus, such as weighing machines, dry cells, and glass U-tubes, he convinced himself that table levitation was only possible thanks to the materialization, from the medium's body, of an ectoplasmic lever that could reach the underside of the table and thus cause the levitation. This became known as the "cantilever theory."

"Do you honestly believe that everything you have experienced through your contact and experiments with the girl is absolutely genuine?" Houdini asked him.

"I am positive in my belief," answered Crawford.

In private, Houdini noted: "On Feilding speaking of materializations and the brutal manner in which Eberhart was exposed by another medium, who found two wigs and a few masks in the chair, and Mr. Chambers'

Kathleen Goligher during a séance. The sheets tied
to the table and to her legs are supposed to be "ectoplasmic rods."
(J. W. Crawford, *The Psychic Structures at the Goligher Circle*, 1921)

written confession, the talk turned on the work, and I mentioned that no one had done anything worth while. Crawford said 'Yes, Crookes had,' and he believes implicitly in Crookes. That made me falter *re* Crawford, and I wonder if he is being deluded. *I think so.*"

A few years later, he was even more straightforward in his book *A Magician Among the Spirits*: "He seems mad to me. . . . To me his credulity seemed limitless."

Crawford committed suicide that same year, leaving a note saying that his research into Spiritualism had nothing to do with his self-murder.

The Goligher case, meanwhile, was drawing to a close. Just before his death, Crawford was working on a second book dealing with the Golighers; finding himself with an incomplete manuscript, Crawford's literary executor asked E. E. Fournier d'Albe to conduct some more tests with the Circle, with the object of obtaining an independent confirmation

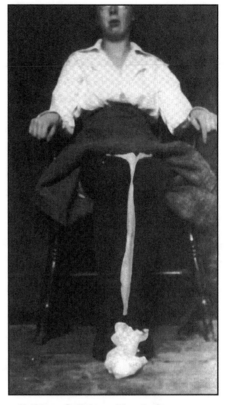

Kathleen Goligher with ectoplasm . . . or is it gauze? (J. W. Crawford, *The Psychic Structures at the Goligher Circle*, 1921)

of the results and of completing the book. D'Albe's conclusions, however, were not the ones that the Spiritualists were hoping for:

> I had gone to Belfast fresh from Eva C's séance, with a strong conviction of reality and with firm faith in Dr. Crawford's reliability and accuracy. I expected a gifted medium surrounded by her honest folks, but then came the blows: first, the contact photographs, then the evidences of trickery. The sight of the "medium" raising a stool with her foot, filled me with bitter disappointment. The simple honest folks all turned out to be an alert, secretive, troublesome group of well-organized performers. . . . The Goligher Circle has repeatedly been urged, by myself and others, to submit to further investigations by a fresh investigator, but so far without success. If it does consent, I can predict two things with confidence:
>   A. No genuine psychic phenomena will be observed.
>   B. No evidence of fraud will be obtained, as the members of the

> Circle are exceedingly wary, and the evidence of trickery which I
> obtained was gathered under conditions which they had not fore-
> seen, but which they will doubtless avoid in the future
> I also feel safe in predicting that if Miss Goligher's feet and hands are
> controlled, and the cooperation of the other sitters eliminated, there will
> be no levitation of any kind.[12]

Houdini kept in touch with d'Albe, who would later write him: "Yes,
the Goligher legend has lost its glamour. I must say I was greatly surprised
at Crawford's blindness." This is what Houdini thought of the researcher:
"I sat with d'Albe at one of Mlle. Eva's séances. I liked his methods and
believe him to be a sincere investigator."[13]

And this is what Houdini thought about ectoplasm after his personal
experiences with both Eva C. and another materializing medium, Eva
Thompson: "Bear in mind, I am not a skeptic. It is my will to believe and if
convincing evidence is brought forward I will be the first to acknowledge my
mistake, but up to the present day nothing has crossed my path to make me
think that the Great Almighty will allow emanations from a human body of
such horrible, revolting, viscous substances as Baron Von Schrenk Notzing
claims, hideous shapes, which, like 'genii from the bronze bottle,' ring bells,
move handkerchiefs, wobble tables, and do other 'flap-doodle' stunts."[14]

Needless to say, Conan Doyle's view on ectoplasm was totally different.
"Personally," he wrote, "the author is of the opinion that several different
forms of plasma with different activities will be discovered, the whole forming
a separate science of the future which may well be called Plasmology."[15]

THE FAIRY PHOTOGRAPHS

Houdini had asked Conan Doyle whether one or more of Crawford's photographs might be procured, and it was in reply to this query that Sir Arthur mentioned to him, for the first and only time, the famous "fairy photographs":

> The Crawford photos—the best of them—are away. I'll send them when I
> hear how long you will be in town. They are too precious to have lying
> around. . . . But I have something far more precious—two photos, one of
> a goblin, the other of four fairies in a Yorkshire wood. A fake! you will say.
> No, sir, I think not. However, all inquiry will be made. These I am not
> allowed to send. The fairies are about eight inches high. In one there is a
> single goblin dancing. In the other four beautiful, luminous creatures. Yes,
> it is a revelation.

The pictures had been taken by Elsie Wright and Frances Griffith, two
girls living in Yorkshire who enjoyed playing in the outdoors. One day they

asked Elsie's father if they could borrow his new Midg camera, with which they took some pictures of themselves with what appeared to be little fairies and goblins. When the pictures came into the hands of Conan Doyle, first he had them examined by experts and, although the Kodak people told him they could undoubtedly reproduce similar effects, he preferred to believe a photographer who claimed that he would have been able to spot any tricks immediately. Since he could not spot any camera trick in the fairy photos, he declared them genuine and Conan Doyle believed him.

His good friend and spiritualist Sir Oliver Lodge refused to accept the photos as genuine. It seemed to him that some Californian classical dancers had been superimposed against a rural British background. Conan Doyle replied that similar tricks would have been impossible for two "working-glass Yorkshire girls."

He could not bear to entertain the possibility of fraud on the part of two young girls: the very idea offended his notions of chivalry. He considered the photos an "epoch-making event" and declared so to the world, first with articles in *Strand* magazine, and then with a book, *The Coming of the Fairies* (1922), that contained all five photographs. He saw himself as a pioneer: "The discovery of Columbus of a new terrestrial continent," he wrote in the book, "is a lesser achievement than the demonstration of a completely new order of life inhabiting the same planet as ourselves."

The reaction of both the public and the journalists was one of amusement, if not downright scorn: "Poor Sherlock Holmes," ran one headline, "Hopelessly Crazy?" and phrases like "easily duped" and "sad spectacle" began to appear in the papers.

Doyle's only worry was that the fuss over the pictures might damage his work in promoting Spiritualism: "I should be sorry if my arguments in favor of the latter should be in any way weakened by my exposition of this very strange episode, which has really no bearing upon the continued existence of the individual."[16]

It was only in 1982, when most of the people involved in the fairies saga had died, that eighty-one-year-old Elsie and seventy-five-year-old Frances felt ready to reveal the truth behind a "practical joke" that had confounded so many people. The fairies were cut-out drawings: "From where I was," Frances said, "I could see the hatpins holding up the figures. I've always marveled that anybody ever took it seriously."

Elsie explained that they had agreed to keep silent because they were "feeling sad" for Conan Doyle. "He had lost his son recently in the war, and I think the poor man was trying to comfort himself in these things, so I said to Frances, we are a lot younger than Conan Doyle . . . so we will wait till they die of old age and then we will tell."

For his part, Houdini did not comment on the subject in any of his letters: perhaps because he could not bring himself to discuss it seriously. Or, possibly, because he could well understand what it meant to live in grief after having lost a beloved family member.[17]

As for Conan Doyle, he would maintain the genuineness of the pictures until his death. Shortly before his death, in fact, he wrote a letter, dated September 19, 1929, to Harold Kellock, author of a biography on Houdini. In it he took Kellock "to task," since he thought that the book was filled with errors (and up to a point he was right). Regarding the fairy photographs, he reasserted that no one at Kodak could find trickery on the plates and wondered: "Why not consult my book *The Coming of the Fairies*, which gives all the facts,—none of which have been controverted? There is no doubt at all that the photographs are perfectly honest."

DISCUSSING FAMOUS MEDIUMS

Before returning to the United States, Houdini met other times with Doyle and, notwithstanding their different approaches to Spiritualism, their friendship continued unabated and unaffected.

"Is luncheon at the Automobile Club, Pall Mall, at one o'clock, on Tuesday next, a possibility?" wrote Doyle on one occasion.

"Your luncheon invitation for Tuesday next has been received with much pleasure," replied Houdini, "and on behalf of Mrs. Houdini, her cousin and myself, shall be delighted to accept." And he added: "If you would care to see the performance at the Palladium, please let me know how many seats you want, and for which performance."

Houdini remembered that lunch at the Automobile Club, where they also had a picture together taken by a photographer: "Sir Arthur called my attention to the fact that a few days previously they had been sitting at the same table with a powerful medium, and he told me in a very serious tone, which was corroborated by Lady Doyle, that the table started to move all around the place to the astonishment of the waiter, who was not aware of the close proximity of the medium. All the time he was relating it, I watched him closely and saw that both he and Lady Doyle were most sincere and believed what they had told me to be an actual fact."

They also continued exchanging books, clippings, and other data. On June 19, 1920, Houdini wrote: "I have just received a lot of stamps, and happen to 'remember' that Lady Doyle collects stamps, so I am taking the liberty, which I hope you will pardon, of mailing them to you."

Their exchange of information continued as well. Just before leaving England, Houdini asked: "Do you know the ultimate finish of the medium Eglinton? According to Dean Harry Kellar, he must have been good."

To which Sir Arthur replied: "Eglinton was a great medium, and was long above suspicion. Then one or two cases arose—his power may have declined—

which were suspicious. Finally, he married money, forswore the occult, and now lives somewhere up the Thames, and is, I hear, the owner of a rich collection of Oriental bric-a-brac. Yes, Kellar endorsed him in Calcutta. . . ."

William Eglinton (1857–1933) was a famous English medium who specialized in physical phenomena, like the materialization of ghosts, or the levitation of his body. Harry Kellar (1849–1922) was, at the time of his meeting with Eglinton, the leading American illusionist. They met in Calcutta, India, in 1882: Kellar had challenged Eglinton in the newspapers and the medium duly invited him to a séance. The magician did not impose any form of control, but just sat in the dark with the others attending. However, although he couldn't see anything, he convinced himself that Eglinton had levitated and declared so publicly: "I went as a sceptic, but I must own that I have come away utterly unable to explain, by any natural means, the phenomena that I witnessed on Tuesday evening."

Houdini was also fascinated by Daniel Dunglas Home (1833–1886), probably the greatest medium who ever lived. "Regarding D. D. Home," wrote Houdini to Conan Doyle in one of his first letters, "I have hundreds of clippings of the trial—possess a number of his private letters—and believe he is one of the few mediums who was not properly, if I may use the word, 'exposed.'"

"No," Doyle had replied, "Home was never exposed, 'properly' or not. He was, I think, above suspicion." In truth, Home was caught a few times cheating, however he was smart enough to operate only when his conditions were met, namely: no controls whatsoever and admittance to the séance room of only those he "liked"; in this way, he could keep the skeptics out of sight.[18] One of Home's most celebrated feats was a "levitation" he performed floating out of one window and in at another. The windows were reputedly eighty-five feet above the ground. "Tall stories," Houdini remarked of Home's witnesses of this unique event, "appear to have been a specialty of these remarkably observant gentlemen."

"I offered," reads an entry in Houdini's diary for May 6, 1920, "to do the D. D. Home levitation stunt at the same place that Home did it in 1868, and G—— shirked and messed it up. He is a fourflusher of the dirtiest kind." It is not known who this "G" was who refused to assist Houdini in the stunt.

Another famous case Conan Doyle and Houdini discussed was that of Henry Slade (1840–1905), the leading expert in "slate writing." He would hold a slate under the table and, after a few minutes, the sound of "writing" would be heard. When the sound stopped, Slade would remove the slate and show that a message from the spirits had appeared upon its surface. "It is extremely doubtful," wrote Houdini, "if the present generation would have known anything about Dr. Slade had the perpetuation of his name been left to the quality of his mediumship, for he was only one of a large number of conjuring fakirs who bamboozled the credulous of his day.

However, he was brought into the limelight on two notable occasions: first by being exposed and criminally prosecuted in London; and second when poor old Professor Zollner [sic], a noted German astronomer and physicist, 'fell' for his simple conjuring and fell so hard that he made Slade the hero of his great (?) work, *Transcendental Physics*."[19]

Although to Conan Doyle Slade was one of the most remarkable mediums of his time, he was also undeniably caught many times in trickery. The one instance mentioned by Houdini refers to the time when Sir E. Ray Lankaster and his friend Sir Horatio Donkin brought Slade to court for obtaining money under false pretenses. Houdini had met Donkin on May 13, 1920, and Lankaster on June 26. "He (Lankaster) told me," wrote Houdini in his diary, "how he caught Dr. Slade. Kidded him along. Pretended he was simple. Asked if the spirits would write for him if he had the slates. Led S. on. S. got *very* careless. Told L. to come next Tuesday. Got Donkin and when S. had written on slate L. held it and took slate away. This at second sitting. . . ."

Lankaster had in fact seized the slate which, on examination, was found not to be clean, as it was supposed to be, but to bear an already written message. Slade was thus prosecuted, found guilty, and sentenced to three months' hard labor. However, he escaped by a legal technicality. He left England and went to Germany, where he was studied by Professor Johan Karl Friedrich Zöllner (1834–1882). Houdini considered the "poor old Professor" to be half-blind and doddering at the time of his experiments with Slade and considered his testimony as valueless. Conan Doyle did not agree: "Zöllner had never a day's illness till six years after his tests with Slade. . . . Zöllner died in 1883 [sic], from an attack of apoplexy." However, he admitted that Slade was "capable of cheating, but I am sure he did not always cheat. The Ray Lankaster conviction seems to me a just one, but on the other hand his work before Zöllner, Weber, Scheibner and the Court Conjurer Bellachini was, I think, beyond all doubt."[20]

Houdini commented on the reliability of scientists: "In all my tests in Germany the great Scientists were so extremely honest that they reminded me of country boys, who have had a strict bringing-up and had their Dear Mother's respect."

While researching material for *A Magician Among the Spirits*, Houdini would later find in Philadelphia a man by the name of Remigius Weiss, who had been able to expose Slade and to obtain from him the following written confession:

> The undersigned, Henry Slade, known professionally as Dr. Henry Slade, —the powerful Spiritistic medium—by reason of the force of unfavorable circumstances, years ago became a Spiritualistic slate writing (etc. etc.) medium, and Spiritistic lecturer and he herewith confesses that all his pre-

tended Spiritualistic manifestations were and are deceptions, performed through tricks.

(Signed) H. Slade

Houdini Returns Home

On July 3, 1920, Houdini sailed for New York. Once back home, he planned to stop performing for at least a year and a half to devote his time to his research in Spiritualism and, probably more important to him at that time, to the production of his own motion picture, *The Man from Beyond*. Unlike the previous series, *The Master Mystery*, this new cinematic venture was going to be produced by the newly created Houdini Picture Corporation.

In a few weeks after his return he wrote to Conan Doyle:

My dear Sir Arthur,

Been busy trying to get back to home life, after my trip abroad, and am just commencing to feel "at home."

The house has all fix't up, and, if you will honor us, by making this our home when you visit New York City, I know you will be comfortable.

If you will accept our invitation, please let me know ahead of time, so that you will find yourself right at home.

The American papers are reprinting Vale Owen's article,[21] and it is causing a lot of talk.

If time permits, I shall go to Lily Dale, and look around at the various mediums and their work. I'll report to you in detail.

By the way, will you please tell me who made that photograph of your boy? You spoke to me one time about this, and the thing made quite an impression on my mind.

Had he ever posed in the position which was shown to you and was there any evidence it was taken from any paper?

I remember you telling me that the case was remarkable, and was telling it to some of my friends, when I was asked who took it, and I was "stalled."

I am on the track of one here who has, so 'tis said, given great satis-faction, and am arranging for a séance some time this coming month.

Remember us kindly to all your folks, from Mrs. Houdini and Miss Karchere.

Sir Arthur replied:

Glad to hear you are safe back among your books. . . . Don't neglect the proofs you have had, for evil lies that way.

It was good of you to send me the N. Y. H. contradiction of that impu-dent lie. A French paper, *La Liberté*, started it. A confounded Liberté, I call it!

They said a medium had been convicted in England, and had said she had personated my son, and I had seen him and recognized him. I have never seen him and there has been no such incident. I have heard him and he has touched me, but that was under test conditions with an amateur. . . .

I remember your kind invitation, but you will understand that I have to be semi-public for my job's sake. But I want to see your psychic library and I want still more to see you.

. . . All good wishes to you, my dear Houdini. Do drop these dangerous stunts.

CONAN DOYLE IN AUSTRALIA

Since 1917, when he had publicly declared his belief in Spiritualism, Conan Doyle's life had radically changed. To no avail his physician would ask him to take it easy at his age. What age, he would ask? The fact that he had passed his sixtieth birthday didn't mean much to him: he felt at the beginning of a new life with a new mission to accomplish. The whole world had to be illuminated with the new revelation of Spiritualism and he had decided to do all that was in his power to help reach that goal.

His writings, however, were not enough: he had to carry the message in person. That is why he accepted an invitation by the spiritualist fraternity of Australia to give a series of talks across the continent and in New Zealand, which would take him away from England for nearly six months, from August 1920 until January 1921.

Although the local spiritualists and some of the press greeted his arrival with enthusiasm and filled his lectures, Conan Doyle frequently felt uneasy at the skepticism shown by others of the press, and he expresses well his feelings in a letter to the *International Psychic Gazette* dated November 3, 1920:

Just a line to show you that I am not done for, in spite of some ups and downs over here! The ups are permanent and the downs temporary, so all is well. Amid the former are my full audiences, their sympathy and acquiescence, and the large amount of interest and consolation which has come with my mission. Of that I have ample proofs. Amid the downs are a Press boycott here, caused partly by ignorant want of proportion, and partly by moral cowardice and fear of finding later that they have backed the wrong horse, or even given the wrong horse fair-play. They are very backward and far behind countries, like Iceland or Denmark, in the knowledge of what has been done. They are still in the stage when folk imagine it's all a sort of three-card trick, and that a clever conjurer could suddenly cry "Hey, Presto!" and in a moment put Crookes and Lombroso and Lodge and all the poor simpletons into their places! It would be comic if it were not so sad. They are dear folk, these Australians—kind, hospitable, straight—but Lord! They do want spirituality and dynamiting out of their grooves of thought. They are where England was before the war. But the tidal wave will strike them—perhaps is striking them. They are actually in the stage when meetings of business men are held at lunch hour to pray that I may be confounded! They prayed when I was on the seas—the Presbyterians did—that I might not reach the country! It was rather near murder, if they really thought their rotten prayers would avail. The result was that we had an excellent voyage!

Well, goodbye. I open in Sydney presently and will have a very lively time by all account. I hope so. It's the unliveliness, the spiritual deadness of this place, which gets on my nerves. It's a great country and worth helping.

While in Australia, Conan Doyle received by the news that his mother had died. Mary Doyle was a strong woman who had objected to various choices of her son: when he wanted to "kill" Sherlock Holmes after the first series of adventures she convinced him to do otherwise, and when he embraced Spiritualism she didn't show much sympathy, actually considering it a load of rubbish. Sir Arthur tried to come to terms with her, after her death, in *The Wanderings of a Spiritualist*, a book detailing his travels through Australia. "For my own psychic work," he wrote, "she had, I fear, neither sympathy nor understanding, but she had an innate faith and spirituality which were so natural to her that she could not conceive the needs of others in that direction."

Also, he had her spirit return. His wife, Jean, had recently discovered that she was gifted with mediumistic powers which manifested themselves through automatic writing. This meant that she had only to hold a pen, keep it poised over a blank sheet of paper and wait for psychic inspiration to come: then messages would come through "from the other side." After Mary Doyle's death, Jean received messages from her expressing encouragement and, as expected, apologies for the skepticism shown during her life: "I ought to have trusted your judgment, my own son" read one of the messages.

Conan Doyle ended his Australian tour, first visiting New Zealand, then Sri Lanka, and, traveling through the Suez Canal, eventually reaching France. Here he met more spiritualists and medium and finally had a chance to sit with Eva C. "The ectoplasm which I saw upon Eva," he would later write, "the much-abused medium, took the form of a six-inch streak of gelatinous material across the lower portion of the front of the dress. Speaking as a medical man, I should say that it was more like a section of the umbilical chord, but it was wider and softer. I was permitted to touch it, and I felt it thrill and contract between my fingers. It seemed to be breaking through the cloth and to be half embedded in it."

Sir Arthur Shows Common Sense

Once back home, Conan Doyle began making plans to bring his Spiritualist crusade to America. Before doing that, however, he resumed his correspondence with Houdini: "I have had some great psychic experiences since Australia. In a fair light I saw my dead mother, as clearly as ever I saw her in life. I am a cool observer and don't make mistakes. It was wonderful—but it taught me nothing that I did not know before."

In another letter, Conan Doyle wrote more about his Australian experience:

> Only just home after many adventures. I shall soon bring out a book, "Wanderings of a Spiritualist," which will recount them. We were 7 in party, but not one day in bed for any of us, which was a miracle in itself, with 3 children in the tropics. I did not come back by America or would certainly have come to see you, tho' we could in any case hardly have taken possession of your house. Thank you all the same—and for Davenport's photo. His brother lies at Sydney. I can't think it was a trick and not spiritual, or he would not have engraved the Cabinet, ropes, etc., on his brother's grave.

Houdini did welcome the opportunity to correspond again with Conan Doyle and the usual exchange of information and comments started anew. In the following letter, for example, Houdini asks Conan Doyle's advice about an odd picture he chanced upon. However, it looks more like an excuse to update Conan Doyle on his accomplishments and to keep their exchange alive:

> Along with this letter am sending you a photograph which I think will interest you. This photograph was secured about four months ago, while my new photoplay called *Haldane of the Secret Service* was in the making. In this photoplay I portray the son of a murdered high police official, and, in one of the scenes, while on my way from the Club, I meet a young lady who is running madly down the street before pursuing thugs. She runs into my arms for protection.
>
> We had a cameramen on the scene, to make an instantaneous photograph of the action, and the result was the picture I am sending to you. This is not a trick picture, that I know. It is not a double exposure, yet how would you explain it? Does it look like ectoplasm?
>
> The gentleman with the straw hat is your good friend Houdini. The girl, whose face is unfortunately turned away from the camera, is Miss Gladys Leslie. She also cannot account for the picture.
>
> You will note that the figures of the persons making up the crowd on the sidewalk are sharply defined. They are watching the action and, as you can see, were greatly interested. I should like to have your opinion regarding the picture.

Am playing a brief tour, but letters directed to my home address will always reach me.

With very best regards and with heartiest greetings for the New Year.

Curiously, in his reply Conan Doyle didn't jump to a spiritualistic explanation, possibly because he wanted to show Houdini that he really was a "cool observer" who doesn't "make mistakes." "The effect," he wrote, "is certainly produced by the whisk of the lady's dress as she rushed into your protective arms. It then wrapped itself 'round her legs. It is certainly not ectoplasm!"

On another occasion, evaluating another picture that had baffled Houdini, Conan Doyle showed some common sense. Houdini had been shown a picture, taken inside the First Spiritualist Temple in Los Angeles, depicting an open coffin with Mrs. Mary Fairfield McVickers inside. In the background of the picture there appeared to be some faces. While there on a tour, Houdini went to the Temple along with a photographer to examine the place.

He studied the wall that was pictured behind the coffin and realized that it was probably its irregular surface that had created the illusion of the faces. He thus had some pictures of himself taken while, with a pen, he pointed to various "faces" on the wall. When the plates were developed, however, one showed a streak of light that really surprised Houdini. He appeared not to have an explanation for the event and wrote so to Conan Doyle. Uncharacteristically, Conan Doyle acted the part of the skeptic:

> Many thanks for the photos. The so-called "faces" are obviously produced by the distemper wash upon the wall. The streak of light, however, is more interesting, though I am by no means convinced that it is a psychic effect. The plate may have been scratched in some way—indeed the way that the line broadens out at the end suggests a scratch.
>
> Many thanks for the photos from Los Angeles. I won't call them "spirit" photos, for they were very unconvincing to me. The faces on the wall seemed quite absurd.

MIRACLE MONGERS AND THEIR METHODS

While Conan Doyle had been touring Australia, Houdini hadn't been idle and, among other things, had published in 1921 a fascinating book, *Miracle Mongers and Their Methods*. It opened with these lines: "My professional life has been a constant record of disillusion, and many things that seem wonderful to most men are the every-day commonplaces of my business. But I have never been without some seeming marvel to pique my curiosity and challenge my investigation. In this book I have set down some of the stories of strange folk and unusual performers that I have gathered in many years of such research."

Six chapters of this fascinating book on sideshow performers and freaks are devoted to "fire miracles": incombustible ladies, fire-eaters, fire-walkers. The remaining chapters deal with other seeming miracle-makers: sword-swallowers, stone-eaters, poisonous-snake handlers, and strongmen.

In the foreword to the first reprint of the book,[22] James Randi, the magician, author, and Houdini expert, writes: "There is a certain amount of naiveté apparent in the text, as if Houdini was not completely confident that some of the methods he describes would really work. Certainly, and it must be stressed to all readers who might be tempted to experiment, formulas given here are largely inventions straight from the imaginations of charlatans who would not have risked trying their own prescriptions for *any* reward. A good example of the fallacy involved is in the various formulas given to desensitize the tongue against the pain of red-hot metal. Painless it might be, but the experience would result in a cooked tongue, pain or not!"

In this book Houdini expresses clearly, for the first time in print, his opinion on the occult and on those scientists who let their reasoning powers be clouded by their will to believe:

> The great day of the Fire-eater—or, should I say, the day of the great Fire-eater—has passed. No longer does fashion flock to his doors, nor science study his wonders, and he must now seek a following in the gaping loiterers of the circus side-show, the pumpkin-and-prize-pig country fair, or the tawdry booth at Coney Island. The credulous, wonder-loving scientist, however, still abides with us and, while his serious-minded brothers are wringing from Nature her jealously guarded secrets, the knowledge of which benefits all mankind, he gravely follows that perennial [*sic*] Will-of-the-wisp, spiritism, and lays the flattering unction to his soul that he is investigating "psychic phenomena," when in reality he is merely gazing with unseeing eyes on the flimsy juggling of pseudo-mediums.

Notes

1. Harry Houdini, *A Magician Among the Spirits* (New York: Harper & Row, 1926).

2. The majority of quotes from letters exchanged between Conan Doyle and Houdini have been taken from Bernard M. L. Ernst and Hereward Carrington, *Houdini and Conan Doyle* (New York: Albert and Charles Boni, 1932). This is the source of quotes in this chapter unless otherwise noted.

3. Houdini met Ira Davenport in July 1910, and not in 1909. In Houdini's book *A Magician Among the Spirits*, a picture that shows Houdini and Ira together, "the last picture of the old showman," bears another mistake: "taken on July 5,

1911." Again, the picture was taken in July 1910, during what appears to have been Houdini's only visit with Davenport.

4. Samri S. Baldwin (1848–1924), aka "The White Mahatma," was a magician who is credited with the invention of the "question and answer" act, in which he would respond from the stage to questions only "thought" by the audience. He was also one of the first magicians to introduce in his show the escape from handcuffs. In his book *the Secrets of Mahatma Land Explained* (1894), he revealed some of his tricks.

5. Harry Houdini, *A Magician Among the Spirits* (1926; reprint, New York: Arno Press, 1972).

6. Kenneth Silverman, *Houdini!!! The Career of Ehrich Weiss* (New York: HarperCollins, 1996).

7. Houdini, *A Magician Among the Spirits.*

8. It is more likely that she was asked to drink coffee so as to test the theory of regurgitation, that is, the ability to bring up certain material from the stomach and eject this from the mouth. Should Eva bring out her alleged "ectoplasm" through regurgitation, in fact, the coffee would have colored it brown.

9. Silverman, *Houdini!!!*

10. From a letter from Eric J. Dingwall to James Randi, dated October 23, 1978. Reprinted with permission.

11. Silverman, *Houdini!!!*

12. Houdini, *A Magician Among the Spirits.*

13. Ibid.

14. Ibid.

15. Arthur Conan Doyle, *The History of Spiritualism* (London: Constable, 1926).

16. Arthur Conan Doyle, *The Coming of the Fairies* (London: Hodder & Stoughton, 1921).

17. Houdini's only mention of the pictures takes place in his book *A Magician Among the Spirits*, where, in a footnote, he writes:

> In speaking of Spirit photography, Sir Arthur Conan Doyle usually brings up as proof positive, that his fairy photographs are genuine. According to the *London Star*, December 20, 1921, there were many interesting developments regarding these: "Messrs, Price and Sons, the well known firm of candle makers, inform us that the fairies in this photograph are an exact reproduction of a famous poster they have used for years, to advertise their night lights. 'I admit on these fairies there are wings, whereas our fairies have no wings,' said a representative of the firm to a *Star* reporter, 'but, with this exception, the figures correspond line for line with our own drawing.' "

For a detailed analysis of the fairies episode, see James Randi's *Flim Flam! Psychics, ESP, Unicorns and Other Delusions* (Amherst, N.Y.: Prometheus Books, 1982).

18. For more on D. D. Home see: Trevor H. Hall, *The Enigma of Daniel Home* (Amherst, N. Y.: Prometheus Books, 1984); and Gordon Stein, *The Sorcerer of Kings: The Case of Daniel Dunglas Home and William Crookes* (Amherst, N.Y.: Prometheus books, 1993).

19. Houdini, *A Magician Among the Spirits.*

20. Doyle, *The History of Spiritualism*.

21. The Rev. Vale Owen was a clergyman of the Church of England who became converted to Spiritualism, and published a number of books dealing with the subject.

22. Harry Houdini, *Miracle Mongers and Their Methods* (1921; reprint, Amherst, N.Y.: Prometheus Books, 1981).

Friends in America 3

Once Conan Doyle had decided that, for the cause of Spiritualism, it was necessary for him to take advantage of his own vast popularity and bring the message directly to the public through a series of lectures, he could not stop at touring Australia and New Zealand, or limit himself to the European countries. It was America, where it all started, that appeared to need him. Especially now that, with the entrance of Houdini into the debate, the voices of the critics started to get stronger.

When Sir Arthur confirmed his plans for his American tour during the spring of 1922, Houdini wrote:

> Awfully pleased to hear definitely that you are coming to America and anticipate the pleasure of greeting you.
>
> I wonder if you could possibly spend an hour as a guest of the Society of American Magicians? I know that, in London, you attended a meeting of the English Society, and it would be a wonderful thing for the American Mystifiers to know you personally.
>
> Did you hear of this girl in Omaha,—Gene Dennis,—who is being watched by Abbott? He claims that it is the first time in his life he has run across the genuine thing. . . . I am sure that you will have a highly interesting and pleasant journey in America.[1]

Conan Doyle replied with a letter dated March 14, 1922:

> My dear Houdini:
>
> I shall not be available for any meetings until my book is done, which will carry me well into May—possibly all May. But I shall always be ready to see you. I have no belief in Mr. Abbott and these other exposers. They ruin their own results and are often as much objects of suspicion as anyone they investigate. We have been infested by several of them on this side. This talk of "fake" is in most cases perfect nonsense, and depends upon our own imperfect knowledge of conditions and of the ways of the Con-

trols, who often take short cuts to their ends, having no regard at all for our critical ideas. This is shown very clearly by the Psychic College report on Miss Besinnet, which I am just reading in proof. If that had not been in the hands of really experienced and sympathetic people, it would have seemed like a huge exposure, and yet it is clearly shown how honest the medium is, how true are her phenomena, and how, in trance, she is certainly at the mercy of her control who mixes the normal and the supernormal. After I had seen my mother in her presence I did not want any proof as to her powers.

In closing his letter, Conan Doyle again pleaded with his friend to abandon his escapes: "Our best remembrances to your wife and self. For God's sake be careful in these fearsome feats of yours. Surely you could retire now."

Finally, all was set for the departure of Conan Doyle and his family on board the White Star Liner *Baltic*. Just before they set sail, Houdini sent them a wire: "Good Luck. Best wishes."

A Tumultuous Welcome

The Conan Doyles arrived in New York on April 9 and received the warmest welcome since another literary genius, Oscar Wilde, had visited America in 1882. As soon as the family arrived at their hotel, they were faced with a crowd of journalists. "They perched themselves round our sitting-room as best they might," Conan Doyle recalled, "and I, seated in an arm-chair in the centre, was subjected to a fine raking fire which would have shot me to pieces had I been vulnerable."

The tone of the questions by the reporters, however, was not what he had hoped for: How is it in the afterlife? Do the spirits have fun? Do they drink wine and liquors? Do they have sex? Although he did his best to answer every question and to bring more seriousness in the discussion, next day's newspapers appeared with such irreverent headlines as: "Doyle Says They Play Golf in Heaven" or "High Jinks in the Beyond."

Conan Doyle gave the first of four scheduled lectures in New York, at Carnegie Hall, on April 12. So many people came to hear him that three more lectures had to be added. "I'd give family, title, whatever fortune I possess, my literary reputation," he told the crowd, "they are all as mud in the gutter to what this thing is to me. I know that it explains all of life to me, and know how inexplicable life was before."

Doyle's manner was calm and reassuring, especially to the many mothers and widows who had lost a son or a husband during the war. Doyle explained why he believed there was no such thing as death. When a man died it was not his material body which survived, it was his etheric body; that is, the soul clothed in its bodily likeness at the best period of its earthly life. To prove his point, Doyle showed a series of slides depicting both great mediums and "real" spirits: the ghost of Katie King with Sir William Crookes, Eva C.'s and Kathleen Goligher's ectoplasms, and many spirit pictures of common people.

These photos made a big impression on his audiences, and everybody, reporters included, were captivated by Conan Doyle's authority and manners. The *New York World* of April 13 wrote about the first of Doyle's lectures:

> Sir Arthur is distinctly of our own world of matter. He is of the flesh to the extent of 200 pounds or more. His utterance is without distinction. His figures of speech are generally commonplace. Some of his reasoning is trivial and much of it illogical. Neither eloquence, grace nor poetry is in his message, and yet it seemed to us extraordinarily convincing.

Houdini did attend one of the lectures, but did not get in touch with Conan Doyle, complying with his requests. However, Houdini filed all the newspaper clippings that appeared related to the tour and looked forward to the possibility of meeting him before he returned to England. The desire was shared by Conan Doyle as well and, in fact, he soon wrote Houdini: "Until Thursday is over I shall be in turmoil. Then, when I can breathe, I hope to see you—your normal self, not in a tank or hanging by one toe from a skyscraper."

SPIRIT PHOTOGRAPHY

Like the rest of the audience attending Conan Doyle's lectures, Houdini had been struck by the mysterious pictures projected by Sir Arthur—not the ones showing mediums and spiritualists, but those mysterious "ghost faces." He had already started collecting material on spirit photography for a book he planned to write on Spiritualism tentatively titled *So This Is Spiritualism* (it would turn out to be *A Magician Among the Spirits*). He had discovered, for example, that spirit photography was born in 1862, when William H. Mumler, a Boston photographer, discovered in a self-portrait the image of his dead cousin.

At the time, photographic techniques were still at a rudimentary stage; the first working photographic process, the "daguerreotype," had been obtained only twenty-two years before by Louis-Jacque-Mandé Daguerre. Photography, then, was a relatively young art, and when Mumler announced that he had been able to capture a ghost on film the public had rushed enthusiastically to his studio to get pictures of their dead relatives.

The fundamental technique, followed by every spirit-photographer, simply involved taking a picture of the client: when the film was developed, however, along with the picture of the client there appeared one or more "extras," that is, ghostly looking faces. Usually, the clients would recognize in these images a dead relative or friend.

When it was discovered that in some of the most famous pictures taken by Mumler some of the "extras" were the faces of people quite alive, even believers became suspicious. Even one of the most touching photos, displayed by Conan Doyle during his lectures, was later shown to be a fake. It showed a crowd of mourners at the London Cenotaph on Armistice Day: above the crowd was a fog of spirit faces, those of fallen heroes it was supposed. However, it turned out that some of the spirits were those of living football players and one belonged to the also living African boxer Battling Siki.

Mumler's trick was to use double exposures—a technique almost unheard of in those days—by which he had been able to superimpose onto the pictures of his clients the faces of anybody else taken from other pictures. He was accused of fraud and taken to court; at the trial, however, he was acquitted. He died penniless in 1884.

THE CASE OF THE CREWE CIRCLE

At the time of Conan Doyle's lectures, one of the most famous spirit photographers was William Hope (1863-1933), a member of the "Crewe Circle," a group of spiritualists from Crewe, England. Hope appeared to be able to register on photographic plates the faces of spirits even without a camera, just by holding the plate in his hands: furthermore, the plates could be furnished by the clients themselves. Doyle had thus obtained a picture resembling his dead sister.

Houdini heard that, in February 1922, his friend Harry Price (1881–1948), of the Society for Psychical Research, and fellow magician Mr. Seymour had conducted an investigation into the methods of the Crewe Circle. Along with Eric J. Dingwall and magician William S. Marriott, they had devised a plan which consisted in presenting Hope with a set of glass negatives that had been secretly marked with X rays. The trap worked: when Hope returned the plates, the one containing the "extra" spirit image showed no sign of the markings; this meant that Hope had switched a prepared plate for the secretly marked one furnished by Price. "In the above case," Price accused in the *Journal* of the SPR, "it can, we think, hardly be denied that Mr. William Hope has been found guilty of deliberately substituting his own plates for those of a sitter . . . it implies that the medium brings to the sitting a duplicate slide and faked plates for fraudulent purposes."

The Spiritualists denounced a conspiracy against Hope, and Conan

Doyle, who was then vice president of the Society for the Study of Supernormal Pictures, leaped to the defense of the Crewe Circle. He begged Price to reconsider his position, hoping to settle the controversy "in some honorable fashion." "At present," he wrote, "it makes an open sore in the movement." Price, however, refused, so Conan Doyle started working on a pamphlet on spirit photography detailing his own side of the affair. While in America, he discussed the case with Houdini in a letter he wrote on April 13, 1922:

> My dear Houdini:
>
> We are living in a shack on the shore—no servants, telephone, telegraph or any other of the inconveniences of civilization. One needs to live thus to get in real touch with one's own family. I am a nailer at peeling potatoes.
>
> I have written a book on Psychic Photography with special reference to the Crewe Circle. The evidence in their favor is overwhelming, tho' what happened on a special occasion with 2 amateur conjurers, out for a stunt, and a third (Dingwall) behind them is more than I can say. We find that another test was independably carried out about the same time, when the Kodak Co. marked a plate. The mark was found by them all right afterwards, and also an extra. Our opponents talk of one failure and omit the great series of successes. However, truth wins and there's lots of time.
>
> I expect I'll be with you again in April.

Houdini had tried to get an audience with Hope in December 1921, but was informed that the medium's engagements would keep him busy for months and that he had to wait. So he asked a fellow British magician, DeVega (Alexander Stewart, 1891–1971), if he would sit for a photograph with Hope. During the sitting, DeVega was sure that the slide he had loaded had been changed for another one, and he told Houdini so. His skepticism about Hope, then, seemed to be justified.

In a letter dated July 8, written when he was back in England, Sir Arthur returned to the subject of the Crewe Circle:

> Here things are in some confusion. I have already written a letter to the Magic Circle tackling their Report, which is a flimsy and ill-informed document. I shall then turn to the more formidable task of Hope and the S.P.R. I know Hope to be a true psychic and will give my reasons when I treat of it; but you can give no man a blank check for honesty on every particular occasion; whether there is a temptation to hedge when psychic power runs low is a question to be considered. I am for uncompromising honesty—but also for thorough examination based on true knowledge. . . .

And again, in a letter dated August 6:

We seem to have knocked the bottom out of the Hope "exposure." The plates were marked by X-rays and we find by experiment that X-ray marks disappear on a 20-second exposure, which was the exact time given. Our time is continually wasted over nonsense of this sort, but I suppose it has to be done. . . .

This information did worry Houdini, since he had already started to talk publicly about the "unmasking" of the Crewe Circle. He kept in touch with Harry Price, who at the time was experimenting to see whether X-ray markings do really disappear on exposure. At first the results seemed to confirm Conan Doyle's theory; however, further experimentation proved that X rays do not simply disappear, thus proving the switching of plates.

While this was going on, Conan Doyle kept on working on his pamphlet, which would eventually be published by Conan Doyle himself under the title *The Case for Spirit Photography*. He mentioned the case again to Houdini in a letter dated August 22:

I am very busy doing a pamphlet on psychic photography, with reference to Hope's powers. The evidence for that power is quite final, but when one comes to individual cases it is not so easy. The present case is in such a snarl that Solomon himself could hardly make head or tail of it. . . .

Hope is a perfectly genuine medium, as I can and do prove in a dozen different ways, but he is a fanatic, and in my opinion would do anything his "guides" had ordered him to do, which has led him into some very queer and dangerous positions. He practically charges nothing and lives in a hovel—still wears the same suit as when I first saw him. He is a great character—and a great medium.

Having lost one possible explanation for the disappearing marking, the Spiritualists had to account for it in another way. One possible solution was that the investigators did not actually give Hope the marked plate, in an attempt to frame him, and this is what Doyle suggests to Houdini in his letter of October 29:

The Hope case is more intricate than any Holmes case I ever invented. I am sure now that there was trickery on the part of the investigators and that the marked plates were not in the packet when taken to the dark room. One of them was returned by post anonymously *undeveloped* to the S.P.R.

Now, since Hope and the College people knew nothing of the test, until four months later, how could they return an undeveloped plate, for how could they pick it out as a marked one, since the marking only shows on development? Clearly it was done by one of the Conspirators, and he could not have picked it out of all the other plates in the dark room, even if he had access to it. It is clear to me therefore that it never went to the dark room at all, but was taken out before. My pamphlet is ready but I hold it back in the hope of learning who the rascal was. . . .

After receiving this letter, but without revealing his source, Houdini wrote to Harry Price on November 18, asking whether these allegations were true or not:

My dear Price,

There is a rumor afloat here that the Crewe circle were "framed." There is talk about an undeveloped negative being sent back anonymously. Have they any reason at all to claim that they were "framed"?[2]

Actually, the return of the undeveloped plate could be explained by Price's hypothesis of fraud: if Hope had switched the marked plate for a previously exposed one, he would still own the plate that Price had originally brought. The disagreement between Doyle and Price about Hope would resurface during the following months, and Houdini would find himself right in the middle of the controversy.

Price, for example, reprinted in a booklet, *Cold Light on Psychical Research*, the results of his experiments with the Crewe Circle that had been published in the SPR *Journal*. "Owing to the fact," he explained in the preface, "that the *Journal of the Society for Psychical Research* is printed only for circulation among its Members and Associates." The booklet caused quite a stir among Spiritualists, and Conan Doyle would try for years to have Price take it out of circulation: "I do feel strongly that the popular six-penny pamphlet designed to ruin a man who had 17 years of fine psychic work behind him is wrong . . . my belief is that you yourself did not write it. However so long as your name is on we can only go for you."

Price later recalled in his autobiography, *Confessions of a Ghost Hunter*, that "Arthur Conan Doyle and his friends abused me for years for exposing Hope."

"TELEPATHY" ACCORDING TO THE ZANCIGS

Besides lecturing on his American tour, Doyle had the occasion to visit a number of mediums. On April 14 he attended a séance with the Italian medium Nino Pecoraro (1899–1973), who would later become the subject of a more thorough investigation by Houdini. The séance had been arranged by Hereward Carrington (Hereward Hubert Lavington Carrington, 1880–1958), a well known psychic investigator, a prolific writer, and a former member of the SPR. Nino was tied with picture wire and placed in a darkened cabinet. There were shrieks, a toy piano on the table tinkled, and, between hymns, Sir Arthur spoke with the spirit of Eusapia Palladino, the most famous medium at the turn of the century.

"I who used to call the spirits back," said Palladino speaking through Nino, "now come back to be a spirit myself."

Houdini and the ghost of Abraham Lincoln "spirit photograph" taken by Harry Price. (Library of Congress, Prints and Photographs Division, LC-USZ62-26516)

"Is that you, Madame Palladino?" asked Carrington.

"Yes," came the whispered reply.

"The power is getting stronger, Palladino," interjected Conan Doyle. "We send you our love and our best encouragement."

Conan Doyle was particularly impressed by a private demonstration he obtained from the Zancigs, Julius and his wife, Ada, a couple of vaudeville mind readers. "No word passed at all," he wrote to Houdini, "but Mrs. Zancig, standing with her face turned sideways at the far end of the room, was able to repeat names and to duplicate drawings which we made and showed to her husband. . . . Possibly it is a real ectoplasmic formation, like the figures of Eva. Telepathy has been imagined by some spiritualists to be a real carrying of messages by some familiar. This is certainly so." He seemed to be particularly impressed by a story that Mrs. Zancig told him about an occasion, in Cambridge, when she had been unable to get her husband's message because her mind was full of the letter *T*. It turned out, she told him, that a group of students had united in thinking of *T*s to play a joke on them. "This surely is proof positive of telepathy," declared Doyle, "for there was no reason for her to tell me this story."

He was so convinced that he wrote a letter of endorsement for the Zancigs:

> I have tested Professor and Mrs. Zancig to-day and I am quite sure that their remarkable performance, as I saw it, is due to psychic causes (thought transference) and not to trickery.

Washington, April 30, 1922

Arthur Conan Doyle

Actually, the Zancigs were just very clever magicians who had worked out a well-honed code through which they could signal each other names, objects, numbers, and so on. Houdini knew very well how they got their results, but kept silent with Doyle, at least for a while. In his book *A Magician Among the Spirits*, he would write: "I want to go on record that the Zancigs never impressed me as being anything but clever, silent and signal codists. . . . In passing I would note that in 1906 or 1907 I engaged Zancig to go with my show. I had ample opportunity to watch his system and codes. They are swift, sure, and silent, and I must give him credit for being expertly adept in his chosen line of mystery, but I have his personal word, given before a witness, that telepathy does not enter into it."

Conan Doyle, as usual, didn't worry much about suspicions (or proofs) of trickery, and so wrote to Houdini: "The only thing I can't understand is why Z. should wish to hide it [his telepathic gift] from you, and mislead you, but I suppose people do try to cover the trail of how they do things, and give fake information rather than true."

He granted that they may use codes, but only "when their powers are low." This attitude brought him many attacks. Joseph F. Rinn for one, a produce merchant and amateur magician who was a longtime friend of Houdini, scorned the Spiritualist in the newspapers. "Poor old Conan Doyle!" he told a reporter of the *Brooklyn Daily Eagle*. "Poor credulous old man! Because he wrote some clever detective stories, people give him credit for having a keen mind. Well, he hasn't. He is gullible and has been made the dupe of mediums."

Sir Arthur, for the moment, refused to fight back: "My attention," he stated in an interview to the same newspaper, "has been called to these various attacks made by Mr. Rinn, and my feeling is that I don't want to throw any brick-bats during my visit in America. I think it would be a mistake for me to answer these attacks and embark in an endless controversy. I prefer to lay the truth before the great American public and leave the case in their hands. If they accept this truth, I shall return to England a happy man; if they reject it, I shall return with the feeling that I have done my duty to the best of my ability." By the time of his second tour the following year, however, his attitude would be much different, and he would answer every criticism made of his statements on Spiritualism.

The Doyles Visit Houdini

"May 10, 1922. To-day at 11 o'clock Sir Arthur and Lady Doyle came up to 278, for a visit." This is how Houdini meticulously started his description for his diary of the Doyles' visit to his elegant brownstone at 278 West 113th Street in Manhattan.

"Sir Arthur was very anxious to see my collection of books," he continued, "and became very much interested." It can easily be imagined that Houdini was far more anxious to show his friend how enormous and valuable was his collection. "I went all over the house and got together all my rare tracts, and he seemed very much surprised at my collection of literature on Spiritualism. I gave Sir Arthur one of the pamphlets given to me by Ira Erastus Davenport, with which he was greatly pleased, and also gave him duplicate of 'Cotton Mather' and a biography of Davenport. Showed him the various letters of D. D. Home and also Davenport."

Doyle certainly seemed impressed by the letters, but less by his books: "Your collection is very short of positive books," he would write him, "you have very few of the really classic and interesting books of the great pioneers, or their modern followers. But these are what really count."

Houdini seemed to be honestly impressed by this comment: "There are a number of books that you mention as being missing which we overlooked, but your letter has given me a thought. I am going to take the floor upstairs and devote it entirely to Spiritualism, and think that, in a week or two, I will cart up all the books from my downstairs office and bring everything upstairs and will have it card-indexed. This will give me a better idea of what is there."

"They stopped for lunch and we enjoyed the visit very much," wrote Houdini in his diary. "There is no doubt that both Sir Arthur and Lady Doyle believe absolutely in Spiritualism, and sincerely so. They related a number of incidents which they accepted without proof." The Houdinis were particularly pleased by Lady Doyle's comment that their house "was the most home-like home that she had ever seen."

After lunch, a cab was called and the Houdinis took the Doyles to the Ambassador Hotel. While in the taxi, Houdini performed a very simple trick, usually done by kids, in which one apparently removes the first joint of his thumb, shows it separate from the rest, then replaces it. Lady Doyle "nearly fainted," remarked Houdini, and Sir Arthur later wrote him: "Just a line to say how much we enjoyed our short visit yesterday. I think what interested me most was the little 'trick' which you showed us in the cab. You certainly have very wonderful powers, whether inborn or acquired." Once again, Houdini could not believe how easy it was to fool Conan Doyle, a man who liked to think of himself as "a cool observer" who doesn't "make mistakes."

THE SPIRIT MOLDS

Among the subjects that Houdini and Doyle discussed during their visit at 278 West 113th Street were "spirit molds," that is, paraffin-wax molds supposedly modeled around materialized "spirit hands" during séances.

The process, invented by William Denton in 1875, consisted in having a basin of hot water, on top of which melted paraffin would float, and a basin of cold water. Once the séance room was darkened, the presumed entity would immerse his/her hand or foot in the hot water, so that the paraffin would stick to it and completely cover it, and would then put it in the cold water to have it solidify quickly. At the end of the séance, empty paraffin molds could be found lying on the table. The general thought was that the molds could still be intact only because the hands around which the wax solidified had dematerialized.

After a period in which the interest in these phenomena faded away, spirit molds made a comeback with Polish medium Franek Kluski (Teofil Modrzejeweski, 1874–1944) and others, and the general public was made

Houdini demonstrates, ca. 1923, how to mold fake spirit hands: first, dip a hand in molten paraffin and then in cold water to cool the paraffin. (McManus-Young Collection, Library of Congress, Rare Books and Special Collections Division, LC-USZ62-112391)

better aware of their existence thanks also to articles in popular magazines such as the *Scientific American*.

Conan Doyle was fascinated: what better proof could there be of the spiritistic nature of a phenomenon that could not be duplicated by men? The molds, in fact, often showed fists, or clasped hands, and sometimes the opening at the wrist seemed too narrow for a living hand to be withdrawn from it. "There seems to have been no explanation open," Conan Doyle would comment, "save that the hand or foot had dematerialised."[3]

Houdini's opinion was different. He knew, in fact, of a simple explanation put forward by some: the medium arrived at the séance with a rubber glove; when darkness was made he would blow air into the glove and then immerse it in the paraffin. When this solidified he could let the air out of the glove and withdraw it from the cast. Conan Doyle found this explanation ridiculous. French researcher Gustave Geley, who had experimented with Kluski at his Institut Métapsychique International (IMI), had tested this hypothesis with thin rubber gloves. The imprints showed typi-

**Houdini demonstrates
how clasped hands
can be made.
(McManus-Young
Collection, Library of
Congress, Rare Books
and Special
Collections Division,
LC-USZ62-112389)**

cally sausage-shaped fingers, clearly revealing that they were made with an inflated rubber glove and not with a real or ghostly hand.

At the time Houdini didn't press the argument further, but later on, experimenting with paraffin, he found that no artifice was needed to duplicate Kluski's molds. As a series of pictures for a newspaper of the time shows, he immersed his hand in the hot paraffin, let it dry, and then carefully removed the hand from it. When one experiments with this technique, one realizes that it is not the plaster cast that has to be removed from the thin wax mold, which would be impossible to do without breaking the mold. One almost forgets that what has to be removed is the living hand, possibly the best-suited object to slip out of a mold without damaging it. In fact, a real hand is even more effective than any other artifice dreamed up to substitute for it. First, the paraffin doesn't stick to skin, only to quite long hair. Nonetheless, if one moves the fingers very slowly, one will realize that every small bit one pulls out will gradually allow the rest of the hand to be removed; that's similar to what happens when one pulls off a tight glove.[4]

Houdini with various examples of fake spirit hands. (McManus-Young Collection, Library of Congress, Rare Books and Special Collections Division, LC-USZ62-112381)

ADA BESINNET

Doyle had quite a low opinion of American mediums, which he had expressed to Houdini: "I fear there is much fraud among American mediums, where Spiritualism seems to have deservedly fallen into disrepute. Even when genuine, it is used for Stock Exchange and other base, worldly purposes. No wonder it has sunk low in the very land that was honored by the first spiritual manifestation of this series."

However, he considered Ada Besinnet one of the most powerful and reliable materializing mediums; he said to Houdini that he was "convinced that Mrs. Besinnet was genuine in everything she did." In her thirties, and good-looking, Besinnet had already sat with the Doyles four times when she had visited England. They had been particularly impressed by the medium because she was the first to produce a materialization of Sir Arthur's mother: "At the end of a very wonderful sitting came my mother's face," he would recount during his lectures. "My wife and I could count the very wrinkles in her face and the gray hairs at the temples during the five or six seconds or more that the face was visible."

On May 20, 1922, Conan Doyle went to Toledo, Ohio, to lecture, but mainly to sit again with Besinnet. Two days later, the *Toledo News-Bee* printed a complete description of the séance: in the darkness lights appeared, tambourines played, voices sang, and spirits appeared—first, Lady Doyle's mother, then the famous spirit of Katie King, and then various others. At one point Conan Doyle exclaimed: "Are we not in danger of overworking the medium? We cannot be too careful of her. Her gift is too valuable to be endangered by overwork." Conan Doyle then saw his mother and heard the voice of his son, Kingsley, which informed him that "Oscar and Uncle Willie are both here with you."

At the end of the séance, Conan Doyle remarked that it had been "one of the most remarkable experiences" he had ever had. "Miss Besinnet's powers were great when I first saw her work in England and were stronger before she left England, but they were much stronger tonight than I had ever seen them before. She should be guarded and looked after very carefully, for she is very valuable. . . ."

"Miss Besinnet is a truly wonderful medium," added Lady Doyle, "and so fine a character that the work produced carries weight. . . . She is simply wonderful. She is such a splendid character that she lends great value to what is obtained through her mediumship."

Doyle also wrote about her to Houdini: "Mr. Keedick came with me last night to sit with Miss Besinnet. Shackleton[5] rose up before him. You should have heard his cry, and he is not a nervous man. It was his first séance, and he knows now how true is all that I have said."

Houdini had tried to sit with Besinnet but she had refused. He had been particularly impressed by a formal investigation, conducted during 1909–1910 in seventy test sittings, by Prof. James H. Hyslop (1854–1920), founder of the American Society for Psychical Research. Hyslop had concluded that the medium created the phenomena herself, but while in a "hysterical state of secondary personality." Other researchers as well had manifested strong doubts about her honesty, particularly because the faces materialized often bore a resemblance to her own face. Hereward Carrington said of her: "My own sittings with this medium left me entirely unconvinced of their genuineness."

Houdini tried to get a séance with her through the help of Sir Arthur. Conan Doyle agreed, asking Besinnet the favor of including Houdini, whom he recommended as a "patient and sympathetic observer," among her sitters in one of her next séances. At the same time he wrote to Houdini:

> I have gone far in giving you that letter to Miss B., for you have the reputation, among Spiritualists, of being a bitterly prejudiced enemy, who would make trouble if it were possible. I know that this is not so, and I give you this pass as a sign that I know it. She is safe in your hands.

Houdini was particularly interested in going to a séance with Besinnet because he probably felt sure that he could trap her. A friend of his, Samri Frikell, had in fact recently attended a séance with her and was convinced he had discovered her tricks. When the room was darkened, he heard the medium leave her chair. To be sure, he kicked out his foot "in the dark and ran the heel of my shoe over the seat of the chair to ascertain whether the lady was where she ought to be, or where she pretended not to be. I am ready to swear that she was not where she ought to have been." Also, when a spirit hand touched his cheek he leaned back his head and touched a lady's bosom, "and a pretty hefty one at that." While a spirit was supposedly walking about the room, Frikell stuck out his foot: the next moment "Miss Besinnet tripped over my foot and fell suddenly into her chair."[6]

However, notwithstanding Doyle's intervention, the proposed séance never materialized. Over the next few years, Houdini would try various times to sit with her. "Regarding Ada Bassinette [sic]," he wrote to Harry Price, "thru a friend of mine I have offered as high as five hundred dollars for a séance and I am willing to lose a weeks pay for two séances." And in a further letter to Price: "I have offered Ada Besinnet five hundred dollars for one or two séances thru the editor of a prominent newspaper and she has refused to let me attend her séances. I believe she is the best known medium we have in America, unexposed. I cannot understand why she will not permit me to attend her séances as I always go into a séance room fully prepared to believe."[7]

An Impossible Demonstration

Possibly hoping to show Sir Arthur how easy it can be to be fooled by mediums, Houdini once gave an extraordinary demonstration, in his own home, in the presence of Conan Doyle and Bernard M. L. Ernst, Houdini's friend and lawyer. Ernst remembered the encounter:

> Houdini produced what appeared to be an ordinary slate, some eighteen inches long by fifteen inches high. In two corners of this slate, holes had been bored, and through these holes wires had been passed. These wires were several feet in length, and hooks had been fastened to the other ends of the wires. The only other accessories were four small cork balls (about three-quarters of an inch in diameter), a large ink-well filled with white ink, and a table-spoon.
>
> Houdini passed the slate to Sir Arthur for examination. He was then requested to suspend the slate in the middle of the room, by means of the wires and hooks, leaving it free to swing in space, several feet distant from anything. In order to eliminate the possibility of electrical connections of any kind, Sir Arthur was asked to fasten the hooks over anything in the

room which would hold them. He hooked one over the edge of a picture-frame, and the other on a large book, on a shelf in Houdini's library. The slate thus swung free in space, in the center of the room, being supported by the two wires passing through the holes in its upper corners. The slate was inspected and cleaned.

Houdini now invited Sir Arthur to examine the four cork balls in the saucer. He was told to select any one he liked, and, to show that they were free from preparation, to cut it in two with his knife, thus verifying the fact that they were merely solid cork balls. This was accordingly done. Another ball was then selected, and, by means of the spoon, was placed in the white ink, where it was thoroughly stirred round and round, until its surface was equally coated with the liquid. It was then left in the ink to soak up as much liquid as possible. The remaining balls Sir Arthur took away with him for examination, at Houdini's request.

"Have you a piece of paper in your pocket upon which you can write something?" asked Houdini of Conan Doyle. He had a pencil.

"Sir Arthur," continued Houdini, "I want you to go out of the house, walk anywhere you like, as far as you like in any direction; then write a question or sentence on that piece of paper; put it back in your pocket and return to the house."

Conan Doyle obeyed, walking three blocks and turning a corner before he wrote upon the paper. When he returned Houdini invited him to take a spoon and remove the cork ball, which had been soaking in the white ink, then to touch the ball to the left side of the slate. The ball "stuck" there, seemingly of its own volition. Slowly, it began rolling across the surface of the slate, leaving a white track as it did so. As the ball rolled, it was seen to be spelling the words: "Mene, mene, tekel upharsin," the very same words that Conan Doyle had written. The guests were speechless.

Houdini turned to Conan Doyle and said: "Sir Arthur, I have devoted a lot of time and thought to this illusion; I have been working at it, on and off, all winter. I won't tell you how it was done, but I can assure you it was pure trickery. I did it by perfectly normal means. I devised it to show you what can be done along these lines. Now, I beg of you, Sir Arthur, do not jump to the conclusion that certain things you see are necessarily 'supernatural,' or the work of 'spirits,' just because you cannot explain them. This is as marvelous a demonstration as you have ever witnessed, given you under test conditions, and I can assure you that it was accomplished by trickery and by nothing else. Do, therefore, be careful in future, in endorsing phenomena just because you cannot explain them. I have given you this test to impress upon you the necessity of caution, and I sincerely hope that you will profit by it."

"Sir Arthur," remembered Ernst, "came to the conclusion that Houdini really accomplished the feat by psychic aid, and could not be persuaded otherwise."

Conan Doyle's reaction, and the refusal to consider trickery even when admitted by the trickster, was so typical, noted Houdini, that "there is little wonder in his believing in Spiritualism so implicitly."

The secret of the trick had remained a mystery for years, until magician and historian Milbourne Christopher revealed it in his book _Houdini, A Pictorial Life_. "Neither Doyle nor Ernst," wrote Christopher, "could fathom this mystery. They might have been less startled had they seen Houdini's friend Max Berol perform in vaudeville." Berol had been performing for years, both in Europe and America, an act in which a ball dipped in ink would spell on an isolated board the words called out by members of the audience:

> Berol did this by switching a solid cork ball for one with an iron core. A magnet at the end of a rod, manipulated by an assistant concealed behind the board, caused the ball to adhere and move—apparently under its own power. After Berol retired Houdini purchased the equipment. An assistant in the room adjacent to Houdini's library had opened a small panel in the wall and extended the rod with a magnet through it. The ball on the slate had an iron center, of course.
>
> Ernst had not remembered that when Doyle returned to the room, after writing the words outdoors, Houdini had checked to make sure the slip of paper on which Doyle wrote was folded, then immediately returned it to his friend. Before doing so, the magician has switched slips. While Doyle was busy retrieving the ball from the inkwell and taking it to the board, Houdini read the words. His conversation cued his hidden assistant. Once the message had been written on the slate, Houdini asked Doyle for the folded slip to verify his words. He opened the blank paper, pretended to read from it, then switched it for the original as he returned the paper to his friend. Later, Houdini explained this switching process during his public lectures on fraudulent mediums.[8]

The Society of American Magicians' Banquet

As previously mentioned, when Conan Doyle was still in England, Houdini had written to him about attending a meeting. But Doyle, then busy planning his American tour, answered that: "I shall not be available for any meetings until my book is done, which will carry me well into May."

Now that May had come, Houdini again invited Sir Arthur to the most important social occasion of the American conjurors:

> I am sending you an official invitation for the Society of American Magicians' annual banquet. You will meet some notable people and, incidentally, this is quite an affair to our organization, as some of the city officials and big business men will be there. . . . I know that you will be interested in witnessing the magicians' performance from a looker-on viewpoint.

Sir Arthur replied:

I fear that the bogus spiritual phenomena must prevent me from attending the banquet, which you have so graciously proffered. I look upon this subject as sacred, and I think that God's gift to man has been intercepted and delayed by the constant pretence that all phenomena are really tricks, which I know they are not. I should be in a false position, for I must either be silent and seem to acquiesce, or else protest, which a guest should not do.

Houdini had made a wrong step when he had announced to Conan Doyle that he had in mind an after-dinner show of Spiritualist-like magic effects. Upon realizing his error, he immediately wrote back to Conan Doyle on May 24:

My dear Sir Arthur:

I am very sorry indeed to note that you would not care to be my guest Friday June 2, at the Society of American Magicians' Annual Banquet, on account of some of the entertainment which was to take place.

I assure you it was only with a view of letting you see mysterious effects and only for your special benefit that this was being put on; therefore I assure you as a gentleman that there will be nothing performed or said which will offend anyone. My motive was a sincere desire from the heart and an expression of good will.

The Society of American Magicians is composed of gentlemen who would not stoop to any indignity to an invited guest. I trust you will reconsider, under the circumstances, and please tell me that Lady Doyle and yourself will honor us that evening.

In passing, would like to inform you that the big literary men will be present, Mr. Ochs of the N. Y. *Times*, Postmaster Morgan, Mr. E. F. Albee [sic] and J. J. Murdock, the heads of the Keith interests, Mr. Bernard Gimbel of Gimbel Brothers and Mr. Howard Thurston, one of the representative magicians of America who is a firm believer in spiritualism.

Regards to Lady Doyle and yourself, in which Mrs. Houdini joins, and awaiting your reply, I beg to remain,
     Sincerely yours,
     Houdini

Evidently satisfied by Houdini's assurances, Conan Doyle replied the following morning with a telegram: "We shall be delighted to come," followed the next day by a letter: "My dear Houdini: Of course we will come. All thanks. But I feel towards faked phenomena as your father would have felt towards a faked Pentecost." To which he added a postscript concerning his heavy tour schedule: "Nearly through—thank God!"

The evening went fine and the after-dinner magic show was full of surprises. Among the magicians who took center stage were big names like Horace Goldin (Hyman Elias Goldstein, 1873–1939), who had perfected the "sawing through a girl" illusion; Max Malini (Max Katz Breit, 1873–1942), a great manipulator; and Houdini, of course, who, along with Bess, presented his famous Metamorphosis illusion. This was the very first act that he had presented when debuting with his wife and that he would occasionally perform during his shows. In it Houdini would be tied in a sack and locked in a trunk; a curtain would be drawn across the trunk, and Bess, standing at the open curtain, would announce: "Now then, I shall clap my hands three times, and at the third and last time I ask you to watch closely for the effect." At this point she would rapidly close the curtain and vanish from sight; instantly the curtain would be reopened, this time by Houdini himself. The trunk would be rapidly unroped and unlocked only to find Bess inside the sack that just a moment before had secured her husband.

Sir Arthur himself, however, had prepared a surprise for his magical audience. He stood up for a brief and mysterious speech:

> These pictures are not occult, but they are psychic, because everything that emanates from the human spirit or human brain is psychic. It is not supernatural. Nothing is. It is preternatural in the sense that it is not known to our ordinary senses.
>
> It is the effect of the joining on the one hand of imagination and on the other hand of some power of materialization. The imagination, I may say, comes from me—the materializing power from elsewhere.
>
> There would be great danger if the original were shown instead of the counterfeit, but what you will see is a living presentment.
>
> I would like to add, to save myself from getting up again, that, if permission is granted for me to show this, they will speak for themselves. I will answer no questions regarding them either for the press or the others present.[9]

Having said that, he sat down and a projector started showing a silent movie depicting . . . live dinosaurs in their native haunts!

The following day the event made the front page of the *New York Times*:

DINOSAURS CAVORT IN FILM FOR DOYLE
Spiritist Mystifies World-Famed Magicians
With Pictures of Prehistoric Beasts

> Monsters of several million years ago, mostly of the dinosaur species, made love and killed each other in Sir Arthur's pictures. . . . His monsters of the ancient world or of the new world which he has discovered in the ether, were extraordinarily lifelike. If fakes, they were masterpieces.

Conan Doyle had refused to comment on what those impressive images really were but, the following day, could not resist in explaining his little game to Houdini and to the press:

> My Cinema interlude, upon the occasion of the Magician's dinner, should I think be explained now that its purpose was fulfilled. That purpose was simply to provide a little mystification for those who have so often and so successfully mystified others. In presenting my moving Dinosaurs, I had to walk very warily in my speech, so as to preserve the glamour and yet say nothing which I could not justify as literally true. Thus, I was emphatic that it was not occult, and only psychic in so far as all things human come from a man's spirit. It was preternatural in the sense that it was not nature as we know it. All my other utterances were, as I think you will agree, within the facts.
>
> The Dinosaurs and other monsters have been constructed by pure cinema art of the highest kind,[10] and are being used for "The Lost World," a picture which represents prehistoric life upon a South American plateau. Having such material at hand, and being allowed by the courtesy of Mr. Watterson Rothacker to use it, I could not resist the temptation to surprise your associates and guests. I am sure they will forgive me if, for a few short hours, I had them guessing.
>
> And now, Mr. Chairman, confidence begets confidence, and I want to know how you got out of that trunk!

A day or so later, Houdini wrote to Sir Arthur:

> There is one thing positive, and that is that the little stunt at the banquet created a great deal more newspaper talk than anything on the program. I am very much obliged to you for your kindness in doing it, and trust that Lady Doyle and yourself had an enjoyable evening. It is the most historic dinner we have ever had, and this is our eighteenth annual dinner. . . . I ran a moving picture, taken at the banquet, and if you desire a copy, I shall be pleased to let you have one. It is a remarkably good picture of Lady Doyle, and you have a very amused expression on your face as if you were in a good humor—and I hope you were!

NOTES

1. The majority of quotes from letters exchanged between Conan Doyle and Houdini have been taken from Bernard M. L. Ernst and Hereward Carrington, *Houdini and Conan Doyle* (New York: Albert and Charles Boni, 1932). This is the source of quotes in this chapter unless otherwise noted.

2. Gabriel Citron, *The Houdini-Price Correspondence* (London: Legerdemain, 1998).

3. Arthur Conan Doyle, *The History of Spiritualism* (London: Constable, 1926).

4. See also M. Polidoro and L. Garlaschelli, "Spirit Moulds: A Practical Experiment," *Journal of the Society for Psychical Research* (July 1997).

5. Sir Ernest Shackleton, who had been a famous Antarctic explorer, had apparently materialized during the séance and was identified by Lee Keedick, who had been his personal friend and was attending his first spiritualistic séance.

6. Samri Frikell (Fulton Oursler), *Spirit Medium Exposed* (New York: New Metropolitan Fiction, 1930).

7. Citron, *The Houdini-Price Correspondence.*

8. Milbourne Christopher, *Houdini: A Pictorial Life* (New York: Thomas Y. Crowell, 1976).

9. *M.U.M. (Magic Unity Mighty)* 2, no. 72 (June 1972).

10. The creatures had been created by Willis O'Brien, the master of special effects who would later bring his talent to *King Kong.*

THE RIFT 4

FUN IN ATLANTIC CITY

THE SUMMER SEASON STARTED EARLY in Atlantic City, one of America's most popular family resorts. Sir Arthur Conan Doyle and his family were there to examine a huge amplifier installed in the city, which could pick up messages from some three hundred miles away. Radio, Conan Doyle thought, might prove useful in communicating with the dead. Actually, he had jumped at the idea of spending some time at the seashore and getting some rest from his heavy schedule.

He started feeling relaxed and, on June 9, wrote to the Houdinis: "Why not come down—both of you? The children would teach you to swim! and the change would do you good."

To which Houdini immediately replied:

> Mrs. Houdini joins me in thanking you for the invitation to come to Atlantic City, and if you will be there next Saturday or Sunday, Mrs. Houdini and I would like to spend the week-end with you. . . . Most important of all, if the kiddies want to teach me to swim I will be there, and in return will show them how to do one or two things that will make it very interesting.[1]

Conan Doyle confirmed his presence during those days: "Yes, we shall certainly be there. There will be a few Spiritualistic friends from Brooklyn (barristers) but you won't clash."

Houdini and Bess reached the Doyles at the Ambassador Hotel, were they stopped for the weekend of June 17–18. They spent part of Saturday afternoon in the hotel swimming pool, where they played with the children. Then they joined Lady Doyle on the beach and talked about spirit photography. The children played in the sand and Houdini was touched by their tender relationship with their mother. Ever conscious of the importance of his meetings, later in the day Houdini wrote down in detail a description of the day:

June 17, 1922
Atlantic City, N.J.

Today, at 4:30, Sir Arthur, Dennis, McHolm, the two boys, and myself met in the swimming pool of the Hotel Ambassador.

I taught the boys how to dive properly and then taught one of them how to float on his back. Sir Arthur, who was in the tank with us, greatly enjoyed my under-water endurance, and he watched carefully how I inhaled and exhaled when I get ready for a long endurance plunge.

When I arose, after remaining under water about two minutes, he asked me why I inhaled as I did, and I explained to him my secret of endurance,—the inhaling and exhaling six or eight times seems to give oxygen in the lungs.

As there was to be a swimming contest that evening, we left at five o'clock, dressed and went out on the beach. . . .

Lady Doyle was there with us and, while they were exercising physically, Sir Arthur and I sat in beach chairs and spoke of spiritualism. He related a number of incidents of the wonderful way in which Mrs. Deane of London gave a friend of his, who had just landed, a marvelous spirit photo, and all the time I knew that the "Magic Circle" of London had apparently trapped Mrs. Deane with marked plates. One *flagrante delicto* case where she exchanged a plate in her bag.

Sir Arthur told me that he had over 25,000 pounds which he had earned on his lecture tour, and which he was going to give to the spiritualists of England, for the cause.

I noticed that, at a séance, Sir Arthur would ask a question and then change his mind and ask another one. Eventually, when he would get an answer to a question, he had evidently forgotten that he had asked that specific one, and, on receiving a reply to same, would naturally think that he had never spoken on the subject before. All during the séance he was willing to believe. It was not a case of being deceived, but merely a case of religious mania, and in knowing, in his own mind, according to his powerful deductions, that he was in the presence of the Almighty or that he was holding communion with the dead.

His voice and mannerisms are just as nice and sweet as any mortal I have ever been near. Lady Doyle told me that he has never spoken a cross word in his life. He is good-natured, very bright, but a monomaniac on the subject of spiritualism. Being uninitiated in the world of mystery, never having been taught the artifices of conjuring, it was the simplest thing in the world for anyone to gain his confidence to hoodwink him.

He showed me a photograph of a coffin, covered with flowers, from under which the pale, eerie face of a dead woman of past middle age was visible, and there were two "spirits," of a man and of a woman, one on each side of the coffin. Lady Doyle said that no one could be so despicable as to do anything by fraud in such an environment. I replied that I could not conceive how any human being could be so sacrilegious as to delude anyone by doing such a thing, and as I looked at the photograph I did say to myself "although these photographs look to be real, they have been obtained by some legerdemain." I cannot see how anyone would be so vile and despicable as to do such a thing.

It seems that, in speaking to Doyle, he showed me a letter from his friend in England in the newspaper called *Light* which informed him of the "reported" exposé of Hope and Mrs. Buxton at Crewe.

What I can remember of the letter which Sir Arthur read to me was that Hope and Mrs. Buxton are with him. They have come to him for assistance and wished that he was there in order to give them his aid. Using the American idiom, I believe that this is all a "frame-up."

Sir Arthur asked me to give him what assistance I could, and that he had this money which he was taking back to England and would spend it. From the letter it seems that he will give it to the law courts.

I told Sir Arthur that I was positive it would be a great big case and in fact a historical event, on a par with the D. D. Home affair. Personally, I believed that the Crewe mediums, as well as Mrs. Deane, would be shown up publicly through the newspapers, but that, as usual, they would find willing believers in the genuineness of their tests. At this late date, Home is still supposed to be a genuine levitator, able to float from one end of the room to another. Scientists still say that Palladino, although exposed, and although she cheated at times, nevertheless was honest sometimes,— about the wind that came from the top of her head which was supposed to be something psychic.

Dr. Sulzberger told me of a case of a boy who had fractured his skull, and, this fracture never properly healing he was able to blow wind right through the back of his head.

There was a freak appearing at Huber's Museum who could blow balloons through his eyes. There is no doubt in my mind that Palladino had some special freak make-up, which enabled her, in a natural way, to do some of the things attributed to her. My contention is that they actually thought that what they wrote about her was true, but it couldn't possibly be exactly as they described it,—although, from their manner of investigation, it was exactly as they claimed.

Sir Arthur told me of a séance he had with Mrs. Pruden of Cincinnati, Ohio, an old lady who held the slates under the table and brought back writing on same. He asked a number of questions, so he tells me, of which no one else knew. Especially about the investment of some money which he called the spiritualist money, in this doctor (?) proposition. The answer came back, I forgot just from whom it was, but I believe it was from Sir Arthur's son, that it was quite all right, for the doctor was an honest man.

Sir Arthur told me of a number of cases, and he assured me that they were actually done without illusion.

Sir Arthur asked Lady Doyle who was standing alongside of me, and was it my mother? Lady Doyle's hand struck the table three times, signifying "yes," that my mother was alongside of me. I tried to imagine that

Harry Houdini with his wife, Bess (at right), and his mother, Cecilia Steiner Weiss, in 1907. Houdini wrote on the photograph: "My two sweethearts." (McManus-Young Collection, Library of Congress, Rare Books and Special Collections Division, LC-USZ62-112416)

my dear mother, whom I worship and always will, was alongside of me, and tried all I possibly could to think of a number of trivial things of which my mother and I often had spoken, and if she had been actually present she would have given me some sign.

The children are unafraid of death, believing implicitly in the teachings of their parents,—that even if they are dead, they still live, and hold conversation with their dead relatives. Death doesn't mean anything to them,—except to live on a higher plane of life.

The children are very bright, very affectionate, and one of the boys came up to his mother in the midst of his play, saying, "Mother, I was so lonesome I came over to give you a kiss."

He kissed her caressingly on the mouth, picked up her hand and kissed each finger in as courtly a manner as any prince kissing his queen's hands. They are wonderful children, both in mind and body.

Saturday evening we attended the swimming contest which was very interesting, but which after a while became tiresome, on account of the great length of the program.

Miss Bleibtrey, the swimmer and champion, gave a number of exhibition sprints. Three other girls swam with their hands and feet tied. Sir

Arthur was bored and wanted to get up and leave the place, but we told him that they were working expressly for us, and as long as they lived they would look upon it as a slight.

He was very nice about it and we sat through the performance until Miss Bleibtrey said, "that's all there is, there ain't no more." He then excused himself, saying he had a headache and retired.

The Fateful Séance

The following day, things took a different turn and the description of what happened exactly became, in the following months, more and more detailed and more and more different whether it was Houdini or Conan Doyle who wrote or talked about it.

Here is the earliest version of the story, written by Houdini on June 18, the same day when it happened:

> I was seated in one of those comfortable chairs facing the beach, with Mrs. Houdini, when a small boy came along with Sir Arthur Conan Doyle, showing him where we were sun-bathing.
>
> It appeared that Lady Doyle wanted to give me an automatic writing séance, in order to see whether it was possible for her to give me some indication from the spirit world, and she had sent Sir Arthur to find me.
>
> Sir Arthur apologized to Mrs. Houdini for not inviting her to the séance, saying that two people who were of the same mind, either positive or negative, would possibly hurt, and if this was so Lady Doyle would not be able to get any writing from any of the spirits who would control her. So I followed Sir Arthur, but not until the boy who had found me for him had taken a snapshot of both of us, ere we left.
>
> We went to the Hotel Ambassador, where we all were stopping,—for, at the invitation of Sir Arthur, Mrs. Houdini and myself went to Atlantic City for the week end. Our room was next to their suite.
>
> Lady Doyle was very charming. Curtains were drawn, writing pads placed on the table and also two pencils of the ordinary kind. Sir Arthur, with his head bowed down, just like a simple child, uttered a prayer, calling upon the Almighty to let us have a sign from our friends from beyond.
>
> He placed his hands caressingly upon Lady Doyle's, to give her more power. I closed my eyes and eliminated from my mind all thoughts but those of a religious order, so that I could help as much as possible.
>
> She took a pencil and, with spasmodic jerks of her right hand, in no gentle way, started to strike the table, explaining that the force had taken hold of her in the most energetic manner that they had ever done at any séance at which she was doing the automatic writing.
>
> For a few moments she seemed to be struggling with it, but then the pencil began to move. She asked of the spirit, "Do you believe in God?"

Upon having her hand beat the table three times she said: "Then I will make the sign of the cross."

She did so, marking the sign of the cross on the edge of the pad on which she was writing.

I think that, in her heart of hearts, Lady Doyle is sincere, and I am positive that Sir Arthur is just as religious in his belief as it is possible for any human being to be. As from time to time Lady Doyle started to write, he would soothe her as if admonishing the spirit not to be too forcible with her. These two spoke as if there was someone in reality standing alongside of us.

Eventually, in asking the question, "who was there," and whether it was my mother, her hand struck the table three times signifying "yes." She then wrote:

> Oh, my darling, thank God, at last I'm through.—I've tried so often—now I am happy. Why, of course, I want to talk to my boy—my own beloved boy—Friends, thank you, with all my heart for this.
>
> You have answered the cry of my heart—and of his—God bless him—a thousand fold, for all his life for me—never had a mother such a son—tell him not to grieve, soon he'll get all the evidence he is so anxious for—Yes, we know—tell him I want him to try to write in his own home. It will be far better so.
>
> I will work with him—he is so, so dear to me—I am preparing so sweet a home for him which one day in God's good time he will come to—it is one of my great joys preparing it for our future—
>
> I am so happy in this life—it is so full and joyous—my only shadow has been that my beloved one hasn't known how often I have been with him all the while, all the while—here away from my heart's darling—combining my work thus in this life of mine.
>
> It is so different over here, so much larger and bigger and more beautiful—so lofty—all sweetness around one—nothing that hurts and we see our beloved ones on earth—that is such a joy and comfort to us—Tell him I love him more than ever—the years only increase it—and his goodness fills my soul with gladness and thankfulness. Oh, just this, it *is* me. I want him only to know that—that—I have bridged the gulf—That is what I wanted, oh so much—Now I can rest in peace—How soon—

When we got as far as "I wanted, oh so much—Now I can rest in peace," Sir Arthur requested me to ask some sort of a question, as a test that it really was my sainted mother at my side.

Lady Doyle did not seem to think that the spirit would answer direct questions, and I purposely evaded asking anything which might embar-

Harry Houdini at his mother's grave. (Edward Saint Collection,
Library of Congress, Prints and Photographs Division, LC-USZ62-79680)

rass the medium, as I wanted to help all I could, so I thought of the question proposed by Sir Arthur, "Can my mother read my mind," in this way answering any question of which I might think.

So I just thought of the question in the ordinary way, and before I had the question firmly formed Lady Doyle started to write.

> I *always* read my beloved son's mind—his dear mind—there is so much I want to say to him—but—I am almost overwhelmed by this joy of talking to him once more—it is almost too much to get through—the joy of it—thank you, thank you, thank you, friend, with all my heart for what you have done for me this day—God bless you, too, Sir Arthur, for what you are doing for us—for us over here—who so need to get in touch with our beloved ones on the earth plane—
>
> If only the world knew this great truth—how different—life would be for men and women—Go on, let nothing stop you— great will be your reward hereafter—Goodbye—I brought you, Sir Arthur, and my darling son together—I felt you were the one man who might help us to pierce the veil—and I was right— Bless him, bless him, bless him, I say from the depths of my soul—he fills my heart and later we shall be together—oh, so happy—a happiness awaits him that he has never dreamed of— tell him I am with him—just tell him that I'll soon make him

know how close I am all the while—his eyes will soon be opened—Goodbye again—God's blessing be on you all.

There is no doubt in my mind that questions are asked and answered in this self-same way, and as the questioning goes on eventually some one happens to think of something that has not been answered, and in this way the "spirits" answer questions which no one else knew about.

After the séance was over, and I had asked about trying out the automatic writing in my own home, I took a pencil and wrote the name "Powell." It was like an electric shock to Sir Arthur, for a friend of his by that name, the editor of *The Financial News*, of London, had died about a week previously.

I wrote the name because I was thinking of Powell, the magician. It seems that he had been the subject of conversation between Mrs. Houdini and myself. Mrs. Powell being very ill, the question arose as to whether he ought to work with a young woman as his assistant.

Mrs. Houdini said it was not fair, but she did not want me to interfere. I think it is perfectly all right for a magician to have young blood in his act, when his wife cannot assist him, and, when I took up the pencil, very likely this discussion was very keen in my mind. This being the most prominent thing in my mind, I wrote out "Powell."

Sir Arthur asked me a number of questions, all of which I answered to the best of my ability. He thought that the spirit of his friend "Powell" was trying to come through to him, but I am certain it was simply for the sake of writing something that I wrote this name,—just the same as when I am waiting for a telephone message, with the receiver in my hand, my other hand is marking down numerals and letters.

I explained things thoroughly to Mrs. Houdini, as she is just as keen an observer at séances as I am. We both came to the conclusion that it was because of our discussion regarding Powell that I had written the name.

Houdini was sure of his motives for writing "Powell" and, when he returned home from Atlantic City, wrote to Sir Arthur:

June 19, 1922

My dear Sir Arthur:

On my return home I found the enclosed letter from my friend, F. E. Powell, whom I evidently meant when I wrote that name. I judge it was just one of those coincidences; and there is also a personal matter in connection with Powell which I must explain privately.

Apparently, Houdini did write again to Conan Doyle explaining the problem of the young female assistant, but this letter has now been lost. However, Houdini's reasoning did not convince Sir Arthur who promptly wrote back:

No, the Powell explanation won't do. Not only is he the man who would wish to get to me, but in the evening Mrs. M., the lady medium got "there is a man here; he wants to say that he is sorry he had to speak so abruptly this afternoon." The message was then broken by your mother's renewed message, and so we got no name. But it confirms me in the belief that it was Powell. However, you will no doubt test your own powers yourself. I'd like to see that report on Hope's mediumship, or anything about Marriott when I come.

William S. Marriott was a London professional magician who performed under the name of "Dr. Wilmar" and who, for some time, interested himself in Spiritualism. In 1910 he had been asked by the SPR to take part in a series of sittings with Italian medium Eusapia Palladino, and had concluded that all he had seen could be attributed to fakery. That same year he published four articles for *Pearson's* magazine in which he detailed and duplicated in photographs various tricks of self-claimed psychics and mediums. He is also famous for having located and made public a copy of *Gambols With the Ghosts: Mind Reading, Spiritualistic Effects, Mental and Psychical Phenomena and Horoscopy*, a secret catalogue of spiritualistic-paraphernalia and tricks then circulating among mediums. A copy of the catalog is still preserved in the Harry Price Library of Magical Literature at the University of London.

Marriott, along with Harry Price, was also involved in the Crewe Circle drama, thus explaining Conan Doyle's interest in the man. In 1921 James Douglas, editor of the *Sunday Express*, had a photo of himself taken by William Hope that, when developed, showed the presence of a spirit extra. Douglas was so impressed by the phenomenon that he issued a public challenge to anyone who could duplicate the feat without using psychic powers. Marriott accepted the challenge and performed not only in front of Douglas but also in front of Conan Doyle and Everard Feilding. He produced a picture of Douglas and Conan Doyle with a young woman and a picture of Conan Doyle with little fairies dancing in front of him. He then explained in detail how he had tricked them and Conan Doyle felt compelled to write a public statement: "Mr. Marriott has clearly proved one point, which is that a trained conjurer can, under the close inspection of three pairs of critical eyes, put a false image upon a plate. We must unreservedly admit it."

While his lecture tour was drawing to a close, Doyle had a chance to see Houdini's film *The Man from Beyond*, which he warmly praised. "I have seen the Houdini picture *The Man from Beyond*," he wrote in an open letter, "and it is difficult to find words to adequately express my enjoyment and appreciation of it. I certainly have no hesitation in saying it is the very best sensational picture I have ever seen. It is a story striking in its novelty, picturized superbly and punctuated with thrills that fairly make the hair stand on end."

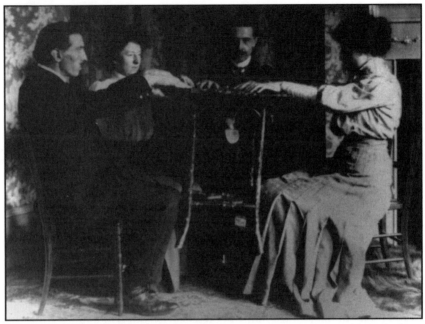

Magician William S. Marriott (second from right) shows how to fake a table levitation by raising it with his foot. (*Pearson's* magazine, 1910)

He later took time to write to Houdini, whom he was already seeing on his way to conversion after the séance in Atlantic City, to tell him about further contacts they had had with his mother:

> I can see you sometime, as your true experiences accumulate, giving a wonderful lecture, "Phenomenal Spiritualism—True and False," in which, after giving an account of your adventures with fakes, you will also give an account of those which bear inspection. It would be a very great draw. Fake photos and true ones. I could fit you up with a few of the latter. But you have other things to do at present. I may say that your mother again came back with words of passionate love through Mrs. M—— of Brooklyn last night. She said, "My son has now told his wife that he is mentally convinced of the truth of this revelation, but he does not see his way and it is dark in front of him. He is now seated in his room thinking it over." That would be about 11, or between 11 and 12 on Sunday night. I give it as we got it. . . .

A SURPRISE GOOD-BYE

As Conan Doyle was preparing for his return to England in a few days, he received a new invitation from Houdini:

> Mrs. Houdini and I are going to celebrate our twenty-eighth marriage anniversary June 22nd. Would you care to join us in a little box party? If so, we will go to see our friend Raymond Hitchcock, who was the Master of Ceremonies at the Magician's dinner, and who, at the present time, is starring at the Carroll Theater in his own Company, which he calls *Pinwheel*, a hodge-podge of good-natured stuff.

The twenty-second was the Doyles' last night in New York, for they would leave on the following day; however, despite tiredness, he gladly accepted Houdini's invitation. What happened that night can better be gathered by the following report, which appeared the next day:

> Sir Arthur Conan Doyle and Lady Doyle, who are sailing for England tomorrow on the *Adriatic*, unconsciously became the central actors in an extraordinary scene at the Earl Carroll Theatre last night.
>
> The distinguished English visitors, with Mr. and Mrs. B. M. L. Ernst, were the guests of Houdini and Mrs. Houdini at the theatre party, to witness Raymond Hitchcock's "Pinwheel Revue." It was an opportunity that the irrepressible Hitchcock, with his manner of intimacy with his audience, could not overlook. He called the attention of his audience to the presence of the noted author, and then, turning to Sir Arthur himself, inquired of him if he thought Sherlock Holmes could tell what Margaret Asquith herself wanted.
>
> Having made his start, Hitchy kept right on going. He announced the presence of Houdini and asked the arch-mystifier to come to the stage and do a little stunt. Houdini arose and boxed his acknowledgments to the applause that followed, but Hitchy was not satisfied with acknowledgments and insisted that Houdini help him make good his promise. Cries of "The Needle Mystery" came from the house. Houdini sat down; the audience continued to clamor while Hitchcock pleaded. In his plea he had an able backer in Sir Arthur, who literally pushed the unwilling Houdini upon the stage.
>
> What followed is a chapter for theatrical history. Houdini explained he had come to the theatre not to work but to be entertained. The cry for "the needle mystery" again arose, and Houdini finally announced that to make good Hitchy's promise he would do just one stunt—either the needle or the rope mystery. He left the audience to choose, and it decided upon the needle trick.
>
> The performance of "Pinwheel Revue" was stopped. Stage carpenters and electricians, principals and chorus people who, according to the rules of the theatre, should have been in their dressing rooms, flocked out on the stage.

Anything that the stage manager of the show may have done to time the performance was work done for nothing—at least on this occasion.

At Houdini's request, a Committee of three came upon the stage, and Houdini performed his needle mystery of swallowing five packages of needles and twenty yards of thread and bringing up the needles threaded.

Seldom has there been heard such applause as that with which Houdini was greeted at the conclusion of the mystery. He finally made his way to his seat, but, with the audience speculating on the mystery, the "Pinwheel" performance was curtailed and the show swung into its closing number. Such an incident is unique, for, though theatrical history records instances of artists "stopping the show" in which they were appearing, it contains no mention, in the memory of the theatrical historian, of the feat of an artist not only stopping but curtailing a show in which he was not programmed to have a part.

The next day Sir Arthur and his family sailed for England accompanied to the ship by the Houdinis. Before leaving them, Houdini took pictures of the Doyles and had some taken of himself with Sir Arthur. Then, as they were leaving, Houdini sent him the following telegram: "Bon Voyage. May the decree of fate send you back here soon for another pleasant visit. Regards. Houdini."

Later, he would send copies of the pictures with a brief note:

> Enclosed you will find two snapshots taken on the steamer the day you sailed away. I am pleased to see that there is a photo of Lady Doyle smiling. She told me it was very hard to get a good-natured photograph of herself, but you will agree with me that both of you are beaming with joy!

And a day or two later, Houdini would write again:

> I have mailed you a number of articles which appeared in the New York papers, as you might be interested in what they said after you sailed. . . . Every big newspaper man I have spoken to complimented you, to me, on the dignity with which you carried on your lecture tour. . . . I hope you had a pleasant trip.

During his stay with the Houdinis, Conan Doyle had also met Bernard M. L. Ernst, Houdini's lawyer and friend, and it was to him that he wrote, possibly regarding the "Pinwheel Revue" episode: "It was a pleasant evening that we had together, tho' poor Houdini had needles instead of a liqueur."

**Houdini says good-bye to the Doyles on board the *Adriatic*,
which would return them to England. (© Patrick Culliton)**

A Small Controversy

Despite the wealth of material and work that had accumulated during his
absence, Conan Doyle found time to write Houdini a brief note on the day
of his arrival, and a longer letter a couple of days later:

My dear Houdini:

I have a moment to look Westward instead of downwards, and I think of you among the first. . . .

What about Bert Reese? Is he the medium whom you quoted as having been exposed by Dingwall at your prompting? Because I hear stories of his proof in court to a New York magistrate, and also to Edison, which don't seem to fit into fraud.

There are the usual futile bickerings here—mere waste of breath and ink. I had a sitting with Mrs. Silbert,[2] an Austrian, who could talk no English, and we had (six of us) plenty of ectoplasm in a good light—the substance which the four professors of the Sorbonne have been unable to see! I daresay Eva is getting rather played-out. . . .

I had to write to the New York *Times* the other day about conjurers. Some fellow, whose name I have forgotten, had questioned my facts, which is always a dangerous thing to do, for I have chapter and verse fairly ready.

In his letter he said that you had "exposed" Eva. Of course I know that you have made no such claim, though you can truly say that you got no results from her. Madame Bisson also, in her private sittings, has recorded in her book that she frequently got no results. The word "exposure" is used in the most ridiculous way, but I am quite sure that you have never made such a claim.

The letter that Doyle had written to the *Times*, and that was published by the newspaper on June 18, ran as follows:

A CORRECTION

To the Editor of the New York *Times*:

Would you kindly note that it was Houdin, not Houdini, whom I quoted as having supported psychic phenomena. The latter is, I believe, quite open-minded on the subject.

After reading Doyle's letter and his correction published in the *Times*, and presumably to clear his position on the Eva case, while doing everything in his power to maintain smooth relations with Conan Doyle, Houdini too wrote a letter to the *Times*, which was published on July 5:

To the Editor of the New York *Times*:

Have read the letter of H. Edwards-Ficken and believe it calls for an explanation on my part. I did not expose Mlle. Eva, the protégée of Mme. Bisson, and had given my promise not to do so to the Hon. Everard Feilding, during the eight séances at the rooms of the Psychic Research Committee, in London, at which I was his guest.

I gave him my word that nothing would be published by me until after the Psychic Research Committee had published its proceedings regarding its séances. They were published about a month ago, which released me from my promise, and I can now give my views publicly. I feel that it is necessary to explain that I did not expose Mlle. Eva in London.

In the majority of these séances I was one of the Committee to examine and hold Mlle. Eva in the cabinet. Each séance lasted three hours, so I had ample opportunity in the twenty-four hours, which were spread over a period of at least one month, to carefully note what the medium was trying to do.

She positively did not do anything that would cause me to believe she was doing something which was not produced by natural means.

Have made minute detailed notes of the hundred séances which I attended and participated in on my last trip abroad, and although those present saw and heard extraordinary things, I was not convinced.

Am afraid that the greater part of things we read about in full-page articles are very much like Sabonee's materialization, which is now being so vigorously denied. At the time it appeared I knew it was not possible, and having gone carefully through Schrenck-Notzing's book, all I can say is that to my belief it could not have happened, but it might have happened in the minds of some who were there, or their confidences have been betrayed.

I have one of the largest libraries in the world on psychic and spiritualistic data; have personally met all the great mediums and am yet open to be convinced. I want to be put on record that I do not say there is no such thing as spiritualism, but state that, in the thirty years of my investigation, nothing has caused me to change my mind.

Having dealt with this, he wrote to Sir Arthur answering his latest letter:

You have heard a lot of stories about Dr. Bert Reese, but I spoke to Judge Rosalsky and he personally informed me that, although he did not detect Reese, he certainly did not think it was telepathy. I am positive that Reese resorts to legerdemain, makes use of a wonderful memory and is a great character reader. He is incidentally a wonderful judge of human beings.

That he fooled Edison does not surprise me. He would have surprised me if he did not fool Edison. Edison is certainly not a criterion, when it comes to judging a shrewd adept in the art of pellet-reading.

The greatest thing Reese did, and which he openly acknowledged to me, was his test-case in Germany when he admitted they could not solve him.

I have no hesitancy in telling you that I set a snare at the séance I had with Reese, and caught him cold-blooded. He was startled when it was over, as he knew that I had bowled him over. So much so that he claimed I was the only one that had ever detected him, and in our conversation after that we spoke about other workers of what we call the pellet test,— Foster, Worthington, Baldwin *et al.* After my séance with him, I went home and wrote down all the details.

I am looking up the report of the man I sent to Crewe, and who brought back photographs with spirits on them. I instructed this man to let Mr. Hope and Mrs. Buxton go as far as they liked. The method of manipulation, as described, is very interesting. It is too bad you were so rushed when you were in America; otherwise, I could have shown you the report. . . .

I believe you will find my answer in the *Times*, informing the gentleman who said I exposed Eva, that such was not the case. It was necessary for me, however, to make the statement that there was nothing there to convince me, or that she had, during the eight séances I visited, caused me to change my mind.

The other night I delivered a lecture on some slides which I had made, and notice that the papers put words in my mouth which I never used, which as usual I must get up and deny, as half the words attributed to "yours truly" were never said. . . .

To this, Conan Doyle replied:

Many thanks, my dear Houdini. If you say you *know* Reese to be a trickster, I shall take him as such. I hear he is in London, but have not seen him. . . . I shall have the pleasure of seeing you both again soon, as we return (the whole tribe) to finish my job in America. Then I am ready to sing *"Nunc dimittis, domine!"*

WRITING TO A FRIEND

During their friendship, Houdini would frequently write Conan Doyle to update him on some of his experiences, or to inform him of some curious news. It was a gentle way of keeping their relationship alive, also at times when they were both busy with their careers.

Once, for example, Houdini ran across a case of Out-of-Body Experience (although this kind of experience was not called this at the time) involving a man named Edward H. Morrell. The man had been confined in a straitjacket and, while struggling to get free, probably fell unconscious and had the feeling that his "soul" was leaving his body. He described to Houdini how he stood apart from it and could watch it objectively as one might view the body of another. The case impressed Houdini, who interviewed Morrell and later reported to Conan Doyle: "I have given a letter to Mr. H. Morrell, the original of Jack London's *Star Rover*, a man who has had the most unique position of having sensitized his faculties to a higher degree than is the opportunity of anyone."

Another time, while Conan Doyle was at sea, on his way back home from America, it was a book on poetry that prompted Houdini to write to his friend:

Something interesting has just occurred. When I was a boy at school in Appleton, Wis., my school teacher, a Miss Sanborn, was a great friend of Alice and Phoebe Cary, who, as you know, wrote some rather exquisite poems. I received a book with all the poems in it, but in the progress of time it was lost.

Last week, while browsing around a book stand, I happened to find a book, and if it is not the same one it must be an exact duplicate. I did not know that the girls were spiritualists but, on looking through the book, two nights ago, I ran across the enclosed copy of a poem written by Alice Cary, who was a firm believer in communication with those who have gone before.

Am sending it on to you, as Alice Cary must have written it with her heart. Hope you are having a nice trip. With kindest regards and best wishes.

> Laugh, you who never had
> Your dead come back; but do not take from me
> The harmless comfort of my foolish dream:
> That these our mortal eyes,
> Which outwardly reflect the earth and skies
> Do introvert upon eternity;
> And that the shapes you deem
> Imaginations just as clearly fall,
> Each from its own divine original,
> And through some subtle element of light,
> Upon the inward spiritual eye,
> As do the things which round about them lie,
> Gross and material, on the external sight.

On another occasion, Houdini ran across some documents that would have made Conan Doyle very happy:

It may interest you to know that I have just obtained a collection of over 100 autographed letters written by your father, Charles A. Doyle, to F. S. Ellis; all written in a humorous vein and relating amusing social experiences and exhibitions, with a great many clever pen-and-ink and watercolor drawings. The letters are dated from 1845 to 1853.

There is one letter in particular, which has two wonderful drawings and is highly interesting. He writes: "My dear Ellis: Here is a design for an historical picture. The subject is a battle in which the souls of the dead rose into the air and renewed the fight. If you like the subject, I think I will do a picture of it as large as life. Only I am afraid no one will appreciate its fineness and the grandeur of the two principal groups. Here is the night after the battle. What do you think of it? Have you read the last number of Dombey and if so how did you like it; is not the description of Mr. Goot's dog capital? It is the very image of our old dog Prinnz, especially in his propensity to bark in his sleep, which he used to do in a manner that was enough to make a horse laugh."

I do not know whether you know of the existence of this collection.

After Houdini's death, Bess sent the letters to Conan Doyle: "Houdini always intended to present it to you, that was the one thing in his huge library that was sacred and marked 'not to be sold at any price' . . . the letters are so beautifully sketched and you will find, as Houdini did, many beautiful forms of angels. My great grief is that my dear one was called before he himself could give it." Conan Doyle was touched by the gift: "It is beautiful and will mean much to the family, but it really seems like a series of miracles,—first that it should exist still, then that it should cross the Atlantic and finally that it should come back to me."

SPARRING WITH A FRIEND IN PRIVATE

Houdini and Conan Doyle's correspondence continued, with the exchange of a letter every few weeks. But something had changed between them, as Houdini's position as the chief opponent of Spiritualism came to be better defined and he found himself more and more in the limelight. Accustomed at booming his exploits as a master escapist, he may have slipped a few words on his "exposures" to a journalist, here and there, which, later, he had to correct unless he wanted to create a rift between himself and Conan Doyle. However, he had to express his opinions in clear terms and felt certain that his honesty would be appreciated by Sir Arthur.

In October, the *New York Sun* published an article by Houdini titled "Spirit Compacts Unfilled," in which he updated his readers on his investigations into the world of Spiritualism, and explained that his mind "is open. I am perfectly willing to believe, but . . . I have never seen or heard anything that could convince me that there is a possibility of communication with the loved ones who have gone beyond."

When Conan Doyle read this sentence he jumped up from his chair: how could Houdini say this after the séance he had with his wife in Atlantic City? Conan Doyle was certain that Houdini had then been convinced of the reality of the contact with his mother and could not believe that now Houdini denied as much. He considered this a personal affront and an insult to his wife. He immediately sat down to write to Houdini:

> They sent me the New York *Sun*, with your article, and no doubt wanted me to answer it, but I have no fancy for sparring with a friend in public, so I took no notice.
>
> But none the less, I felt rather sore about it. You have all the right in the world to hold your own opinion, but when you say that you have had no evidence of survival, you say what I cannot reconcile with what I saw with my own eyes. I know by many examples the purity of my wife's mediumship, and I saw what you got and what the effect was upon you at the

time. You know also that you yourself at once wrote down with your own hand the name of Powell, the one man who might be expected to communicate with me. Unless you were joking when you said that you did not know of this Powell's death, then surely that was evidential, since the idea that out of all your friends you had chanced to write the name of one who exactly corresponded, would surely be too wonderful a coincidence.

However, I don't propose to discuss this subject any more with you, for I consider that you have had your proofs and that the responsibility of accepting or rejecting is with you. And it *is* a very real lasting responsibility. However, I leave it at that, for I have done my best to give you truth. I will, however, send you my little book on Hope, but that will be my last word on the subject.

Meanwhile, there are lots of other subjects on which we can all meet in friendly converse. I hope your fine film will make your fortune, and that you will then cut the whole manufacturing side of it out, for it will bring you annoyance and loss and divert your mind from bigger things.

Houdini, however, did not want to "leave it at that," and proceeded to explain his motives in a letter dated December 15:

My dear Sir Arthur:

I received your letter regarding my article in the New York *Sun*. You write that you are very "sore."

I trust that it is not with me, because you, having been truthful and manly all your life, naturally must admire the same traits in other human beings.

I know you are honorable and sincere, and think I owe you an explanation regarding the letter I received through the hands of Lady Doyle.

I was heartily in accord and sympathy at the séance, but the letter was written entirely in English, and my sainted mother could not read, write or speak the English language. I did not care to discuss it at the time because my emotions, in trying to sense the presence of my mother, if there was such a thing possible, kept me quiet until time passed and I could give it the proper deduction.

Regarding my having written the name Powell. Frederick Eugene Powell is a very dear friend of mine. He had had two serious operations. He was financially embarrassed. Furthermore, Mrs. Powell had had a paralytic stroke at that time. He was practically stranded in a lone Texas town, and, although he never asked for any assistance, it was on my mind to financially aid him onto his feet,—he having been one of our star performers in his particular line when I was a struggling mystifier,—he having played the finest theatres in America, giving an entire performance,—he having been a professor of mathematics in the Pennsylvania Military College and now, with all his ability, education and experience he was unable to make both ends meet.

That was in my mind, and I cannot make myself believe that my hand was guided by your friend. It was just a coincidence.

I trust my clearing up the séance from my point of view is satisfactory, and that you do not harbor any ill feeling, because I hold both Lady Doyle and yourself in the highest esteem. I know you treat this as a religion, but personally I cannot do so for, up to the present time, and with all my experiences, I have never seen or heard anything that could really convert me.

Trusting you will accept my letter in the same honest good faith and feeling as that in which it was written.

With best wishes to Lady Doyle, yourself and the family, in which Mrs. Houdini joins.

Just to avoid any possible misunderstanding in the event of his death, Houdini decided a few days later to put in writing the details of the séance with Lady Doyle and have the document signed and witnessed before a notary public:

THE TRUTH REGARDING SPIRITUALISTIC SÉANCE GIVEN TO HOUDINI BY LADY DOYLE

Fully realizing the danger of statements made by investigators of psychic phenomena, and knowing full well my reputation earned, after more than thirty years' experience in the realm of mystery, I can truthfully say that I have never seen a mystery, and I have never visited a séance, which I could not fully explain; and I want to go on record regarding the séance given to me by Lady Doyle in the presence of Sir Arthur Conan Doyle, at Atlantic City, June 17, 1922.

Lady Doyle told me that she was automatically writing a letter which came through her, and was guided by the spirit of my beloved, sainted mother. Every boy who has ever had a worshipping mother and has lost earthly touch knows the feeling which will come over anyone at the thought of sensing the presence of his mother.

There was not the slightest idea of my having felt my mother's presence, and the letter which follows I cannot possibly accept as having been written or inspired by the soul or spirit of my sweet mother.

And the more do I refuse to accept the above letter, as, although my mother had been in America for almost fifty years, she could not read, speak or write English, and spiritualists claim that when you are possessed by the same spirit, who does not speak the language, they automatically write, speak or sing in the language of the deceased.

Regarding my having automatically written the name "Powell" on a piece of paper, I must emphatically state that this was written of my own volition; I knew what I was doing. I had the name in mind, and there was not the slightest chance of it having been more than a deliberate mystification on my part, or let us say a kindlier word regarding my thoughts, and call it "coincidence."

I put this on record so that, in case of my death, no one will claim that the spirit of Sir Arthur Conan Doyle's friend Ellis Powell guided my hand.

(Signed) Harry Houdini
State and County of New York,
Sworn to before me this 19th day of Dec., 1922
Agnes P. R. Boyd,
Notary Public Bronx Co., No. 141,
Certificate filed in N. Y. Co., No. 819
    Witnessed by,
    James A. Jackson
    220 W. 42nd, St., N. Y. C.

Notes

1. The majority of quotes from letters exchanged between Conan Doyle and Houdini have been taken from Bernard M. L. Ernst and Hereward Carrington, *Houdini and Conan Doyle* (New York: Albert and Charles Boni, 1932). This is the source of quotes in this chapter unless otherwise noted.

2. Maria Silbert (?–1936) was an Austrian physical medium who specialized in apports and psychokinetic phenomena. She claimed that a "Dr. Franciscus Nell" was her control, and one of his curious demonstrations was the engraving of cigarette cases, held under the table, with his name. It was only thanks to an investigation by Walter F. Prince, in 1927, that her real modus operandi was discovered: she had in fact developed the ability to maneuver a stiletto using only her feet and was thus able to write names on cigarette cases held under the table.

THE SCIENTIFIC AMERICAN COMMITTEE

5

T HE YEAR 1923 BEGAN IN the best of ways for Houdini and Conan
Doyle's friendship; however, by the end of the year their relationship would come to an end.

On January 1, Conan Doyle wrote to Houdini: "The best of wishes to
you and your dear wife from all of us for 1923. April 3 should see me in
New York, and April 6 I hope to face the music once more."[1]

Conan Doyle's 1922 American lecture tour and his upcoming new tour
in 1923 revived a strong interest by the public in psychic matters and
prompted the popular magazine *Scientific American* to take a public stand
on the subject. It had published various articles dealing with spiritualism
and "psychic sciences" ranging from hypnosis to auras, ectoplasm and the
Goligher Circle, table tipping and spirit photography. Now, it was time to
face these phenomena directly. The December 1922 issue ran the following
editorial:

> Is the *Scientific American* too ambitious in imagining that séances carried
> out under the immediate supervision of its editors, observed by them,
> reported by them at first hand in its columns, will be any more determi-
> native than the procedure which has heretofore ruled? We believe that per-
> haps we are not; that we stand so conspicuously as a disinterested party
> seeking only the truth and willing to give both sides a square deal, that our
> negative findings would get attention from those eager to believe and our
> affirmative ones from those inclined to scoff.

Having said that, the magazine announced the establishment of a prize
of $5,000 "to be awarded for conclusive psychic manifestations." In partic-
ular, $2,500 would go to the first person who could produce a psychic pho-
tograph under test conditions, and the other $2,500 to the first person who
could produce a visible psychic manifestation of other character. All of the
contestants would have to stand the scrutiny of a specifically established
committee.

Malcolm Bird with "spirit extra" in a
picture taken by William Hope in London.
(*Scientific American*, June 1923)

The January 1923 issue presented in detail the *Scientific American* psychic investigation; "its scope, conditions and procedure"; the names of the judges forming the committee; and the reasons for their selection. William McDougall, professor of psychology at Harvard University, and president of the American Society for Psychical Research (ASPR), was chosen because "a psychologist of repute must be on our committee," and "the name that occurs before all others" is his. Daniel Frost Comstock, formerly a member of the faculty of the Massachusetts Institute of Technology, noted inventor, and member of the Advisory Scientific Council of the Society for Psychical Research, was included since "there must be a physicist of the modern school, skilled in the design and use of special apparatus." Walter Franklin Prince (1853–1934), minister and pastor of numerous churches and principal research officer for the ASPR, was selected as one of "our experienced psychical researchers" along with Hereward Carrington as another, "particularly in the physical field." J. Malcolm Bird, a member of the editorial board of the *Scientific American*, and from the Department of Mathematics at Columbia University, would act as permanent secretary to the committee.

Houdini's presence as a member of the committee was explained in the magazine: "Houdini is so very well known in connection with his escape specialties that some of us may have overlooked his standing as a master of the more conventional sides of the magician's profession. At the same time he is deeply interested in psychic phenomena. He has wide experience in séance work, as well as in the detection of fraudulent mediumship." Furthermore, Houdini would serve "as a guarantee to the public that none of the tricks of his trade have been practiced upon the committee."

"The truth is," observed Edmund Wilson, ". . . that in a committee of scientists of which Houdini is a member it is Houdini who is the scientist. Doctors, psychologists and physicists are no better qualified to check up on spiritualistic phenomena than lawyers, artists or clergymen."

Aware of the risks of staking his reputation on the judgments of a committee, Houdini had agreed to lend his name and his services on the condition that he reserved the right to reject appointments to the committee. "Men easily deceived might be selected," he said in an interview in the *New York Tribune*, "and if a medium's work should be accepted by them, I would be the laughing stock of the public."

This was agreed to by the editors of the *Scientific American*, but when Houdini heard that they had selected a committee without consulting him he wrote the following letter:

November 13, 1922

Dear Mr. Bird,

I have just been informed by Mr. Hopkins that you have already selected a committee to serve as investigators for the $5,000.00 offered to the mediums.

So, that there is no mistake in this, I would like to have it understood emphatically, that when I consented to be one of your committee, it was under the condition that,

A. I am to know each and every man so selected.
B. That all conditions placed before the mediums should be thoroughly gone over with me, so that there could be no loop-hole for anyone to misconstrue the conditions of the manifestations required.
C. Another condition is that the selected committee will go to a number of séances for investigation purposes, so that we could get a line on each other regarding the capability of actually recording in writing what was seen, as mal-observation is the curse of all descriptions.

It was also stipulated in my conditions that we are to hold conferences to see whether all the committee are agreeable to each other, because we must work in harmony.

I have more at stake than the money you are offering, and that is, my reputation as a psychic investigator, and I, therefore, ask you to give me your full confidence, as I am giving you mine. I intend to serve you faithfully, and with all the knowledge I possess, but I ask to be fully protected in this.

May I suggest that it might be advisable for us to get together again before publicity is given, so as to prevent any mistakes on all our parts. I am keenly and intensely interested in the subject and will deem it a compliment to be on the committee, but if any of the above conditions do not meet with your approval, please count me out.[2]

Apparently, Houdini's conditions were approved and the committee formed. Not that Houdini was satisfied with all of the other members, however. For example, he had known Carrington for at least fifteen years, had discussed magic various times with him, and had warmly praised at least one of his books, *The Physical Phenomena of Spiritualism* (1910). "Your book," he had written to him, "is certainly the best ever written on the subject,—at least that I have ever read." However, he had doubts about Carrington's sincerity, since he had acted as a personal manager for Eusapia Palladino, one of the most famous, and probably the most frequently exposed medium of all times. According to Malcolm Bird, during a preliminary meeting, Houdini and Carrington's differences emerged from the beginning, when they argued "well into the night" about some technical problem related to the investigations.

When Houdini informed Conan Doyle of his new position as an official "psychical investigator," he played down his role:

> The *Scientific American* has asked me to act as one of the five on the Committee to investigate mediums accepting some kind of a challenge which they are supposed to have issued. Not knowing exactly what the challenge is, and thinking it would be best for me to be "among those present," I willingly accepted.

Doyle immediately wrote back and expressed his doubts as to the committee and, particularly, as to Houdini's place upon it:

> I see that you are on the *Scientific American* Committee, but how can it be called an impartial Committee when you have committed yourself to such statements as that some Spiritualists pass away before they realize they have been deluded, etc.? You have every possible right to hold such an opinion, but you can't sit on an impartial Committee afterwards. It becomes biased at once. What I wanted was five good, clear-headed men who would stick to it without any prejudice at all—like the Dialectical Society of London, who unanimously endorsed the phenomena. However, it may work out all right. . . .

MALCOLM BIRD AND SIR ARTHUR

Conan Doyle also wrote a letter to Orson D. Munn, editor of the *Scientific American*, advising against the risk of offering money for some mediumistic demonstration because, he opined, this would "stir up every rascal in the country." "I don't understand the necessity or wisdom," he also declared to the *New York Times*, "of publicly offering prizes for conclusive manifestations of psychic photographs. This is a direct invitation to the rogues of two continents." He thus offered his cooperation to the magazine, suggesting that he put them in touch—for free—with the best European mediums. Since it would have taken some time to properly set up the committee, receive the letters of the first claimants, and arrange for the tests, the editor decided that, in the meantime, the magazine could start publishing a series of articles dealing with direct observations of famous mediums. Malcolm Bird was assigned to the project.

Bird left for England on February 10, 1923, and when he met Sir Arthur he found him very charming and courteous: a feeling reciprocated by Conan Doyle. Bird, in fact, appeared to lean more toward belief than skepticism and Doyle certainly appreciated that fact. Later, he would express this appreciation by declaring: "They cannot continue to think I am a credulous fool so long as my observations are corroborated by such [a] man as Bird." His opinion was that Bird was "rapidly acquiring so much actual psychic experience that if he should criticize our movement he

Photo of Bird (right) and Conan Doyle in London, taken by William Hope. (*Scientific American*, June 1923)

is a critic to whom we shall be obliged to listen with respect—which is not too common an experience."

Bird was admitted to his first séance on February 23, when he met John C. Sloan, a voice-medium who performed in the dark. During the séance Sloan spoke with different voices and phosphorescent lights could be seen blinking in different spots in the room. Considering the absence of controls, Bird failed at first to be impressed, but was more convinced when the lights appeared far from the medium.

In March they met Evan Powell, whom Conan Doyle considered one of the best living mediums. From inside a cabinet, where he was strapped, Powell was able to ring bells, have flowers fly out of it, and produce other physical manifestations. Bird described this as "the best séance that I had in England," adding: "After attending this and other séances, the occurrence of genuine psychic phenomena of a physical character impresses itself upon me as less improbable than I should have judged it to be in the absence of experience."[3]

Bird also had a chance to sit with William Hope, of the notorious Crewe Circle, and with Mrs. Gladys Osborne Leonard (1882–1968), the medium who had convinced Sir Oliver Lodge that his son, Raymond, killed during the war, could still talk to him. With Hope, Bird first had his picture taken sitting beside Conan Doyle; then, in a picture in which he was alone, two extra faces appeared. After discussing all the possible explanations, Bird concluded: "I will say that to me the probabilities seem good that the Hope picture . . . constitutes a genuine psychic phenomenon."[4]

He then interviewed Charles Richet and Gustave Geley in Paris and saw the famous spirit-molds preserved at the Institut Métapsychique International. In Berlin he inspected Dr. Grünewald's remarkable laboratory for tests of physical phenomena with no mediumistic candidates for testing. While in Germany, he also had the opportunity of having a sitting with Maria Vollhardt, a medium who specialized in obtaining strange stigmatas in her hands. Bird suggested that the "angry-looking pricks" could be made with the use of a battery of three or four forks or a section of a nutmeg-grater.

All of the articles by Bird, later collected in a book titled *My Psychic Adventures*, however, bore a very cautious statement from the editors that probably made Houdini happy and Sir Arthur annoyed:

> Apart from what he may have learned regarding advantageous séance procedure, it is to be emphasized that Mr. Bird's mission in Europe has no connection with our American investigation, with our offer of $5000 for genuine physical manifestations of psychic powers, or with the work of our Committee of Judges in that investigation. Mr. Bird went to Europe merely to get, for presentation to our readers, first-hand personal impressions as to the nature of these physical phenomena, about which so much has been written and so little really understood. His mere description of the wholly unscientific conditions under which he sat would alone make it plain that nothing further than this could come out of his experiences.

In April, Bird and the Doyle family boarded the White Star Line ocean liner *Olympic*—very similar to another tragically famous White Star liner, the *Titanic*—to reach New York. Conan Doyle, in fact, was going to start a second lecture tour of the western states of the United States.

Houdini had already begun a new tour with his magic show for the Orpheum Circuit (this was a theater circuit, another was Keith's), but had agreed with the other members of the committee that he was ready to cancel any show should his presence be needed for a specific investigation. The main reason why he was performing escapes onstage once again was that he needed the money to finance his cinematic ventures.

Upon learning of his new tour, Conan Doyle, despite their now-increasing differences, had written to him: "For goodness sake take care of those dangerous stunts of yours. You have done enough of them. I speak because I have just read of the death of the 'Human Fly.'[5] Is it worth it?"

CONAN DOYLE STARTS HIS SECOND TOUR

On April 8, Conan Doyle delivered his first lecture, as he had done the previous year, at New York's Carnegie Hall. In it, he told the audience of the recent talk he had had with the spirit of his friend W. T. Stead, who had died on the *Titanic* eleven years before. He also showed slides of spiritistic wax gloves and, despite his talks with Houdini, declared that it was impossible to withdraw a human hand from it without breaking the mold. The Society of American Magicians offered to show him how the trick could be done: "The spirit glove in boiling paraffin can be reproduced in a material manner," explained illusionist Servais Le Roy. Conan Doyle never replied to the offer.

Joseph F. Rinn, the Houdini friend and skeptic, was present at the lecture. Rinn offered Conan Doyle $5,000 if he would agree to be shown how he had been tricked by mediums. "I think that Sir Arthur has been buncoed again," said Rinn to the *New York Herald*. "He had some more trick photography imposed upon him. But I believe he is sincere, even if he is deluded. What he believes is evidence cannot be called that."

The *New York American* asked Rinn to attend a number of Doyle lectures and then write a critical analysis of them for the newspaper. That analysis appeared on April 29, 1923, and prompted Sir Arthur to write a long and angry reply: "I do not as a rule answer articles which contain personal attacks, for I am indifferent to them. But I feel that indifference might be mistaken for weakness, and that it is my duty to expose the ignorance and malevolence of the writer." Conan Doyle then continued to reply to the various critiques invented by "Mr. Rinn's fanciful brain." The following day he wrote to Houdini: "I wasted a whole day yesterday in answering an article of Joseph F. Rinn. I think it broke the record of all the fallacious statements which I have ever had to correct." In a letter to Bird, Conan Doyle also wrote: "My answer to Rinn's broadside appears on May 27 in all the *Herald*'s 4,500,000 readers. I think my gunnery is better than his."[6]

During his tour, Conan Doyle also had a chance to sit once more with Ada Besinnet, in Toledo, Ohio. After his first visit, during the previous year, Besinnet had been accused of fraud by publisher Fulton Oursler, who had attended a séance and caught her doing tricks. Conan Doyle did not care for the exposé and called Oursler a "hostile witness." On April 26, he brought along to the séance his new friend, J. Malcolm Bird. "We were greatly favoured that evening," wrote Doyle later, "for we had the whole gamut of the medium's powers, the powerful voices, the wonderful musical performances, the brilliant lights, the fitful materialisations, the written messages, the continuation of the songs even when a bandage was over the lady's lips, and finally the whole heavy table was lifted bodily onto the air. It was a very impressive exhibition, and Mr. Bird was as interested as I was."

"The voices," confirmed Bird to the *New York Times*, "came from the centre of the table at first and then moved about the room. One bass voice was tremendous; it would have filled a church. There was also whistling in accompaniment to the music, very clear, loud whistling of extraordinary quality, the best I ever heard in my life."

HOUDINI AND CONAN DOYLE IN DENVER

Houdini's and Conan Doyle's paths crossed in Denver, Colorado, on May 8. The Doyles attended a performance by Houdini at the Orpheum Theatre. "We sent them a bunch of violets and five pounds of candy for little Billy, the little tom-boy daughter of the Doyles," wrote Houdini in his diary. "They sat in a box and certainly enjoyed the show."

Between acts, Conan Doyle went to Houdini's dressing room and had a long chat with him, detailed in part in Houdini's notes:

> I showed him a number of books that I was reading, relative to the power of the mind and the body.
>
> Sir Arthur said that he was capable of detecting trickery, and we had a discussion in which I said that I did not think he could. He looked amazed at me, and I said, "Why, Sir Arthur, I have been trained in mystery all my life and every once in a while I see something I cannot account for."
>
> He replied, "I am perfectly willing to stand by my offer of two thousand pounds if Rinn will produce spirit photographs under test conditions the same as Hope's."
>
> I said: "But then it is a simple matter to get figures on a plate."
>
> He said: "Yes, but I shall ask him for one of my relatives."
>
> I said: "You might be able to take care of yourself, but when it comes to trickery, you can rely on me for any assistance in my power."
>
> "That is very nice of you, Houdini, and I will remember it."

They met again the following morning, took a car, and, after an hour's drive, sat in a park. All the while, they discussed various subjects. One of these was Father de Heredia, a Jesuit priest who was at that time touring the country, giving lectures on Spiritualism, and showing demonstrations of some tricks of the mediums. Doyle insisted that de Heredia was no match for real mediums. He had tried to demonstrate fake spirit photography at the offices of the *Scientific American* but had been caught hiding something in his hand: "He asked someone to write the name on an exposed negative first," wrote Houdini in his notes, "and then said 'I might as well sign it'. As we [sic, should read "he"] put his hand on the plate, someone in the office saw that he had some object in his hand. Father Heredia is supposed to have said: 'Let us go through with this now.' "

They also talked about Carl Wickland of Los Angeles, who claimed to cure cases of spirit possession by spiritual means. "He would lay them down and have the evil spirits go into the body of his wife. The evil spirits would leave the body of the possessed and get into the body of his wife, and the wife, being a very healthy creature, Dr. Wickland easily made the evil spirits leave his wife's body. In this way he cured patients."

Once again, Conan Doyle insisted that the Zancigs were genuine: "He said," wrote Houdini, "that, at the time he gave his lecture, no word was spoken. Mr. Zancig's back was turned and the medium duplicated the ship that Sir Arthur drew. I tried to tell him that Zancig acknowledged to me in front of witnesses that he never claimed telepathy, but all this did not move Sir Arthur or Lady Doyle."

Conan Doyle gave Houdini a letter of introduction to Bruce Kemp, a trumpet medium of Chicago:

Dear Mr. Kemp:

I hope that you will give a sitting to Mr. and Mrs. Houdini, who are deeply interested in psychic phenomena. With Mr. Perlman you will make quite a sympathetic circle. I should much like him to hear "Redfoot's voice."

Kemp, Conan Doyle explained, had a voice so powerful that it hurt his eardrums, and he had to ask the Indian guide to moderate his voice. Also, Conan Doyle added, the hands of the medium were under constant control, rendering it impossible for him to speak into the trumpet. "Of course," noted Houdini in his diary, "this is his description to me and, upon investigation, very likely I shall find things entirely different."

While in the United States, Conan Doyle kept up his correspondence with Malcolm Bird and that same day wrote to him:

I had a talk with Houdini today & he answers me that the papers misrepresent his attitude and that he is not intolerant at all so that made ease [?] things with the Commission. What he really wants is evidence in which he has been singularly unfortunate but my experience with my wife needs me to think that he may reject good evidence when it is put before him. . . . I have given H the address of young Kemp with the noisy control, in Chicago whither he goes next week. If he can get results there it may help him. But he is obsessed by the idea that everyone can be and is fooled bar himself.[7]

Conan Doyle appeared to be very anxious for Houdini to meet Kemp, for he wrote later to the magician: "I wonder if young Kemp gave you a demonstration of his Indian's powers? I had a nice note from him, but he did not mention it." And again later on: "Let me know if you heard from

Bruce Kemp, the young voice medium." It appears, however, that the meeting never took place.

"Doyle Defies Houdini"

Later, on May 8, Houdini picked up the newspapers and found, to his surprise, an article in the *Denver Express* headlined: "Doyle in Denver defies Houdini and offers to bring back dead again." The article ran as follows:

> Sir Arthur Conan Doyle, here to preach his gospel of spiritism, is going to back his psychic forces with $5,000 against the skepticism of Harry Houdini, the magician, who recently asserted that all séance manifestations were fakes. The famous writer so asserted on his arrival from Colorado Springs late yesterday when informed Houdini was also in Denver.
>
> "Houdini and I have discussed spiritism before," said Sir Arthur. "I have invited him to attend a sitting with me, each of us backing our beliefs with $5,000. I have even offered to bring my dead mother before him in physical form and to talk to her. But we have never got together on it."

That evening Beatrice Houdini attended Sir Arthur's lecture. Later she would give her thoughts on the lecture to her husband: "Bess goes to Doyle lectures," read Houdini's diary. "Says mine is more interesting and convincing, but I told her, yes, Doyle is a historical character and his word goes far, in fact much further than mine"—to which Bess added below this entry: "I don't think. B.H."

When Houdini arrived at the lobby of the lecture hall to pick up his wife, Sir Arthur approached him. He "profusely apologized to me," noted Houdini, "for the challenge which appeared in the Denver *Express.*" The magician replied that he was not offended, since "frequently the papers misquote people."

Sir Arthur, however, was still hurt by Houdini's feelings on the Atlantic City séance, and thought that maybe his difficulty in accepting the reality of the message from his mother could be due to a limited understanding of the laws governing the afterlife. Later, in fact, he would write to Houdini:

> Concerning your difficulty about your mother's language, there is really nothing in that. Mrs. Wriedt or any trance or half-trance medium might get the Hebrew through. I don't think a normal automatic writer ever would. It would always come as a rush of thought, which is translated in coming, or else as a message through the Control of the medium. In your case, the great excitement assures me that it was direct.
>
> You will remember that you asked a mental question, and admitted at the time that the answer was to point. Also, that very night, we had allu-

sions to what had occurred through an independent person who knew little of the matter. If all this is coincidence, and Powell a coincidence as well, then it is more marvelous than the very simple explanation that love can bridge the grave and show that it can, if we obey the laws. . . .

By the way, Mr. Bird told me that, in the very complete test given you by your mother, you found it incredible that she, a Jewish lady, should put a Cross at the top. The cross is put by my wife above the first page of all she writes, as we guard against lower influences, and find it protective. . . .

Only a trance medium gets unknown tongues. A normal inspirational medium is used to transmit the thought, and often character and even phrases,—but not unknown tongues. . . .

ON THE HISTORY OF SPIRITUALISM

During their meeting after Conan Doyle's lecture, they discussed various subjects as usual. Houdini told Conan Doyle that he had "a number of extraordinary spirit slate tests of a mechanical order," and that he would allow him to examine the slates thoroughly. He was convinced that any check notwithstanding, it was "impossible to discover the method." Doyle, however, didn't show much enthusiasm at the idea that so excited Houdini. "He did not seem greatly interested in Slate writing," noted Houdini.

Bess observed that such a long lecture could be a strain on Sir Arthur. She suggested that after an hour's lecture Sir Arthur should have a rest period of ten or fifteen minutes, allowing the audience to talk and soft music to play. Conan Doyle thought it was an excellent idea. In his diary, Houdini noted with a bit of not very well hidden pleasure: "In the Denver *Post* there was hardly anything about Sir Arthur's lecture at the Ogden Theatre. The Theatre was comfortably filled but I do not think it was a 'turn away.' In my estimation, if this man was circussed he would be turning away thousands."[8]

The talk then turned to the Fox sisters, who as girls had started the Spiritualism movement in 1848 from their little cottage in Hydesville, New York, where mysterious rappings started to be heard one night. The rappings soon developed into a form of communication, with young Kate and Margaret Fox acting as the mediums, and it was thus "discovered" that spirits could communicate with the living. That was the real beginning of Spiritualism as a mass movement: thanks to those rappings, at first thousands, and then millions, of people came to believe in communication with the afterlife through psychic mediums. When forty years later in 1888, Margaret and Kate admitted publicly that it had all been a fraud, and that they produced the rappings by snapping their toes, the movement had become so large and powerful that the confession didn't matter much to anyone.

Conan Doyle, for example, would not even believe that Margaret, denouncing Spiritualism from the stage of the New York Academy of Music, had really demonstrated how she could rap her toes. "This might be discounted," he wrote in his *History of Spiritualism*, "upon the grounds that in so large a hall any prearranged sound might be attributed to the medium." However, the October 22, 1888, *New York World* had reported on that occasion: "A committee consisting of three physicians taken from the audience then ascended the stage, and having made an examination of her foot during the progress of the rappings, unhesitatingly agreed that the sounds were made by the action of the first joint of her large toe. The demonstration was perfect and complete and only the most hopelessly prejudiced and bigoted fanatics of Spiritualism could withstand the irresistible force of this commonplace explanation and exhibition of how spirit rappings are produced."

In any case, to Conan Doyle the Fox sisters where like saints and Hydesville seemed to him like a sort of shrine. He had even started a subscription among Spiritualists to raise a memorial "to the great occurrence at Hydesville in 1848 which has modified and glorified the lives of so many."[9] While talking with Houdini, he said that he had been too busy, when he had played Rochester, to visit Hydesville. However, he added and Houdini noted in his diary, "he was liable to go at the end of his Lecture Tour, and that it was agreeable to him that we should both visit Hydesville, making a special trip to go there, so we could make the pilgrimage together."

The pilgrimage, as well as the construction of the memorial, never happened. Although Conan Doyle appealed in Spiritualist papers, such as *Light* and the *Two Worlds*, to donate money for the memorial, it appears that the idea did not interest the Spiritualists. On March 10, 1923, in fact, Conan Doyle regretfully wrote to *Light*: "The response to my appeal for some central memorial of our Cause has been so scanty that I cannot bring myself to present it. I am, therefore, returning the money to the various subscribers whom I hereby thank."

Doyle also informed Houdini that he was going to write a history of Spiritualism: "as a start," noted Houdini, "he said he had already a man (Canow) who was 'deviling' for him. He meant the man was doing Research work for him. He said that McCabe[10] had written a History of Spiritualism but like a man half-convinced, and he, Sir Arthur, thought that he could write the book and make it interesting and important."

A last note regarding Doyle and Houdini's stay in Denver occurs in Houdini's diary, under the date of May 11:

> I called Sir Arthur's attention to a book that was loaned to me by a lady stopping at our hotel, Mrs. Eleanor P. C. Lewis: the book called: *Life Understood*, by F. L. Rawson.

I asked Sir Arthur if he was acquainted with this man and he said: "Yes, this man is no good. During the war he would charge the women 30Sh. for a prayer which, he said, would keep the bullets from wounding their sons. He is a bad lot," repeated Sir Arthur. "Any man that does that cannot be good."

I am writing these things in my day-book, realizing that Sir Arthur is a huge success in the literary world, and a great many things he says or does will be of interest at some future time.

Houdini may also have decided to take detailed notes of his meetings with Conan Doyle because he did not want further misunderstandings to arise from what was said during their talks. Despite this precaution, however, misunderstandings would soon appear to be inevitable, as the following episode illustrates.

While chatting in Denver, Houdini had expressed to Conan Doyle his difficulty in finding a copy of his book *Our American Adventure*. Conan Doyle explained that he was still working on it, but had the manuscript in rough form. "When I get the book ready," said Conan Doyle, "I will let you have it. Now it is all scribbled."

"That is the beauty of the MS," replied Houdini.

"As soon as I return, I will send it to you."

"I assure you I will appreciate it very much."

"You will have it on my return," confirmed Doyle.

Some time later, Houdini reminded Sir Arthur of his promise to send him the manuscript. Having forgotten the incident, Doyle replied:

A promise—especially to a friend—is very binding with me, but I wish you could recall more precisely to my memory how I promised you last year to send you the MSS of *Our American Adventure*. I think that you surely confused the book with the MSS. I can't help feeling that the latter should be kept in my family, for my descendants, for if this mission of mine has any appreciable effect in altering the religious opinion of the world, then the time will come when the account of my travels may be very interesting and even valuable to those who follow me. I may say that the value of one of my longer MSS now, in the open market, is several hundred pounds, but that would not in the least prevent my fulfilling a promise if such a promise was made. But I have no recollection of speaking of anything beyond the printed book. Or was it in a letter?

When Houdini recalled the conversation to Conan Doyle, however, he wrote back at once: "You shall certainly have the MSS. You will excuse me if, in the rush of events, I did not carry it in my mind."

In one of his last letters, Doyle commented on one of Houdini's many good actions: "It was good of you to give those poor invalids a show, and you will find yourself in the Third Sphere all right, with your dear wife, world without end, whatever you may believe."

"Pray," he did conclude on a sour note, "remember us all to your wife. Mine is, I am afraid, rather angry with you."

ALEXANDER MARTIN'S SPIRIT PHOTOGRAPHS

On his leave for Salt Lake City, Conan Doyle suggested that Houdini should visit Alexander Martin, a Denver spirit photographer. Houdini went to visit Martin, an elderly, bearded man, accompanied by his trusted assistant Jim Collins: "So I would have a witness if anything of a psychic nature occurred," noted Houdini. This is what happened next according to Houdini:

> When we went into the house I walked right into the dark room but Martin called me saying: "Now don't you go in there, just wait a minute." While we waited outside Martin spent about eight minutes in the dark room. Then he came out and we went into his studio, a simple room with a black background. He had me sit down and placed Collins behind me on my right. As a test I told Collins to step over to the other side as it might look better. Then when he had done so I turned to Martin and asked: "Is that all right or is it better to have him take the original position?"
>
> "I think it would be nicer if he stood where he was in the first place," Martin replied.
>
> This led me to think he was keeping that side of the plate clean for something to appear.[11]

Martin took a couple of photographs, then said: "That is all I can do to-day. Now I must hurry away." On the following day, Houdini returned for a second sitting and Martin gave him the pictures of him and Collins, showing various extra faces, one belonging to Theodore Roosevelt and another one to Italian criminologist Cesare Lombroso (1835–1909), who had been one of the most ardent supporters of Eusapia Palladino, the medium. The odd thing was that three out of the five faces wore glasses: do the spirits have bad eyesight even in the afterlife, wondered Houdini?

"I have not the slightest doubt," wrote Houdini later, "that Mr. Martin's Spirit photographs were simply double exposures. I think his method was to cut out various pictures, place them on a background and make an exposure. His plates were then ready for his next sitter, which in the above instance was myself. . . . I am convinced that the two Spirit photos which he made of me were simply double exposures."[12]

Anxious to inform Conan Doyle about his meeting with Martin, Houdini wrote him: "In my last letter, I believe, I told you that I had two sittings with Mr. Alexander Martin of Denver. I will show you the photographs at the first opportunity." He also added: "I have been invited this evening to a séance of a trumpet medium in the offices of the *Scientific American*. If you will send me your address, I will give you the full facts."

Conan Doyle wrote back:

Five thousand people last night, and a good, psychic, religious atmosphere. It is a really splendid place and fine people. I am very much impressed.

I read the Eddy article.[13] The whole story seems to me an extraordinary example of human credulity, but she must surely have been a very magnetic, remarkable woman, for there are no effects without causes. I can see nothing in the whole business, for "faith healing" is as old as history. And yet they have filled the world with their great temples, while we, with the greatest revelation that the world has ever known, can hardly get a roof to cover us. But poverty wins in the long run!

The "Arena" is not to hand yet, but I have no doubt I shall get it. Our affectionate remembrance to your lady, whom we much admire. You are among the eternity mates—most marriages are temporary.

VALIANTINE ACCEPTS THE CHALLENGE

By May 21 the *Scientific American* finally found a medium who was willing to sit for the judges and try to win the prize. His name was George Valiantine (1874–?), a Pennsylvania voice-medium of some notoriety, the same "trumpet medium" to which Houdini had made reference in his letter to Conan Doyle. Just like other mediums of his kind, Valiantine worked in the dark with zinc trumpets, instruments through which, it was supposed, spirits could make their voices better heard by the sitters.

The first sitting, held without test conditions, so as to get the medium accustomed to the sitters and vice versa, took place in the *Scientific American* library. Malcolm Bird was present as well as Carrington, Prince, various journalists, and a friend of the medium. Once the room was darkened, a few quick phenomena took place: voices were heard and touches felt by some committee members. "All that occurred," wrote Bird in the final report, "came with a suddenness well calculated to startle the sitters into momentary inability to observe closely; and was gone before that ability was regained."[14] Although he never went into a trance, and was vigilant all the time, Valiantine had asked that nobody ever turn the light on while the séance was in progress. This raised suspicions even in Bird, especially after an interesting incident that occurred during the séance, when

Prince had placed his right foot farther forward, and "a spirit (had) trod partly upon it."

For the sitting of May 22, in which magician Fred Keating participated as well, a few luminous buttons had been hidden on some walls and between books. In the darkness Valiantine or his friend, from their positions, could not see them, but the experimenters could and they were placed in such a way as to allow notice of any movement on the part of the medium. When Valiantine asked whether spirit lights were manifesting themselves, Bird explained that those were luminous buttons: but Valiantine could not have seen them without leaving his chair. Later, when the trumpet apparently was floating in the air, Keating raised his hand and grabbed the trumpet. The spirits apparently did not appreciate the unexpected move, and nothing else happened that night.

For the last séance, on May 24, Houdini dropped his other engagements and went to New York. "One of the first things done by the medium," remembered Prince, "was to stand in front of me and ask the entire company not to stick their feet out. But he looked accusingly at me, and it was evident that he knew whose outstretching foot the spirit had stepped on, Monday evening."[15] Other surprises, however, were in store for the medium. Without him knowing it, a new control had been added to the séance room: Valiantine's chair had been wired. Whenever he left his seat a light flashed on in an adjoining chamber and a note was made of the time. For fifteen times, that evening, the light flashed and when, later, the time of the flashes was compared with the time line of the phenomena recorded it was apparent that phenomena took place only when Valiantine left his chair. Confronted with the evidence, Valiantine's only defense was that "the disappearances of the light were caused by his shifting his position in the chair."[16]

The final report, published in the July issue of the *Scientific American*, concluded that "the medium has failed to give any evidence whatever that his mediumship is genuine . . . and that his claim to the prize and to the Committee's further attention stands vacated."

The report, however, came only after Houdini had taken full credit for the exposure. The day following the final séance, in fact, the *New York Times* published an article in which it was revealed that "Houdini denounces as outright fake alleged spirit manifestations by George Valentine [*sic*]." Bird was annoyed and said so to the reporter of the *Times*: "We had an understanding that what occurred at tests was to be kept secret until we published our report." Houdini replied that "there was no string tied to my invitation, and I feel at liberty to tell just what happened. I was not pledged to secrecy, although there has been an awful lot of reticence on the part of those present."

Bird replied by saying to the press that Houdini had been ousted from the committee for betraying its trust. To which Houdini pronounced Bird an "amateur" who could be "fooled by any high class magician." He had revealed the exposure, he said, because he feared he might be seen as a "simpleton" by his friends.

This time the press did not take Houdini's side, as it frequently did, and instead criticized him for revealing the nature of a trap that could have been used with other mediums: "This is a regrettable consequence of Mr. Houdini's hurry to convince his friends that he was not such a 'simpleton,' " wrote the *Times* on May 30, 1923. "Except for that, probably half a dozen Valentines [*sic*] could have been exposed, and the impressiveness of the disclosures would have been greater."

THE FRIENDSHIP IS STRAINED

While the Valiantine tests were going on, Conan Doyle gave an interview to the *Oakland Tribune* in which he replied to certain statements made by Houdini to the same paper. Following the interview, he wrote to Houdini:

> I have had to handle you a little roughly in the Oakland *Tribune*, because they send me a long screed under quotation marks, so it is surely accurate. It is so full of errors that I don't know where to begin. I can't imagine why you say such wild things which have no basis in fact at all. I put the Thompsons down as humbugs. I never heard of my son or brother through the Thomas brothers. They were never exposed. I never said the Masked Medium was genuine. I wish you would refer to me before publishing such injurious stuff, which I have to utterly contradict. I would always tell you the exact facts as I have done with the Zancigs.
>
> . . . I hate sparring with a friend in public, but what can I do when you say things which are not correct, and which I have to contradict or else they go by default? It is the same with all this stuff of Rinn's. Unless I disprove it, people imagine it is true.

Still not satisfied, Conan Doyle wrote another letter the following day:

> Dear Houdini:
>
> In continuation of my letter of yesterday, I must really ask you to deny over your signature these three injurious statements which you have made, none of which have the slightest truth in them—so that this denial may be published in the Oakland or any other paper which has contained such statements.
>
> They are:
>
> A. That I ever endorsed the mediumship of the Thompsons.
> B. That I ever claimed that my son or brother came through the Thomas mediums.
> C. That I ever endorsed the mediumship of the Masked Lady.

I am very sorry this breach has come, as we have felt very friendly towards Mrs. Houdini and yourself, but "friendly is as friendly does," and this is not friendly, but on the contrary it is outrageous to make such statements with no atom of truth in them.

I do not wish to argue the points, but simply that you accept unreservedly my assurance that all three statements are false and that you contradict them.

It was probably a repeat of what had happened in Denver: the journalist who had interviewed Houdini had stretched his replies, filled them with details, so that a series of eight articles could come out of one single interview. Conan Doyle, forgetting that the same thing had happened to himself, had jumped to the conclusion that Houdini wanted to insult him. No wonder he wrote, shortly after this:

Our relations are certainly curious and are likely to become more so, for so long as you attack what I *know* from experience to be true, I have no alternative but to attack you in return. How long a private friendship can survive such an ordeal I do not know,—but at least I did not create the situation.

When Houdini had a chance to reply, he was by that time also being criticized by the New York papers for the interviews in which he had divulged the trap used during the *Scientific American* séances with Valiantine. He felt constrained to write to Sir Arthur to give his side of the case, but did not address the specific points raised by Sir Arthur in his letters:

My dear Sir Arthur:

I am commencing to believe that at last I am "famous"? Newspapers are misquoting me.

There is quite a stir here about a medium who was detected, and it seems that the *Times* had one of their reporters at the séance, with the understanding that the manner in which the medium was detected would not be written until the *Scientific American* had been published. A very big misunderstanding has arisen, in which the giving out of the information is placed up to me, which I can easily explain.

It is too long to write about it, but will tell it to you in person when you arrive.

Mrs. Houdini joins me in sending kindest regards and best wishes to Lady Doyle, the children and yourself.

MEDIUMS AND TRUST

The mediums who provoked the strain between Houdini and Conan Doyle were the Thomas brothers, the "Masked Lady," and the Thompsons.

Tom and Will Thomas were two brothers living in Penylan, a mining village in the south of Wales. Their spirit guide, as was so often the case in those days, was a Native American, by the name of "White Eagle." In a typical séance the two brothers would be tied to their chairs and, when the lights were turned off, objects would fly about the room. Sir Arthur and Jean had participated in a séance with the brothers in 1919. Lady Doyle was asked whether she was cold; on answering in the affirmative a heavy jacket that belonged to Will fell into her lap.

Houdini had questioned Conan Doyle about the manner in which the brothers were bound: "He told me that they were secured so tightly that it was impossible for them to move as they were absolutely helpless. I told him that did not make it genuine, for any number of mediums had been tied the same way and had managed to free themselves."

Conan Doyle had replied that Houdini might be able to release himself by natural means, but that "mediums do not have to, as they always receive Spiritual Help."

"Maybe so," countered Houdini, "but I should like, sometime, to tie them myself and see whether the Spirits could release them under test conditions."

As for the statement that so irked Conan Doyle, Houdini commented: "I never claimed that Sir Arthur's son or brother came through the Thomas mediums in Cardiff. I did state that Sir Arthur said they were genuine and that they, the mediums, were helpless to move because he had tied them and in his judgment if they were tied in my presence I would be convinced of their genuineness."[17]

The "Masked Lady" episode dates back to the same period as that of the Thomas brothers. As soon as the news that Conan Doyle had participated in séances with the brothers became public, the editor of the *Sunday Express*, James Douglas, offered £500 to any spiritualist or medium who could prove beyond all doubt that he or she could make contact with someone recently dead. Conan Doyle was able to convince the Thomas brothers to participate, but the only noteworthy occurrence that took place was that one Spiritualist claimed that a pair of suspenders had landed in his lap. The award was not assigned and Conan Doyle, who had not participated, decided that he had to be present at a future occasion.

A new séance was organized and Conan Doyle joined a committee including Lady Glenconner, Sir Henry Lunn, a superintendent from the Metropolitan Police, and the editors of the *Occult Review* and *Light*. The new medium was introduced by a magician who, in the past, had exposed false mediums but had undergone a conversion and was now convinced of the reality of Spiritualism. The medium to be examined was a London lady who wore a veil like a "yashmak," as the reporters described it. She was tied to a chair and the lights were turned off. She began giving personal details about the sitters and, when it was Conan Doyle's turn, she talked about his son Kingsley.

"She was able," said Doyle to the *Sunday Express*, "to tell me the initials on the ring of my boy—who died some months ago—although the average person examining it would perhaps make nothing of it. It was so worn that it would be excusable if you could not make anything of it even if you had the ring before you. So far as the second part of the programme was concerned, that is a different matter. Before a decision can be made, one must attend several séances with the same medium. One certainly saw a floating light. But although I was sitting in the front row, and was quite close to it, I could not make anything of it. I should have to see it again before passing a definite opinion on it. In any case, I think that the proceedings were instructive and clear. But I have my doubts about the whole thing."

He was right in being skeptical for the séance had been a hoax, staged by the magician to get publicity for a theatrical show that, by the way, never materialized.

"I did not say he endorsed her," stated Houdini afterward, "although I should judge from newspaper accounts he seemed very much impressed." Apparently, Houdini had not seen the *Sunday Express* interview.[18]

The Thompsons incident took place during Conan Doyle's first tour of the United States, in 1922. The Thompsons of New York, not to be confused with the Tomsons of Chicago, who we shall meet later in this chapter, were a married couple, William R. Thompson and his wife, Eva. Mrs. Thompson was considered to be a "materializing" medium, with a "sensitive nature attuned to the finer harmonies of our etherealized dead." Her sensitivity apparently allowed her to bring back the dead "in materialized form, and even make them speak."

In a typical séance, Mrs. Thompson would take a seat in a cabinet while the sitters were instructed by Mr. Thompson to sing hymns throughout the proceedings. The lights were extinguished and, after a long wait, ghostly forms would materialize. When Conan Doyle participated in a séance with them he immediately, "overcome with emotion," recognized his mother and was able to touch her hand. In one version of the episode, Conan Doyle kissed the hand, in another he watered it with his tears.

"The chance to touch my mother's hand," he said afterward, "and feel the substance there; the chance to see her force, was very precious to me."

Only three days later, two undercover policemen participated in a séance and, as soon as a form emerged from the cabinet, they wrestled it to the ground. The lights were turned on and the spirit proved to be Mrs. Thompson dressed in iridescent robes. The couple was arrested for fraud. All the newspapers published lengthy exposes, with titles like "How the Mediums 'Brought Back' Sir Conan Doyle's Dead Mother."

Houdini had participated in a couple of public séances with the Thompsons and, on one occasion, had heard them mention that they had been tested and subsequently endorsed by Sir Oliver Lodge. When Lodge was informed of this he wrote to Houdini: "I would be grateful if you would make it known that any statement that I have vouched for their genuineness, is absolutely false. . . . I only saw them once. . . . I considered the performance fraudulent, but the proof was not absolutely complete because the concluding search was not allowed, and the gathering dispersed in disorder. . . . What I should like the public to be assured of, is that I was *not* favorably impressed, and never vouched for them in any way."[19]

As for Conan Doyle, the incident was particularly troublesome. Although he had expressed great emotion during and after the séance, he would later deny that he had been fooled; he stated that he had known all along they were fakers but did not wish to offend his host by expressing his doubt openly. "Both my wife and I," he would later write in *Our American Adventure*, "were of the opinion that the proceedings were very suspicious and we came away deeply dissatisfied, for there were no test conditions and no way of checking such manifestations as we saw."

By August 4, Conan Doyle had finished his tour of the West and was boarding the ship that was going to take him back to London. This time, however, there was no Houdini at the pier to wish him a good trip and to take pictures. Although they would exchange a few letters, they would never meet again.

Before leaving, however, Conan Doyle clearly expressed to Houdini his views on the *Scientific American* committee:

> The Commission is, in my opinion, a farce, and has already killed itself. Can people not understand that "psychic" means "of the spirit," and that it concerns not only the invisible spirit or the spirit of the medium, but equally those of every one of the Investigators? A delicate balance and harmonious atmosphere are needed. I fear some of your recent comments which I have read would not only keep away every decent medium—for they are human beings, not machines, and resent insult—but it would make spirit approach impossible, for they also do not go into an atmosphere which is antagonistic. Thus a certain class of researcher always ruins his result before he begins. However, no one is the worse, save himself, for there is a huge responsibility in the matter.

FRAUDULENT MEDIUMS FOR THE *SCIENTIFIC AMERICAN*

After the experience that Valiantine had with the *Scientific American* tests, for a while there appeared to be no more mediums interested in the prize. By October, however, two more psychics stepped forward.

The first was a Reverend Josie K. Stewart, a little lady who appeared to be able to obtain writings on cards held in her hands. In a typical demonstration, she would tear off the petals of various flowers and would place them at intervals between cards in the pack, the reason for this being that the petals were assumed to produce the "ink" for the writings and drawings. She would then pick up petals and cards and hold them on top of someone's head that she felt was "receptive." After a while, the cards were checked and usually a few had writings on them.

For the official tests, the medium was given forty-nine blank cards: no messages appeared during the first three tests, but the experimenters noticed that five cards were missing from the pack. Finally, the fourth séance, held in the open air, bore success: messages, purporting to come from the spirits of William James and W. T. Stead, appeared. The medium thought she had won the prize, instead she had been unmasked. Between séances, in fact, Bird had had the cards shortened on one side by a few millimeters: the cards with the messages were longer. This meant that the messages had appeared on the five lost cards that, evidently, had been stolen by the medium during the first séance so that she could prepare them at home. When Reverend Stewart was informed that there was no point in continuing the investigation, she agreed in tears.

The other medium who had agreed to be tested was Elizabeth A. Tomson, of Chicago, a materializing medium who had been expelled by the National Spiritualist Association for fraud. Oliver Lodge, who had sat with her, had commented afterward: "To my mind there was no evidence of anything of a supernormal character."[20]

Houdini as well had a chance to sit with Mrs. Tomson in Chicago, some time before. It was an unfortunate occasion for the medium because a picture was taken in which she could be seen faking phenomena. At the time, Houdini had detailed Conan Doyle about the incident; however, Sir Arthur was not convinced. He wrote to Bird: "He [Houdini] told me that he could see the foot of Mrs. Tomson in the photo taken with him in Chicago but he clearly had never heard of a transformation. I should think the real argument is that where media is faking she would take particular notice that her foot was not visible."

Conan Doyle had explained his theory to Houdini as well, but Houdini didn't seem convinced. "Coming back to the Thomsons [sic]," Houdini wrote in his diary, "I explained to him [Conan Doyle] that, without my permission and sanction, there was a flashlight photograph taken by the photographer. He said he had seen the various photographs and believed positively that what I thought was a veiling was a transfiguration which, he said, meant that the Ectoplasm oozed out of the body of the medium and covered it, while she was in an unconscious state, and would go walking out of the cabinet covered with that ectoplasm."[21]

Conan Doyle had great esteem for Mrs. Tomson's powers, if not for her morality. He admitted to Houdini that the Tomsons "are unscrupulous and posses a lack of morality," but, he added, "I believe they are genuine." And Lady Doyle commented: "There are great opera singers who are immoral, but who have a great voice, and may be compared with unscrupulous mediums."

When addressing someone more "receptive," however, Conan Doyle's thoughts on the medium appeared to be softer. "You'll have to take Mrs. Tomson of Chicago seriously," he wrote to Bird. "I have been examining the evidence & photos and am so impressed that I am as near conviction as can be. It is her fool of a showman husband who queers it all. But she is true to type."[22]

"With all his brilliancy and child-like faith," considered Houdini in his diary about Sir Arthur's reasonings, "it is almost incredible that he has been so thoroughly convinced, and nothing can shake his faith."

As could be expected, when Mrs. Tomson was informed that for the official tests with the *Scientific American* Commission she would not be allowed to conduct the experiments as she pleased, and that fraud-proof conditions would be imposed, she withdrew.

NINO PECORARO: THE ENERGETIC ITALIAN

If there had been no need to call on Houdini to test Valiantine and Tomson, the need soon arose when a third medium came forward. His name was Nino Pecoraro (1899–1973), an illiterate Italian from Naples who could produce physical manifestations after having been tied to a chair. Dr. Anselmo Vecchio, his mentor and interpreter, explained that the phenomena manifested through Nino were due to his "control," the famous Neapolitan medium Eusapia Palladino, who had died a few years earlier.

Carrington, who had introduced Pecoraro to Conan Doyle the year before, had also proposed that the medium participate in the *Scientific American* contest. Pecoraro held four séances for the *Scientific American* judges, on December 10, 14, and 18. During the first séance, Nino was tied to a chair with sixty feet of rope; beside him was placed a table holding tambourines, bells, and trumpets: he was then hidden from view by a curtain. After a while noises were heard from behind the curtain: raps, ringing, and shrieks from Nino. At the end of the séance, Nino was found lying on the floor, still tied to the chair. The same events happened during the second séance.

O. D. Munn, the editor of the *Scientific American,* suspected that Nino had somehow been able to free one hand to play the instruments. Munn wired Houdini, then playing in Little Rock, Arkansas, urgently requesting his presence in New York. Houdini took the first train and, when he arrived at the December 18 séance, he was amazed to discover the kind of controls that had been imposed upon the medium. Nobody, he explained, could be securely fastened with one long piece of rope: it was too easy to get some slack and get free. He cut the rope into a dozen shorter pieces and with those proceeded to tie Pecoraro: it took him almost an hour and forty-five minutes to finish the job, but after that all the phenomena disappeared and Nino did not win the prize.

Houdini described the episode to his friend Harry Price in a letter dated December 19, 1923:

> Last night I tied up a medium for the *Scientific American.* He is called the "boy wonder" but is 24 years of age. There were no manifestations with the exception of raps which he managed to make by striking his foot on the side of the cabinet.
>
> They asked me to tie him up so that he could not move—and he stayed put. Personally, I believe the man is mad and thinks the "spirits" help him.
>
> He is a powerfully built fellow, has great curved shoulders and an enormous amount of endurance—but he did not get out. You will read a detailed account later on.[23]

A fourth séance was held, where Dr. Vecchio did the tying, but though phenomena returned, at the end of the sitting the wires and cords were found forced, the canvas gloves were wet with saliva and showed teeth marks, while the bells were covered with fingerprints.

No formal decision was rendered by the judges, since Dr. Vecchio, who still protested that his medium was genuine, was granted the privilege of more sittings in January. These, however, appear not to have been claimed by Pecoraro.

CONAN DOYLE COMMENTS

Sir Arthur Conan Doyle, in a long article published in the December 22 issue of the Spiritualist paper *Light,* criticized the *Scientific American* tests and defended Mrs. Stewart's honesty; his statements, however, were full of errors and false interpretations, which made his observations useless. "It is an abuse of words," he wrote, "to say that a verdict is impartial if it will cost the judge five hundred pounds to give it." In reality, the money for the challenge, as clearly stated from the beginning, did not come from the judges but from the *Scientific American*, with whom the committee had no connection. Sir Arthur, however, ended his article: "I have slowly and painfully been forced to the conclusion that none of these newspaper inquires are honest or useful. They are not carried out to find truth, but they are carried out to disprove truth at any cost."

Surprisingly, two months later, Sir Arthur returned on the subject of Mrs. Stewart's honesty in a brief letter he wrote for *Light* February 2, 1924:

> In an article in *Light* some weeks ago, I pointed out some weak points in the case made by the investigators of the *Scientific American* against Mrs. Josiah [*sic*] Stewart. I explained at the same time that I had never tested this medium myself, and that I was merely commenting upon the face-value of the report before me. Since then I have had the opportunity of reading the details of an investigation held by the leading Spiritualist authorities of the United States some eighteen years ago, in which they come to the unanimous conclusion that Mrs. Stewart's phenomena were fraudulent. This seems to me quite final and entirely justifies the *Scientific American* in its conclusion.

Although this may seem a brave letter, it contains an inaccuracy, since Conan Doyle's comments on the *Scientific American* tests were not based on "the report before me," but mainly on "an account from Mrs. Stewart's husband," who, by the way, was not at the sittings. Once more, Conan Doyle had showed his readiness to believe blindly what the mediums or other Spiritualists told him, and he had changed his mind only after discovering that Mrs. Stewart had been declared fraudulent, some eighteen years before, *by the leading Spiritualist authorities of the United States.*

A few days after the Pecoraro episode, on December 24, Houdini received one of the last letters from Conan Doyle. It had taken about five months for him to reply to Houdini's previous letter:

> Dear Houdini:
>
> I was surprised and sorry to get your letter because you force me to speak, and I have no wish to offend you. But you can't have it both ways. You can't bitterly and offensively—often also untruly—attack a subject and yet expect courtesies from those who honour that subject. It is not reasonable. I very much resent some of your press comments and statements, and I wrote you from San Francisco to tell you so.
>
> At the same time I wish you personally all good—and your wife most cordially the same.

The end of Houdini and Conan Doyle's strange friendship was now very near.

NOTES

1. The majority of quotes from letters exchanged between Conan Doyle and Houdini have been taken from Bernard M. L. Ernest and Hereward Carrington, *Houdini and Conan Doyle* (New York: Albert and Charles Boni, 1932). This is the source of quotes in this chapter unless otherwise noted.

2. Harry Houdini, *Houdini Exposes the Tricks Used by the Boston Medium "Margery"* (New York: Adams Press, 1924).

3. Malcolm Bird, *Scientific American* (May 1923).

4. Ibid.

5. On March 5, 1923, Harry F. Young, known as "The Human Fly," fell ten stories from a window ledge of the Hotel Martinique, in New York City. About this event, Houdini noted in his book *A Magician Among the Spirits* (1926; reprint, New York: Arno Press, 1972): "For the benefit of those who do not know, 'A Human Fly' is an acrobat who makes a specialty of scaling tall buildings, simply clinging to the apertures or crevices of the outward architecture of such building for the edification of an assembled throng, for which he receives a plate collection, a salary or is engaged especially for publicity purposes. It is not a very lucrative profession and its dangers are many."

6. James Randi Collection. Reprinted with permission of the James Randi Educational Foundation.

7. Ibid.

8. Kenneth Silverman, *Houdini!! The Career of Erich Weiss* (New York: Harper-Collins, 1996).

9. *The Two Worlds*, January 19, 1923.

10. Joseph McCabe was a representative of the British Rationalist Press Organization. He had debated on Spiritualism publicly with Conan Doyle in London, in 1920, and had come out a loser. He had made the mistake of doubting that scientists were really involved in Spiritualism. "I courteously challenge him," McCabe had declared, "to give me in his first speech tonight the names, not of fifty, but of ten, university professors of any distinction who have within the last thirty years endorsed or defended spiritualism." Conan Doyle couldn't ask for a better challenge, and in fact had gone on, to the cheers of the Spiritualists present at the debate, naming dozens of professors who, like Richet, Crookes, and Lombroso, had endorsed Spiritualism.

11. Houdini, *A Magician Among the Spirits*.

12. Ibid.

13. The "Eddy" referred to here is Mary Morse Baker Eddy (1821–1910), the founder of the Christian Science Church.

14. Malcolm Bird, *Scientific American* (July 1923).

15. *Journal of the American Society for Psychical Research* 18, no. 6 (June 1924).

16. Ibid.

17. Houdini, *Magician Among the Spirits.*

18. Ibid.

19. Ibid.

20. Ibid.

21. James Randi Collection. Reprinted with permission of the James Randi Educational Foundation.

22. Ibid.

23. Gabriel Citron, *The Houdini-Price Correspondence* (London: Legerdemain, 1998).

MARGERY THE MEDIUM 6

IN THE CENTURY-LONG HISTORY OF serious psychic research, the "Margery" episode is probably one of the most interesting. No other medium since D. D. Home, not even Eusapia Palladino, had been able to attract as much interest and controversy as Mina Stinson (1888–1941), better known as Margery, the "Blonde Witch of Lime Street." Like Home, Mina (her birth name) didn't ask for money for her demonstrations but, unlike her predecessor, she refused even donations or jewels. No ignorant peasant coming from a country town, like Eusapia, she was the wife of a respected and wealthy Boston physician, Dr. Le Roy Goddard Crandon. By all accounts Stinson was brilliant and quick-witted. In her early thirties, she was described as very attractive, with blue eyes and long brown hair.

LIFE AT LIME STREET

The events that interest us began in the spring of 1923, at Number 10 Lime Street, a four-story brick house in the stylish neighborhood of Beacon Hill in Boston.

Margery's husband was a dour and aristocratic man, with many hobbies and interests beyond medicine, ranging from a passion for the sea to the study of the writings of Abraham Lincoln. It was inevitable that this nimble mind would turn to a subject that interested everybody in the 1920s: psychic research. His interest was sparked by a meeting he had with Sir Oliver Lodge, who had suggested a book to Crandon, *The Physical Structures of the Goligher Circle* by Dr. W. J. Crawford. After reading the story of Kathleen Goligher and her family, strange thoughts crept into the doctor's mind.

Was it really possible, wondered Crandon, that the "psychic cantilevers" that Crawford talked about existed? In Crawford's opinion these were sort of "ectoplasmicrods" emanating from the body of the medium, and considered to be responsible for the movement of objects and lifting of tables in the dark. And if so, how could these "pseudopods" have the strength to lift even a table? Crandon decided to find out for himself and in a few weeks had a table built to the exact specifications of the one that had been used in the Goligher case.

On May 27 Crandon sat around the table with his wife and a few friends on the top floor of the house in Lime Street. The chamber was darkened and following Crandon's instructions, the sitters joined hands and waited. Mina felt silly. "They were all so solemn about it that I couldn't help laughing," she recalled. "They reproved me severely, and my husband informed me gravely that 'This is a serious matter.' "[1]

Suddenly, the table moved slightly. Then it moved again and tilted up on two legs. Someone suggested they try to find out which one of them might be the medium, so each sitter left the room one at a time. Since the table continued to rock and stopped only when Mina departed, there was no doubt: she was the medium.

MINA THE MEDIUM

Mina had originally been married to the owner of a small grocery store, Earl P. Rand, and had always been a vivacious, active woman. She and Rand had a child, but later divorced. As a teenager she had played in professional bands and orchestras, had worked as a secretary, loved sports, and was active in various church social action groups. The marriage to Crandon required that she give up her dynamic lifestyle, in those days not suitable for a physician's wife. The new experience of the May 27 séance provided a pleasant change from the confined life of leisure of a wealthy woman.

For the whole summer the Crandons held private séances in their home. The doctor became more and more excited every time he discovered his wife had a new "power." Her abilities seemed limitless and he only had to read about some new mystery and "Psyche"—as he had begun to fondly call her—would duplicate it at the next séance. Raps and flashes of light were among the earliest phenomena to appear in the darkness of her séances and, along with more traditional effects like the movement of the table, Mina appeared to be able to stop a watch simply by concentrating on it, or to produce dollar bills and live pigeons, things that seemed to be taken directly from the repertoire of a magician. Soon there was a new turn.

Mina had conducted her séances while awake and fully conscious of her surroundings when her husband suggested that she try to fall into a trance. The request met with immediate success and various "entities" started to communicate through the medium. One of these began to appear more frequently and came to dominate. Dr. Crandon and the others agreed that this visitor had to be Walter, Mina's brother. Walter Stinson had died twelve years earlier, at the age of twenty-eight, crushed by a railroad boxcar. Walter's voice, which became Mina's spirit control for the next eighteen years, not surprisingly was the same as Mina's, only a little more hoarse. His language was scurrilous and he had a ready wit and irritable manners, a personality quite foreign to the kind and polite lady medium.

In August of 1923 Dr. Crandon wrote an enthusiastic letter to Conan Doyle, telling him about his wife's wonderful abilities. Before he even met her, Doyle immediately declared that he was convinced the phenomena were genuine "beyond all question." When, in December, Crandon took his wife to Paris and London to build up a consensus of favorable opinions from European experts, Conan Doyle finally had a chance to sit with her. During the séance, held at Conan Doyle's London flat in Buckingham Palace Mansions, Walter came through, a bell rang, and a dried flower fell at Lady Doyle's feet. Conan Doyle declared himself satisfied, "so far as one sitting could do so, as to the truth and range of her powers."[2]

He immediately told J. Malcolm Bird about her, insisting that the committee should investigate her powers. Before that, however, Bird had a chance to sit with her in London, in a sitting given in the rooms of the Society for Psychical Research. Reviewing Bird's account of this sitting, V. J. Woolley, the Society's Honorary Research Officer, writes that this is "the only case in which [Bird's accuracy as a reporter] can be estimated by us in his account of the sitting at the S.P.R. rooms in 1923, in which he describes Mr. 'Feilding' as a conjurer and the table as 'the celebrated trick table of Mr. Harry Price.' In point of fact Mr. Feilding is not a conjurer, and the table is in no sense a trick table and was not designed by Mr. Price."

THE SCIENTIFIC AMERICAN INVESTIGATES

In November 1923 Bird paid a visit to the Crandons in Boston and there he met again what he had found an undoubtedly interesting couple: a somber doctor and a spirited, cheerful, and fascinating woman. Mina's charm clearly affected him, so much so that many would later question the reliability of his observations, as Woolley had done in London. Bird had already given the same impression when he commented with particular kindness on the demonstrations of a medium about whom others had serious doubts. On that occasion, Walter Franklin Prince, reviewing Bird's book, *My Psychic Adventures*, wrote: "Mr. Bird, if he wishes to achieve the authority in psychical research which I invoke for him, must hereafter avoid falling in love with the medium."[3]

Conan Doyle spent four days in Lime Street and became very close to the Crandons, and particularly to Mina, whom he found "an extremely keen person."

Margery with "spirit extra." When this picture was first published in *Scientific American*, Margery's face was cut off in order to protect her privacy. (*Scientific American*, 1924)

Before leaving Boston, Bird invited Mina to enter the contest announced by the *Scientific American*. She agreed and specified that if she won, the prize would go to psychic research. She even insisted in paying all the expenses that might arise from the investigation, including those for the committee's stay in Boston. The only condition that she imposed was that the committee should come to her instead of her going to them. The Crandons would lend their house to the investigators.

An article about the medium, written by Bird, appeared in the July 1924 issue of the *Scientific American*. To protect Mina's privacy, Bird renamed her "Margery"; "Walter" was called "Chester," and Dr. Crandon became "F. H." (Friend Husband). The readers of the *Scientific American* learned that at last a potential winner of the prize had arrived: "With 'Margery,'" Bird wrote, "... the initial probability of genuineness [is] much greater than in any previous case which the Committee has handled."

The committee then moved to Boston; Bird and Carrington, and occasionally the other members of the committee, gladly agreed to be guests of the Crandons during the investigation. William McDougall, living in Boston, remained at his home, while W. F. Prince "preferred to stop at a hotel."

Harry Houdini, the only member of the committee who was not informed about the investigation, had to rely on the newspapers to find out what was happening, and what he read piqued his skeptical interest, to say the least: "Margery, the Boston Medium, Passes all Psychic Tests"; "Scientists Find No Trickery in a Score of Séances"; "Versatile Spook Puzzles Investigators By Variety of His Demonstrations." The surprise was even greater when, opening the July issue of *Scientific American*, Houdini learned that the investigators of Margery's claims were his colleagues on the committee. And newspapers titles like "Experts Vainly Seek Trickery in Spiritualist Demonstration; Houdini the Magician Stumped" didn't help his mood: he was furious. Why hadn't he been informed? Bird tried to explain the position to Houdini in a letter:

My dear Mr. Houdini:

As you will observe when you get your July *Scientific American*, we are engaged in the investigation of another case of mediumship. Our original idea was not to bother you with it unless, and until, it got to a stage where there seemed serious prospects that it was either genuine, or a type of fraud which our other Committeemen could not deal with. Regardless of whether it turns out good or bad, there will be several extremely interesting stories in it for the *Scientific American*; and these will run in the August and following issues.

Mr. Munn feels that the case has taken a turn which makes it desirable for us to discuss it with you. Won't you run in, at your convenience, to take lunch with one or both of us, and have a talk with Mr. Munn?

Better call me in advance, and make sure that he and I will be in at the time you select.[4]

Houdini arrived at the New York's offices and asked Bird directly: "Do you believe that this medium is genuine?"

"Why, yes," answered Bird, "she is genuine. She does resort to trickery at times, but I believe she is 50 or 60 percent genuine."

"Then you mean that this medium will be entitled to get the *Scientific American* prize?" Houdini asked.

"Most decidedly," Bird replied.

Houdini pulled no punches: "Mr. Bird, you have nothing to lose but your position and very likely you can readily get another if you are wrong, but if I am wrong it will mean the loss of reputation and as I have been selected to be one of the Committee I do not think it will be fair for you to give this medium the award unless I am permitted to go up to Boston and investigate her claims, and from what you tell me I am certain that this medium is either the most wonderful in the world or else a very clever deceiver. If she is a fraudulent medium I will guarantee to expose her and if she is genuine I will come back and be one of her most strenuous supporters."

Then turning to Munn he said: "If you give this award to a medium without the strictest examination, every fraudulent medium in the world will take advantage of it. I will forfeit a thousand dollars if I do not detect her if she resorts to trickery. Of course if she is genuine there is nothing to expose, but if the *Scientific American* by any accident should declare her genuine and she was eventually detected in fraud *we would be the laughing-stock of the world*, and in the meantime hundreds of fraudulent mediums would have taken advantage of the error."

"Well," replied Munn, "then you and I will go up together and see."

"All right, I am at your service."[5]

The Wizard and the Witch

Houdini and Munn arrived in Boston on July 22 and took rooms at the Copley Plaza Hotel. Houdini was shocked at hearing that Bird and Carrington had accepted the Crandons' hospitality, or, as Joe Rinn, a friend of Houdini, put it: were being "wined and dined as the guests of Margery and her husband." How unbiased could their judgment be if they were guests of the party that they were asked to investigate? But the accommodations, as later became known, were not the only blandishment offered to the members of the committee. Carrington, for example, had borrowed some money from Dr. Crandon, and Bird had even received a blank check for his expenses. An even more dangerous influence, however, threatened the integrity of the investigators: the attractions of Mina, who wore only a filmy dressing gown and silk stockings during the séances. She obviously enchanted Bird and only many years later was it known that she and Carrington had very likely slept together.[6] "It is not possible to stop at one's house [sic]," Houdini explained, "break bread with *him* frequently, then investigate *him* and render an impartial verdict."[7]

July 23 was the day scheduled for the first sitting with Houdini present. That morning, Crandon wrote Conan Doyle that Margery was "vomiting merrily" at the prospect of meeting the magician.

A feat that had baffled the members of the committee involved the use of a wooden box with an electric switch that when pressed would ring a bell placed inside the box. In the previous sittings the box had been put on the floor between Margery's feet, and the bell had rung even while the medium's hands and feet were supposedly being held. For control there was a member of the committee on the left and her husband presumably doing the same on the right. With the medium so "immobilized," the sitters reasoned that the one responsible for the phenomena could only be Walter the spirit-guide. When Houdini arrived he sat on the medium's left and the box was placed between his feet. His hand held that of the medium while his ankle would control her leg. Houdini picks up the story from there: "All that day I had worn a silk rubber bandage around that leg just below the knee. By night the part of the leg below the bandage had become swollen and painfully tender, thus giving me a much keener sense of feeling and making it easier to notice the slightest sliding of Mrs. Crandon's ankle or flexing her muscles."[8]

The precaution appeared to be crucial when, after pulling up her skirts well above her knees, Margery asked for darkness. In fact, continued Houdini in his account of the séance, "I could distinctly feel her ankle slowly and spasmodically sliding as it pressed against mine while she gained space to raise her foot off the floor and touch the top of the box. To the ordinary sense of touch the contact would seem the same while this was being done. At times she would say: "Just press hard against my ankle so you can see that my ankle is there," and as she pressed I could feel her gain another half inch. When she had finally maneuvered her foot around to a point where she could get at the top of the box the bell ringing began and I positively felt the tendons of her leg flex and tighten as she repeatedly touched the ringing apparatus."[9]

When the bell stopped ringing, Houdini felt the medium's leg slowly slide back to its original position on the floor. Bird sat at her right with one hand free to "explore" and the other on top of the hands of both the medium and Dr. Crandon. Suddenly, Walter asked for an illuminated plaque to be placed on the lid of the box that held the bell. Bird got up to

**Margery and the *Scientific American* Committee: (from left) W. F. Prince,
D. F. Comstock, Margery, O. D. Munn, and Harry Houdini. (Harry Houdini,
Houdini Exposes the Tricks Used by the Boston Medium "Margery," 1924)**

get it and at that moment Walter called for control. Margery placed her free
hand in Houdini's and immediately the cabinet was violently thrown backward. The medium then gave Houdini her right foot and said: "You have
now both hands and both feet." Then Walter called out: "The megaphone
is in the air. Have Houdini tell me where to throw it." "Toward me," replied
the magician and it instantly fell at Houdini's feet.[10]

Despite the clever work of misdirection created by the medium, Houdini had been able to understand what had really happened in the darkness. When Bird had left the room to search for the luminous plaque,
Margery was left with her right hand and foot free. This had allowed her to
tilt the corner of the cabinet enough to get her free foot under it; then,
picking up the megaphone she placed it on her head, dunce-cap fashion.
She was then able to throw the cabinet using her right foot which she
would later give to Houdini. While it would appear that Margery was under
complete control by Houdini, simply jerking her head would cause the
megaphone to fall at his feet. After the séance, Houdini commented: "This
is the *slickest* ruse I have ever detected." He would also express his admiration for Margery's ability, a few weeks later, in a letter to Harry Price: "There
is no doubt in my mind, whatsoever, that this lady who has been 'fooling'
the scientists (?) for months resorted to some of the slickest methods I have
ever known and honestly it has taken my thirty years of experience to detect
her in her various moves. The greatest thing she did was under full control,
where you held both her feet and both of her hands, was to have the megaphone lifted in the air and be thrown in any direction the investigator
desired. Will send you drawings and particulars."[11]

Margery stands at the front door of her home at 10 Lime Street. (McManus-Young Collection, Library of Congress, Rare Books and Special Collections Division, LC-USZ62-99115)

Houdini had seen through deception after just one séance while the other members of the committee hadn't, even after thirty. Bird resented his air of superiority and was close to Dr. Crandon in his dislike of the man. Crandon, as well as Bird, had shown racist hatred for Houdini, when in a letter to Conan Doyle he had expressed his regret that "this low-minded Jew has any claim on the word American."[12]

The Second Séance

The following night, Margery agreed to hold the séance in the hotel suite in which Dr. Comstock stayed. This time, the group sat around a table, with Houdini to the left of the medium. Walter ordered everyone to move back from the table so that he might gather the necessary force to lift it. "This," commented Houdini, "was simply another ruse on the medium's part, for when all the rest moved back she moved back also and this gave her room enough to bend her head and push the table up and over." Houdini could confirm his theory when, after letting go of Munn's hand, he began groping around under the table until he felt the medium's head. The magician whispered to Munn that he could denounce and expose her at once but the editor proposed to wait and the séance continued.[13]

It was then time for the bell-box. Again it was placed between Houdini's feet, again Margery put her ankle against that of the magician, and again, in the darkness, Houdini, who had rolled up his trouser leg like the night before, felt her stretching her foot to ring the bell. The buckle of Houdini's garter, however, had caught the medium's stocking, preventing her from reaching the box. "You have garters on, haven't you?" she asked. "Yes," replied Houdini. "Well, the buckle hurts me." After taking the garter off, Houdini felt the woman's leg stretching again and the bell ringing each

A drawing from Houdini's pamphlet about Margery,
showing the position of the sitters during the first bell-box test. (Harry Houdini,
Houdini Exposes the Tricks Used by the Boston Medium "Margery," 1924)

time her muscles extended. The séance over, the Crandons left the room and the committee discussed what had happened. Houdini told the others about his discovery and gave a practical demonstration. The committee, however, decided to wait until they were back in New York before issuing a press release. Meanwhile, it was necessary that the Crandons be left in the dark about Houdini's discoveries.

Munn and Houdini left for New York and Bird remained as a guest with the Crandons for three more days. Later it became known that he had told Mina and her husband what Houdini had discovered and what the committee intended to do. From that moment on Margery would be on guard. Arriving in New York, Munn spiked an article by Bird for *Scientific American,* already in print, in which Bird praised Margery's abilities. However, he couldn't stop the newspapers from reporting Bird's declarations. Some headlines that appeared in the newspapers of the day read: "Boston Medium Baffles Experts" and "Baffles Scientists with Revelations, Psychic Power of Margery Established."

One of the bell-boxes used during the *Scientific American* tests with Margery.
(© Ken Klosterman Collection)

Conan Doyle commented: "It was a capital error to put Houdini, who has been most violent in his expressions of contempt and hostility, upon such a body. Dr. Carrington, though he acted well in the matter of Eusapia, is not popular with Spiritualists. Dr. Prince, and Professor MacDougal [*sic*] have been so many years without declaring themselves in public that it seems hopeless that they should do so now. There remains only Mr. Comstock and Mr. Bird, open-minded, clear-headed men. But, alas! The mischief is done, and unless some system of travelling sub-committees is arranged the inquiry will end in fiasco."

HOUDINI'S WRONG STEP

When the committee met a month later there clearly was open war between Houdini, who wanted to expose the medium once and for all, and Margery, who wanted to make Houdini look the fool. It was then that Houdini made his worst move, introducing in the experimental setting a ridiculous constraint to control the medium. It was a big wooden box inside which the medium would sit leaving only her head and hands sticking out.[14] The main problem with such an extreme form of control is that it gave the medium the opportunity to complain that the cabinet prevented the materialization of the "pseudopods" needed to perform the phenomena and

A photographic close-up of the bell-box séance that was depicted in Houdini's drawing. (© Ken Klosterman Collection)

gave her an alibi for a possible absence of the same. There was also another drawback: if the cabinet wasn't really fraud-proof as Houdini believed it to be, and Margery could find a way to do some tricks, it could become proof of a true paranormal demonstration. If the fraud were later discovered, Houdini would have appeared incompetent.

Bird had offered to transport Houdini's box to Boston in his car, but Houdini, probably fearing that Bird would allow Margery to examine the box in advance, replied that he would carry it himself. Houdini and his assistant, Jim Collins, arrived at Dr. Comstock's apartment, at Charlesgate Hotel, early on the morning of August 25 to set up the cage. Mina and her husband arrived later that day. After inspecting the contraption, they asked the committee to allow Mina a practice séance in the device, and only in the presence of a few friends, before attempting the actual experiment. The committeemen agreed, but Houdini remained in the room until Margery had got into the cage and the covers had been fastened down, and then he withdrew.

The séance took place behind closed doors while the experimenters waited in another room. After thirty minutes, in which Walter apparently came through, whistled, and said that everything was okay, Dr. Crandon had his friends out of the room and the committeemen in. He asked for the following statement to be put on record: "The psychic does not refuse to sit in the cage made by Houdini for the committee; but she makes the reservation that she knows no precedent in psychic research where a medium has been so enclosed; and she believes that such a closed cage gives little or no regard for the theory and experience of the psychic structure or mechanism."[15]

Shortly after the formal sitting started, and the lights had been turned off, the box with the bell, placed on a table in front of the cabinet, rang; when the lights were turned on, it was discovered that the lid on the cabinet appeared to have been forced open. Houdini suggested that, with the lid open, Margery could have rung the bell by projecting her head forward. The medium denied any responsibility, claiming that Walter had forced open the cabinet-box. The discussion became so heated that, to "clear the atmosphere," a further séance with the medium's friends was promptly organized.

When "psychic harmony" was restored, the committeemen were called back in. Walter started a conversation with Houdini: "Have you got the

**Two drawings from Houdini's pamphlet: Malcolm Bird leaves his place,
freeing Margery's right hand. She can now put the megaphone
on her head and slide the cabinet using her feet. (Harry Houdini,**
Houdini Exposes the Tricks Used by the Boston Medium "Margery," **1924)**

mark just right? You think you're smart, don't you? How much are they
paying you for stopping phenomena here?"

"I don't know what you're talking about," was Houdini's reply. "It's
costing me $2,500 a week to be here." Houdini, in fact, had to pass up a
theater date in Buffalo in order to come to Boston for the séance.[16]

Walter then instructed Comstock to take the bell-box out into the light
and examine it. Comstock did as instructed and, tucked under the flap,
found a small, rubber eraser, off the end of a pencil. Although it did not
make the bell inoperative, Comstock estimated that it would make it about
four times harder to press on the lid and thus ring the bell. Houdini,
smarting from the accusation, stated immediately that he had not put the
eraser there. The séance ended without further phenomena.

THE RULER INCIDENT

The cabinet had proved its uselessness but Houdini wanted to try again. He
had the lid sealed with steel strips and locks and prepared for the next
night. That evening began with the dramatic entrance of Bird, who had
been informed by Mina of the previous night's fiasco. He demanded to
know why he had been left out of the séances. Houdini answered coldly, "I
object to Mr. Bird being in the séance room because he has betrayed the
Committee and hindered their work. He has not kept to himself things told
him in strictest confidence as he should as Secretary to the Committee."
Bird at first denied but then admitted that Margery, worried, had persuaded
him to tell her the facts. He then resigned from the committee and left.

Houdini's explanation of how Margery was able to levitate a table by using her head. (Harry Houdini, *Houdini Exposes the Tricks Used by the Boston Medium "Margery," * 1924)

There and then Prince was elected as the new secretary. Margery was searched by Miss McManama, the stenographer, since Crandon had refused to allow a thorough examination of his wife's body by a competent physician. Then a pillow was placed in the box, under Mina's feet, and the box was closed.

The séance began with Margery confined in the cabinet and Houdini and Prince at her sides, holding her hands as they extended through the holes on the sides of the box. Houdini particularly insisted that Prince never let go of the medium's hand until the séance was over. This provoked Margery to ask Houdini what was on his mind.

"Do you really want to know?" asked Houdini. "Yes," said the medium.

"Well I will tell you. In case you have smuggled anything in to the cabinet-box you can not now conceal it as both your hands are secured and as far as they are concerned you are helpless."

"Do you want to search me?" she asked.

"No, never mind, let it go," said Houdini. "I am not a physician."

Soon after, Walter appeared in the circle saying: "Houdini, you are very clever indeed but it won't work. I suppose it was an accident those things were left in the cabinet?"

"What was left in the cabinet?" asked the magician.

"Pure accident was it? You were not here but your assistant was." Walter then stated that a ruler would be found in the cabinet-box under the pillow at the medium's feet and accused Houdini of having had his assistant put it there to throw suspicion on his sister. Then he finished with a violent outburst in which he exclaimed: "Houdini, you God damned son of a bitch,[17] get the hell out of here and never come back. If you don't I will!"[18]

According to Bird, who got his account of the séance from Mina, "Houdini buried his face in his hands, groaned, almost wept, and cried out: 'Oh, this is terrible. My dear sainted mother *was* married to my father!'"

A search of the cabinet revealed the presence of a new collapsible carpenter ruler, a two-foot-length folded in six-inch sections. But the question remained: who put it there? Comstock suggested that it may have been left there when the box was being repaired. Houdini, however, claimed that it was Margery's. By sticking the rule through the neck opening, the magician explained, she could have easily rung the bell. Also, the medium had suggested that the armholes in the sides of the cabinet be boarded up, which would allow her to move her hands freely and uncontrolled inside the cabinet. Margery rejected the allegations and accused Houdini, suggesting that his assistant, Jim Collins, had hidden the ruler to discredit her.

Collins, however, had been interrogated that same night, in Houdini's absence, and took an oath that he did not place any ruler inside the cabinet, that he had never seen that ruler, and that his ruler was in his pocket. Houdini himself took an oath: "I also pledged my sacred word of honor as a man that the first I knew of the ruler in the cage was when I was so informed by Walter."

According to writer William Lindsay Gresham, Collins had hid the ruler: "I chucked it in the box myself. The Boss told me to do it. 'E wanted to fix her good."[19] Milbourne Christopher, magician and magic historian, expressed his doubts about this incident in his book *Houdini: The Untold Story*:

> The source of this story, though not given by Gresham, was Fred Keating, a magician who had been a guest of the Crandons in their house on Lime Street at the time Carrington was investigating the medium. Keating, however, was not unbiased. Several days before Gresham spoke to him, Keating had seen an unpublished manuscript in this author's collection in which Houdini, while praising Keating as a magician, had commented in unflattering terms on Keating's abilities as an investigator of psychic phenomena. In this writer's opinion, the story of Collins' admission is sheer fiction.

Who put the ruler in the box remains unknown to this day. The mystery could have been solved if at the time a laboratory could have examined the ruler for fingerprints or other useful traces. Evidently the *Scientific American* committee was not that scientific after all.

As soon as Conan Doyle heard the story of the ruler—or, better, as soon as he heard the version given to him by Crandon—he began circulating it. In a letter to Harry Price, for example, he wrote: "I hear from New York—but this is private—that Houdini is accused of dropping objects into a medium's cabinet in order to discredit her. The facts are very clear as stated & I understand that his own committee are against him. He is a very conceited self opinionated man but I should not have thought he would have descended to that."[20] Price, however, didn't seem to be much impressed, and he wrote in his autobiography, *Leaves from a Psychist's Case-*

Book: "The reader will notice that it is always the investigator who is accused of cheating; never by any chance the 'poor medium.' "

Conan Doyle, for his part, did not need too much time to reach conclusions: "It is as clear as daylight," he wrote to Bird, "that the ruler was put in the box, and the rubber in the apparatus by someone who wished to show that the medium was fraudulent. And who could this be save Houdini himself since it only occurred when he was present. Surely the Committee will not stand for this, and will protect a very self-sacrificing lady against such attempts upon her honour. I trust the matter will be most fully ventilated in the Press. It is a complete exposure—but not of the medium."[21]

The Last Séance

A last séance was planned for August 27. That afternoon Munn, Prince, Dr. Crandon, Mina, and Houdini dined together outside Boston. The medium, upon hearing that Houdini was about to denounce her from the stage at Keith's Theatre in Boston, protested that she didn't want her twelve-year-old son to read that his mother was a fraud. "Then don't be a fraud," Houdini told her. To which she said that if he misrepresented the facts some of her friends would come up on stage and give him a good beating.

"I am not going to misrepresent you," Houdini replied, "they are not coming on the stage and I am not going to get a beating."

"Then it is your wits against mine," said Margery slowly as she gave him a furtive look.

"Yes, certainly, that is just what it is," said Houdini.

Dr. Comstock had invented a device to immobilize the medium for the committee's last séance. It was a low box into which Margery and one investigator, sitting one in front of the other, would put their feet. A board, connected to the box, would be locked on top of the knees, preventing withdrawal of the feet. The sides of the box remained open allowing any possible "psychic structure" to operate. Her hands were held by the investigator and the box with the bell was placed outside the control-box; all was ready for the séance to begin. While waiting for something to happen, Dr. Crandon remarked: "Some day, Houdini, you will see the light and if it were to occur this evening, I would gladly give ten thousand dollars to charity."

"It may happen," replied Houdini, "but I doubt it."

"Yes sir," Dr. Crandon repeated, "if you were converted this evening I would willingly give $10,000 to some charity."[22]

It was a "blank séance," that is, nothing happened: Houdini was not converted and Dr. Crandon kept his $10,000 (which Houdini had interpreted as an attempted bribe). Dr. Comstock's device, obviously better than the one used by Houdini, had shown that when the medium was immobi-

**Houdini in the "Margie Box,"
1924. (Library of Congress, Prints
and Photographs Division,
LC-USZ62-26517)**

lized and controlled by an investigator (rather than by her husband) the phenomena never materialized. As usually happens in such cases: when controls are 0 percent phenomena are 100 percent; when controls are 100 percent phenomena are 0 percent. In the eyes of the public, the doubt cast over her honesty by the committee investigation was not enough to destroy her. Malcolm Bird resigned from *Scientific American* after Houdini announced on a radio program: "I publicly denounce here Malcolm Bird as being an accomplice of Margery!" After resigning, Bird spent his time promoting Margery.

DIFFERENT OPINIONS

Houdini, convinced that he had indisputably debunked Margery, announced: "I charge Mrs. Crandon with practicing her feats daily like a professional conjuror. Also that because of her training as a secretary, her long experience as a professional musician, and her athletic build she is not simple and guileless but a shrewd, cunning woman, resourceful in the extreme, and taking advantage of every opportunity to produce a 'manifestation.'"

Carrington, the first to defend her, charged Houdini with being interested only in publicity and declared: "The reason I didn't go to Boston when he held his sittings with 'Margery' was that I knew he distrusted me and I knew that anything he could not explain he would bring to my presence there."[23]

Finally, it comes as no surprise that one of the most strenuous defenders of the medium was Conan Doyle, who was preparing a long article in the hope of discrediting Houdini's accusations: "It is a really bad incident," he wrote to Harry Price, "and needs showing up. It should be the last

**With the panel closed, Houdini shows how a ruler could be used to ring the bell.
(McManus-Young Collection, Library of Congress,
Rare Books and Special Collections Division, LC-USZ62-96053)**

of him [Houdini] as a psychic researcher, if he could ever have been called one."[24]

"[T]his self-sacrificing couple," he would write in his article, "bore with exemplary patience all the irritations arising from the incursions of these fractious and unreasonable people, while even the gross insult which was inflicted upon them by one member of the committee did not prevent them from continuing the sittings. Personally, I think that they erred upon the side of virtue, and that from the moment Houdini uttered the word 'fraud' the committee should have been compelled either to disown him or cease their visits."[25]

According to Conan Doyle, the only honest and trustworthy members of the committee were Carrington and Bird. Regarding Bird, Conan Doyle said that he had a "better brain than Houdini's" because after fifty séances "he was completely convinced of the genuinity of the phenomena." Houdini didn't have an "open mind" as Conan Doyle intended it and he also expressed his surprise that a committee consisting of gentlemen should have permitted an attack on the reputation of a lady, and allowed a man "with entirely different standards to make this outrageous attack."

"I am perfectly certain," wrote Conan Doyle years later, "that it was an exposure, not of Margery but of Houdini. I have not the faintest doubt, from the evidence, that it was he who played the tricks against which 'Walter' so vigorously protested."

As for the other members of the committee, Prince's utility "was seriously impaired by the fact that he was very deaf so that he could hardly check those direct voice phenomena which were an important feature of the case." As for McDougall, he was inclined to credit only negative evidence.

The official report of the committee took six months to be completed. Committee members had been sworn to reveal nothing about the sittings until the publication of the report, while Bird and Dr. Crandon, not restricted by such burden, kept on telling journalists what Houdini considered to be "black lies." They claimed, for example, that Houdini had not allowed anyone to examine the cabinet before the séances and stated that Houdini was the last person who had touched the bell-box when the eraser was found in it.

These attacks elated Conan Doyle, who wrote to Bird: "Congratulations on your stand against Houdini. I have always said that investigators want to be watched just as the mediums are, so as to have even-handed justice. I have known an investigator, whose name is quoted by the public, say in a burst of confidence that he would not hesitate to put muslin in a medium's pockets if thereby he could expose her."[26]

While Houdini's irritation, and the public curiosity for the committee verdict mounted, a preliminary report was published in November in *Scientific American*. It reported only the singular members' views but, at least, freed them from their vow of confidentiality.

"I am compelled," stated Prince, "to render an opinion that thus far the experiments have not scientifically and conclusively proved the exercise of supernormal powers." Comstock was more optimistic: "I have not yet seen in connection with this case such sufficiently definite and often-repeated phenomena in the light; but I have seen enough in the light to awaken a lively interest on my part, and I think the investigation should be continued. My conclusion therefore is that rigid proof has not yet been furnished but that the case at present is interesting and should be investigated further." Carrington needed no further experiments: "The present case is peculiarly difficult, for many reasons; but I am convinced that genuine phenomena have occurred here, and that a prolonged series of sittings, undertaken in an impartial spirit, would demonstrate this." McDougall apparently had been absent and could not be reached in order to secure a formal statement.

As for Houdini, his conclusions were very clear: "Summing up my investigations of the five séances I attended of 'Margery,' which took place

on July 23, 24 and August 25, 26 and 27, 1924, the fact that I deliberately caught her manipulating with the head, shoulders and left foot, particulars of which I have handed to Mr. O. D. Munn with illustrations, and the blank séances and incidents which took place at the last three tests; my decision is, that everything which took place at the séances which I attended was a deliberate and conscious fraud, and that if the lady possess any psychic power, at no time was the same proven in any of the above dated séances."

To make himself clearer, Houdini went so far as publishing at his own cost a pamphlet entitled *Houdini Exposes the Tricks Used by the Boston Medium "Margery"* and started a tour where he completely exposed Margery's act. "Am looking forward with great interest," he wrote to his friend Harry Price in relation to his booklet, "to the alibi the folks interested will make."[27]

Dr. Crandon reacted by attacking Houdini and the others from the pages of the *Boston Herald*: "On paper, this committee could not be improved upon. Our experience, however, has shown this committee to have certain very bad qualities. There has been a lack of harmony and confidence. Houdini will not trust Bird or Carrington, and Bird and Carrington return the compliment." Houdini was ready to answer: "Dr. Crandon states that I do not trust Carrington or Bird and that they return the compliment. Well they might, for they know full well that I, never having been nonplussed by so-called phenomena, would be very apt to detect any trickery in which they might indulge. Possibly that is why Carrington, who knows me better than Bird, kept away from the séances I attended and left it to Bird to assist in fooling the committee. Evidently Bird stupidly thought that I belonged in the same class of believer or easy marks he has been in the habit of sitting with. There is no doubt in my mind that Mr. Bird has been deluded, possibly prior to his European trip as a psychic investigator, for his entire work in this field shows his inexperience and a weakness of the

The cover of Houdini's pamphlet on Margery. (Harry Houdini, *Houdini Exposes the Tricks Used by the Boston Medium "Margery,"* 1924)

willingness to believe, and would seem to justify the thought that in the Crandon case he was sufficiently deluded to help out with little effects at opportune times."

To foster his case, he even had an anonymous scurrilous leaflet printed, *How a Tricky Young Lady Trapped Stupid "Scientists."* In it he describes Margery, the "spirit-fakir," as "a vivacious young lady, happily wedded to a man with a title and a large bank account." Hereward Carrington is described as "the famous cigarette smoker, whose wild spiritistic trash has had so much prominence in the newspapers and magazines as 'scientific research,' " as for "Birdy Malcolm," he is called "the celebrated authority on pre-historic fly-specks." The leaflet accused Carrington and Bird of having been willing accomplices of Margery, in exchange for "three bounteous meals a day," "downy beds to sleep on at night," and "ice cream and hooch." "We can easily see," concluded the leaflet, "Hereward and Birdy, with napkins stuck into their collars, pushing custard pie into their faces with their knives, and wondering how they managed to strike such easy graft. Is it any wonder that they decided in favor of the lady? How could they brand their charming hostess a liar and fraud after she had wined and dined them for so long a time?"

MARGERY'S SUSPICIOUS-LOOKING ECTOPLASM

In 1924, while the discussions continued, Margery had begun to produce ectoplasm during her séances. Like her famous predecessor, Eva C., her substance also was said to pour out from her bodily orifices. This is a supposition, of course, since she, like Eva, used to perform in the dark. Meanwhile, Margery's fame had reached Europe and she was particularly well known in England. Conan Doyle, who was by then a close friend and supporter of the Crandons, expressed the wish to participate in new sittings with the medium, but the séances never took place and the newspapers reported: "Margery Fears Fog May Block London Séances" and "Medium Who Failed to Win $2,500 Prize Not Sure Damp Air Will Agree with 'Walter' Her Control."

The Society for Psychical Research was also interested in the case, and if the medium wouldn't come to the society, the society would go to the medium. This was brought about by Eric J. Dingwall, the research officer for the SPR, who had arranged with Crandon to test Margery in Boston. Dingwall had many sittings with Margery during January and February 1925, and was duly impressed by what he saw. During a séance conducted in the red light of an electric torch which was turned on and off by Dr. Crandon following the orders of Walter, he saw things that looked like materialized hands resting on Margery's lap. Excited, he wrote to psychic researcher Von Shrenck-Notzing: "It is the most beautiful case of teleplasm and telekinesis with which I am acquainted. One is able to handle the teleplasm freely. The materialized hands are connected by an umbilical cord to the medium; they seize objects and displace them. The teleplastic masses are visible and tangible upon the table, in good red light. I hold the hands of the medium, I know where her fingers are and I see them in good light. The control is irreproachable."

The enthusiasm, however, died quickly and Dingwall began to have doubts. He realized that he had never been able to actually see the ectoplasm pouring out of the medium's body. The faint light was not as good as he had earlier enthusiastically described; the hands were partially or completely formed and were static rather than moving. Dingwall remembered that when he was "allowed to hold the materialized substance, the medium at once began to turn in her chair and the mass was pulled out of my hand. It seemed simply an elastic bag and crumpled up as it was pulled away. I tried to follow it when it fell into the medium's lap, but she resisted strenuously, throwing her left leg on to the table and forcing my hand away from it with her own. Another crucial test had failed completely."[28]

The substance was clearly lifeless. At one point, as the materializing ectoplasm was spotlighted, Margery actually put her hand down with Dingwall's hand still controlling it, and threw the mass upon the table.

But what was this substance made from? The pictures taken by Dingwall show a very doubtful ectoplasm. The mass had the appearance of animal tissue and an examination of the enlargements of the photographs displayed certain ring markings that "strongly resembled the cartilaginous rings found in the mammalia trachea. This discovery led to the theory that the 'hands' had been faked from some animal lung material, the tissue cut and joined, and that part of the trachea had been used for the same purpose."[29]

Further examinations of the pictures by biologists at Harvard led to the same conclusion—the ectoplasm "undoubtedly was composed of the lung tissue of some animal."[30] In addition to going to any butcher and obtaining material, Dr. Crandon wouldn't have any difficulty in obtaining the needed substances, since he worked at Boston Hospital.

Dingwall produced a long report of his investigation, published in the 1928 *Proceedings of the SPR*, volume 36, and concluded thus: "I did not succeed in achieving my primary purpose, of coming to a definite conclusion as to the genuineness or otherwise of the phenomena. During the course of the sittings the evidence seemed to me at one time for, and at another time against, their supernormal nature, but never to incline decisively either way."

In the report, however, Dingwall suggested that the medium could hide the faked ectoplasm in her bodily cavities and could expel it afterward by way of muscular contraction. At the time, there were many rumors circulating as to the exact dimensions of Margery's anatomy. An example of this is the following paragraph, taken from a letter written by Grant H. Code, of the Harvard commission that would soon test Margery's powers, to Walter Franklin Prince:

> Do you think there is anything in my idea that in addition to the perfectly obvious reason for never permitting an anatomical examination (i.e. dangerous precedent that might be awkward if appealed to at the wrong séance), Dr. Crandon does not want any investigator to know the precise nature of the surgical alterations he has made in Margery's most convenient storage wharehouse? Second only to Dr. Crandon's description of Margery as a simple, guileless girl, is his oft repeated statement of the normal internal dimensions of that same warehouse. In commenting on her alleged profuse menstrual flow, Margery told me that it was partly occasioned by an operation. Now a slight surgical enlargement of the mouth of the uterus would make it a more convenient receptacle, especially if it is displaced. And on Dr. Fawcett's testimony, Margery's "development" is abnormal.[31]

The Symphony Hall Exposé

Before Dingwall's change of mind, his conviction that Margery's powers were at least partially genuine led him to a confrontation with Houdini. The magician had always considered Dingwall a friend and a fellow-conjuror since the time of Eva C.'s investigation in London. He was then greatly surprised at what happened during his live exposé of Margery's tricks at Symphony Hall.

Exasperated by the frequent attacks by Margery's defenders, and silenced by his vow not to reveal the committee conclusions before publication, Houdini had decided to launch a new challenge to Margery. On December 30, 1924, he traveled to Boston City Hall offering ten thousand dollars in bonds, which he fanned in front of a large crowd, should Margery accept to appear with him at Symphony Hall on January 2 or 3 and produce manifestations that he could not explain. The audience packed the hall both nights, but Margery didn't show up, explaining that a magician and a Spiritualist had nothing in common. Houdini then reenacted all the séances in which he had participated with her; he invited on stage a committee of volunteers who he blindfolded to give them the illusion of being in the darkness of a séance room. Also, this artifice allowed the rest of the audience to see all of the tricks being used by the medium, played in this case by Houdini. He duplicated the megaphone tossing, the table lifting with his head, the bell ringing, and took Margery's place inside the wooden box.

He lectured on Spiritualism, denounced Bird and Carrington as Margery's confederates, and made fun of his ex-friend Conan Doyle: "Sir Arthur states I am a medium. That is not so. I am well done." He also ridiculed him by calling him a "great big boy" but his attacks became vicious when somebody from the audience yelled: "I will tell you one thing, you can't fill a house like Conan Doyle did twice." This comment hit a nerve: "Well, all right, if ever I am such a plagiarist as Conan Doyle, who pinched Edgar Allan Poe's plumes, I will fill all houses. . . ."

"Do you call him a thief?" retorted the heckler.

"No, but I say that his story Scandal in Bohemia is only the brilliant letter [sic] by Poe. . . . I walked into his room at the Ambassador Hotel and I saw twenty books, French, English and German, a paragraph marked out of each one of the detective stories. I don't say he used them. . . ."

Someone else shouted something from the audience, demanding to check a trick bell-box that Houdini had just used to duplicate one of Margery's feats. Houdini was "thunder-struck" to see that the heckler was Dingwall. "Well, Dingwall," he said, "you here and challenging me when you know that any secret I have in Spiritualism is yours simply for the asking? You ought to be ashamed of yourself. You know everything I do is trickery."

"I turned to the audience," continued Houdini, "told them that he had been sent here specially by the Psychic Research Association of England, and here he was sneaking in to see me work, when he was a member of two of the Organizations to which I belong and said, 'Dingwall, this is not cricket'. . . . He was crestfallen, he flushed, and when they yelled for him to stand up so that they could see him he said, 'Kindly address your remarks to the lecturer,' and sank into his seat."[32]

The Last Quarrel

On January 26, 1925, the *Boston Herald* ran Conan Doyle's long article, "Margery Genuine, Says Conan Doyle: He Scores Houdini," written to defend Margery or, as he put it, to "fight for the truth, the exposure of evil and the defence of the honour of a most estimable lady." As predictable, Houdini's accusations kept to center stage in Conan Doyle's article: "Houdini has pushed self-advertisement and defamation to the point of issuing a pamphlet explaining how his skill and his wonderful box had stopped all phenomena." But, he argued, "the investigator who imagines that he disproves phenomena by checking or stopping them, only proves his own ignorance of the subject, though in Houdini's case that has already been amply shown by the innumerable errors in the book which he has put to his name." He went on detailing his fanciful version of the Margery séances, based on Crandon's accounts, in which Houdini played the part of the rogue who had masterminded a "very deadly plot" against the poor medium. Conan Doyle claimed that Houdini left Boston "a very discredited man so far as psychic research is concerned," and hoped the Houdini would "confine himself in future to that art in which he is famous and leave a field for which his strong prejudices and unbalanced judgment entirely unfit him."

Houdini did reply in the same issue of the *Herald*: "My opinion of Sir Arthur Conan Doyle is that he is a menace to mankind, because the public thinks that he is just as great a man in spiritualistic field as he is at writing stories. . . . I have personally warned Sir Arthur of a number of things, but it seems he will not protect himself. He has not enough mentality left to use good judgement. . . . I am really very sorry for him. It is a pity that a man with such a reputation in the literary field should, in his old age, do such really stupid things."

The following day, Houdini's reaction appeared even worse: "Houdini Stirred by Article, May Sue Sir Arthur," headlined one newspaper. The reporter stated that Houdini was contemplating "legal action" as a result of Conan Doyle's remarks: "Houdini said yesterday he does not propose to let Sir Arthur get away with certain harsh remarks contained in the article. He will have a retraction or 'communicate with his lawyers.' " In the article, Houdini is credited with calling Doyle "a bit senile . . . and therefore easily bamboozled"; also he is supposed to have thought "that a bit of the sharpness contained in Sir Arthur's remarks may have been occasioned by the fact that he, Houdini, once expressed the belief that Lady Doyle was not a valid medium either."

"There is not a word of truth in his charges against me," continued Houdini. "Sir Arthur has been sadly misinformed. Anyhow, I fail to see how he, being 3,500 miles away, qualifies as a judge. I have posted $10,000 with Mayor Curley of Boston to be given to charity if she makes good before a committee chosen by Mayor Curley. The truth of the whole matter is that Margery, in my belief, is a social climber."

Conan Doyle would later comment in a letter to the January 14, 1926, *Morning Post*: "There is an abnormal frame of mind which may be called the Conjurer's Complex or Houdinitis. It is based upon several fallacies. The first is that Spiritualism depends upon physical phenomena for its proofs, whereas the more cogent are mental. The second is that mental dexterity bears some relation to brain capacity and enable[s] its possessor to sit in judgment upon the Crookes, the Wallaces, and the Lombrosos. . . ."

Finally, the *Scientific American* Committee issued its official verdict on February 11, 1925. "We have observed phenomena," the report stated, "the method of production of which we cannot in every case claim to have discovered. But we have observed no phenomena of which we can assert that they could not have been produced by normal means." Hardly what Houdini would have liked, but in any case, this at least meant that Margery didn't win the prize.

A NEW AWARD AND A NEW COMMITTEE

On April 1, 1925, the *Journal of Abnormal and Social Psychology* offered an award of $5,000 to any person "claiming to produce supernormal material phenomena who would be the first to demonstrate the actuality of the same under rigid laboratory conditions and by recognized scientific methods, in full light." The committee consisted of five members coming from Harvard University plus Houdini.

The formation of the new committee was a direct consequence of the Margery investigation or, better, of the failure to reach a clear verdict:

> It is safe to say that no conclusions reached, whether favorable or unfavorable, positive or negative, drawn from researches made, as in the case of "Margery," in a dark room, or in such dull red light as to require the use of luminous paint on objects to make them visible, will ever be accepted as final by a consensus of opinion. Those with the will to believe, will believe; those with the will to disbelieve, will disbelieve; those of a critical, scientifically trained mind will remain agnostics. It will be a question of belief not of proof.

To overcome this problem, the *Journal's* conditions were that "the phenomena must be subject to instrumental control and therefore, whatsoever their cause, must be material or physical phenomena; must be visible, produced in full light and subjected to instrumental recording, measuring and testing. Any known physical or chemical means of testing the phenomena must be permitted to be used."

Crandon reacted with fury to the announcement of the prize: "This seems to be an age which has lost interest in priceless things and is only enamored of things with a price." He declared that he was himself ready to offer:

> (1) $10,000 for a full materialization of a spirit-form on the roof of the Copley-Plaza in bright sunlight at noon on any Tuesday.
> (2) $20,000 for the metamorphosis of a larva into a butterfly, without a cocoon, on the north wall of the public library on Dec. 15, 1925, 10 minutes before midnight. . . .[33]

Entries for the prize closed on November 1, 1925. Forty-four persons responded, however, they were thus grouped: one "offer of assistance in investigation"; five letters "asking for information. None of these responded after receiving a copy of the conditions"; nine letters from "persons claiming to have supernormal powers of some sort. . . . None of these individuals replied after receiving copies of the conditions"; fourteen letters from "persons obviously psychopathic. . . . One threatened violence to the committee and stated that she was not above killing the secretary"; seven letters, "probably all from mediums," protesting the conditions: "Houdini came in for his share of the abuse"; five letters from persons "disclaiming any desire to compete for the prize but who wished to tell of their own experiences"; two letters from individuals "with mechanical devices by which they claimed to be able to demonstrate the conversion of psychical energy into physical energy"; and three letters from individuals "backing other persons with mediumistic powers. None of these replied to letters from us."[34]

There were only three persons who made a pretense of seriously entering the competition. One was an individual with the "mechanical device" for converting psychical energy into physical energy, who would later be revealed as unreliable and, thus, was regarded as "ineligible." Two others "went so far as to write second letters stating their intentions of meeting the preliminary requirements, but they did not carry the matter further." "It may be significant," concluded the committee's report, "that no group of investigators of supernormal phenomena produced a candidate."

NOTES

1. Thomas R. Tietze, *Margery* (New York: Harper & Row, 1973).

2. Arthur Conan Doyle, *The History of Spiritualism* (London: Constable, 1926).

3. *Journal of the American Society for Psychical Research* 18, no. 6 (June 1924).

4. Harry Houdini, *Houdini Exposes the Tricks Used by the Boston Medium "Margery"* (New York: Adams Press, 1924).

5. Ibid.

6. In Paul Tabori's book *Pioneers of the Unseen* (New York: Taplinger Publishing Co., 1972), Henry N. Gilroy, a longtime associate of Carrington, has this to say about Margery: "Of course, most people don't know this—but he (Carrington) had a love affair with Margery—on the q.t. They had an understanding that it would not affect in any way the report of the *Scientific American* magazine as to whether her mediumship was genuine or not. Their little love affair went on for several months and he told me how difficult it was to have their little trysts and get-togethers" (p. 40).

7. Houdini, *Houdini Exposes the Tricks Used by the Boston Medium "Margery."*

8. Ibid.

9. Ibid.

10. Ibid.

11. Ibid.

12. Kenneth Silverman, *Houdini!!! The Career of Ehrich Weiss* (New York: HarperCollins, 1996).

13. Houdini, *Houdini Exposes the Tricks Used by the Boston Medium "Margery."*

14. The "Margie Box," as it became known, was preserved at the Houdini Magical Hall of Fame, a museum at Niagara Falls, Ontario, until it was destroyed by fire on April 30, 1995, along with many other unique Houdini belongings and memorabilia, including the Water Torture Cell.

15. Malcolm Bird, *"Margery" the Medium* (Boston: Small, Maynard & Co., 1925).

16. Ibid.

17. According to Bird's secondhand account of the séance, the words used were, "Houdini, you God damned bastard." Houdini, in a pamphlet exposing Margery's tricks, didn't write the exact words but left them to the imagination: "Houdini, you G—d——." According to others, like biographers Milbourne Christopher and Kenneth Silverman, however, Margery's outburst was exactly: "Houdini you God damned son of a bitch." Typically, when Conan Doyle detailed the episode to his friend Oliver Lodge he could not help but clean up the language, and the insult became: "Houdini, you unutterable cad!" which transformed itself again to "Houdini, you—blackguard!" in his book *The Edge of the Unknown*.

18. Houdini, *Houdini Exposes the Tricks Used by the Boston Medium "Margery."*

19. William Lindsay Gresham, *Houdini: The Man Who Walked Through Walls* (1959; reprint, New York: MacFadden Books, 1968).

20. Gabriel Citron, *The Houdini-Price Correspondence* (London: Legerdemain, 1998).

21. James Randi Collection. Reprinted with permission of the James Randi Educational Foundation.

22. Houdini, *Houdini Exposes the Tricks of the Boston Medium "Margery."*

23. Ibid.

24. Citron, *The Houdini-Price Correspondence.*

25. "Margery Genuine, Says Conan Doyle; He Scores Houdini," *Boston Herald*, January 26, 1925.

26. James Randi Collection. Reprinted with permission of the James Randi Educational Foundation.

27. Citron, *The Houdini-Price Correspondence.*

28. Eric J. Dingwall, "Report on a Series of Sittings with the Medium Margery," *Proceedings of the Society for Psychical Research* 36 (1928).

29. Ibid.

30. Tietze, *Margery.*

31. Ibid.

32. Silverman, *Houdini!!!*

33. *Journal of Abnormal and Social Psychology* 20, no. 4 (January 26, 1925).

34. Ibid.

A Magician Among the Spirits 7

Houdini's Lecture Tour

THE EVER-GROWING DISCUSSIONS ABOUT Spiritualism that Houdini presented during his shows had induced him, in February 1924, to sign a contract with the Coit-Alber lecture bureau to undertake a lecture tour on Spiritualism all over the midwestern and southern United States.

He had occasionally talked about the subject to university classes: this was, however, a real tour comprised of twenty-four lectures in twenty-four different cities.

"I am fifty years of age today," he wrote in his diary on April 6. "I can't believe it. But I am!! But not in body and far from it in mind. I believe if I live I'll be better, body and mind, than ever before, and more capable of making a living in my old age. But I must provide now!"[1]

At his age and in his position, Houdini could very well have retired, as he had often claimed he would do, and devote himself only to writing. Although he was the most highly paid performer of his time, and could command any fee he demanded, he elected to tour the country in a series of one-night stands as a lecturer, at a lecturer's wage.

There were probably two reasons that led him to this decision. First, he had a genuine dislike for unscrupulous mediums who took advantage of a gullible public; second, he certainly enjoyed this change in his career. *Billboard* stated this clearly: "Houdini the magician has become Houdini, the educator!"

This new position not only allowed him to mingle with the literati, or to "meet the intelligents" [*sic*] as he wrote in his diary, something that he really enjoyed; also, it made him feel on the same level as Conan Doyle and thus able to counterattack all his claims. "Wait till Sir A. C. Doyle hears of my lectures!" he wrote in his diary.

This is how Houdini opened a typical lecture on Spiritualism:

About thirty years ago in Garnett, Kansas, I was traveling with a small company—the man was a philanthropist—long beard and long hair, and he stood on the street corner and told the people that he would sell them a bottle of medicine worth a hundred dollars for a dollar. And I was the man that sold it for him. Then Wednesday morning at the hotel he said, "Houdini, things are a little quiet in the show business. Can't you do something on a Sunday night of a religious nature so we can get a house?" I said, "There is one thing I can do of a religious nature and that is make a collection." (Laughter)

He said, "You will have to make one for me if business doesn't hurry up. . . . Why don't you do a couple or more tricks and I will advertise it as a spiritualistic séance." I says, "All right, go ahead." He says, "I have got to square the chief of police." That was very easy, thirty years ago, to square the chief of police even in Garnett, Kansas. And he was a very fine chap, really, he was very fine. (Laughter) That Saturday—they had a weekly paper there—that Saturday the paper had great big headlines. "Houdini the World Famous Medium, who only gives séances in largest cities in the world"—and I had just come from Appleton, Wisconsin (Laughter)—"has been prevailed upon by popular request of the public"—that was Dr. Hill—"to give a séance. Pianos will float over the heads of the audience, tables will be levitated by unseen hands, messages will appear." . . . I was good in the newspaper. I still have it in my scrapbook.

Well that Sunday night, ladies and gentlemen, I gave what I believe was the most sensational spiritualistic performance that ever took place in Garnett, Kansas. And I tell you why I was qualified to give that marvelous entertainment. That Sunday morning, accompanied by the sexton and the oldest inhabitant of the town, we walked out to the village cemetery, and I had a notebook, and what was not carved on the slabs of marble or granite tombstones—any information that was lacking, the sexton would tell me the missing data, and the old Uncle Rufus would give me the scandals of everyone sleeping in God's acre. (Laughter) And can you imagine going out there . . . and retailing that terrible stuff. Their eyes stuck out. I know one man named Obermeyer—I had brought back his grandfather, and I said "Obermeyer, you are not doing right by the grandson." He got up and said, "Tell my grandfather I will take care of him in the morning." (Laughter)[2]

It was Houdini's very easy-going and friendly style that immediately conquered the audience. Usually, after an introduction in which Houdini would tell of his past experiences in Spiritualism, there was a part in which slides were projected. There were about fifty colored pictures that Houdini used to tell his own version of the story of Spiritualism. Every now and then, to better exemplify a few points, he would perform some of the tricks he was talking about. It was not enough to say that the medium Henry Slade used tricks to make "spirit messages" appear on his slates: to be more convincing, it had to be shown *how* he did that. Among other things, Houdini would sit at a table and show how to ring a bell with his toes, while giving the impression to the person sitting in front of him that both his hands and feet were under his control.

Houdini's lectures were a success in every city he visited, so much that the tour was prolonged for two months. In addition to his lectures, Houdini was frequently invited to address religious groups, radio stations, public debates, and parties, and journalists would frequently call on him for his opinion on some psychic matter. Houdini was now seen as a real authority on the psychic world, an expert who could really help people not to be taken in by frauds. To complete his background, he only needed a book telling about his experiences in the world of Spiritualism.

A MAGICIAN AMONG THE SPIRITS

The most important book written by Houdini, *A Magician Among the Spirits*, was published during the spring of 1924. It was about three hundred pages in length and was intended to offer, in sixteen chapters, a detailed critical history of Spiritualism from its inception to the present day.

In the past, many other critical books had been published, including: *How to Come Out as a Medium* (1860); *Modern Spiritualism* (1876), by British magician John N. Maskelyne; *Behind the Scenes With the Mediums* (1907), by David P. Abbott; and *Revelations of a Spirit Medium* (1922), edited by Harry Price and Eric J. Dingwall.

None of these books, however, intended to offer a critical history of the movement. The most authoritative book that offered a critical perspective was *Modern Spiritualism* (1902), by Frank Podmore (1856–1910), one of the best-known researchers of the Society for Psychical Research. It was from this book that Houdini had drawn his inspiration while writing *A Magician Among the Spirits*.

The first six chapters in *A Magician* were devoted to the great mediums of the past: the Fox sisters, the Davenports, Daniel Dunglas Home, Eusapia Palladino, Henry Slade, and a third-rate medium, Ann O'Delia Diss Debar, a contemporary of Houdini's. There followed monographic chapters about making messages appear on slates, faking spirit photography, ectoplasm, the dangers of Spiritualism, investigating psychic claims, how mediums obtain information about their clients, and the use of magicians in the investigation of Spiritualism.

An entire chapter was devoted to Conan Doyle. In it, Houdini described in detail exactly what had happened at the Atlantic City séance:

> At the written invitation of Sir Arthur and Lady Doyle Mrs. Houdini and I
> visited them while they were stopping at the Ambassador Hotel in Atlantic

City. One day as Sir Arthur, Mrs. Houdini and I were sitting on the sand skylarking with the children Sir Arthur excused himself saying that he was going to have his usual afternoon nap. He left us but returned in a short time and said "Houdini, if agreeable, Lady Doyle will give you a special séance, as she has a feeling that she might have a message come through. At any rate, she is willing to try," and turning to Mrs. Houdini he said, "We would like to be alone. You do not mind if we make the experiment without you." Smilingly, my good little wife said, "Certainly not, go right ahead, Sir Arthur; I will leave Houdini in your charge and I know that he will be willing to go to the séance." Doyle said, "You understand, Mrs. Houdini, that this will be a test to see whether we can make any Spirit come through for Houdini, and conditions may prove better if no other force is present."

Before leaving with Sir Arthur, Mrs. Houdini cued me. We did a second sight or mental performance years ago and still use a system or code whereby we can speak to each other in the presence of others, even though to all outward appearances we are merely talking, pointing or doing the most innocent-looking things, but which have different meanings to us.

In that manner Mrs. Houdini told me that on the night previous she had gone into detail with Lady Doyle about the great love I bear for my Mother. She related to her a number of instances, such as, my returning home from long trips, sometimes as far away as Australia, and spending months with my Mother and wearing only the clothes that she had given me, because I thought it would please her and give her some happiness. My wife also remarked about my habit of laying my head on my Mother's breast, in order to hear her heart beat. Just little peculiarities that mean so much to a mother and son when they love one another as we did.

I walked with Sir Arthur to the Doyles' suite. Sir Arthur drew down the shades so as to exclude the bright light. We three, Lady Doyle, Sir Arthur and I, sat around the table on which were a number of pencils and a writing pad, placing our hands on the surface of the table.

Sir Arthur started the séance with a devout prayer. I had made up my mind that I would be as religious as it was within my power to be and not at any time did I scoff at the ceremony. I excluded all earthly thoughts and gave my whole soul to the séance.

I was *willing* to believe, even *wanted* to believe. It was weird to me and with a beating heart I waited, hoping that I might feel once more the presence of my beloved Mother. If there ever was a son who idolized and worshipped his Mother, whose every thought was for her happiness and comfort, that son was myself. My Mother meant my life, her happiness was synonymous with my peace of mind. For that reason, if no other, I wanted to give my very deepest attention to what was going on. It meant to me an easing of all pain that I had in my heart. I especially wanted to speak to my Mother, because that day, *June 17, 1922*, was her birthday [This was not known to Lady Doyle. If it had been my Dear Mother's Spirit communicating a message, she, knowing her birthday was my most holy holiday, surely would have commented on it]. I was determined to embrace Spiritualism if there was any evidence strong enough to down the doubts that have crowded my brain for the past thirty years.

Presently, Lady Doyle was "seized by a Spirit." Her hands shook and beat the table, her voice trembled and she called to the Spirits to give her a message. Sir Arthur tried to quiet her, asked her to restrain herself, but her hand thumped on the table, her whole body shook and at last, making a cross at the head of the page, started writing. And as she finished each page, Sir Arthur tore the sheet off and handed it to me. I sat serene through it all, hoping and wishing that I might feel my mother's presence. There wasn't even a semblance of it. Everyone who has ever had a worshipping Mother and has lost earthly touch, knows the feeling which will come over him at the thought of sensing her presence.

The letter which follows purported to have come from my Mother, I cannot, as much as I desire, accept as having been written or inspired by the soul or Spirit of my Sweet Mother. (pp. 63–64)

Then follows the text of the letter, already reproduced on pages 97–98 of this book. At the end of it, Houdini commented:

In the case of my séance, Sir Arthur believed that due to the great excitement it was a direct connection.

The more so do I hesitate to believe and accept the above letter because, although my sainted mother had been in America for almost fifty years, she could not speak, read nor write English but Spiritualists claim that when a medium is possessed by a Spirit who does not speak the language, she automatically writes, speaks or sings in the language of the deceased; however, Sir Arthur has told me that a Spirit becomes more educated the longer it is departed and that my blessed Mother had been able to master the English language in Heaven. (p. 154)

In the same chapter, Houdini quoted various extracts from Conan Doyle's letters. He probably wrote Conan Doyle early in 1924 to ask for permission to reproduce them. What follows is Conan Doyle's reply, and the last letter that he ever wrote to Houdini:

Feb. 26, 1924

Dear Houdini:

I am answering you by the first post. I could not make myself clear in a cable.

You probably want these extracts in order to twist them in some way against me or my cause, but what I say I say and I do not alter. All the world can quote.

What you quote, however, about your own frame of mind is obviously a back-number.

The assertion about the bones in the Fox house should be referred to its origin—*The Boston Journal*, Nov. 23, 1904.

I read an interview you gave some American paper the other day, in which you said my wife gave you nothing striking when she wrote for you. When you met us, three days after the writing, in New York, you said—"I have been walking on air ever since," or words to that effect. I wonder how you reconcile your various utterances!

I observe that, in your letter, you put down my starting my world-mission "in a crisis of emotion." I started in 1916. My son died in 1918. My only emotion was impersonal and the reflection of a world in agony.

Our regards to Mrs. Houdini.[3]

Houdini dealt again with Conan Doyle at the conclusion of the book:

Sir Arthur says: "If you want to send a telegram you must go to a telegraph office. If you want to telephone you must first pick up the receiver and give your message to either an operator or a waiting automaton."

Very well, I have gone to the operator between the Beyond and this earthly sphere, I have gone to the telegraph office that receives the message in code, to the so-called *medium*. What would be more wonderful to me than to be able to converse with my beloved mother? . . . but I have not heard from my blessed Mother, except through the dictates of the inmost recesses of my heart. . . .

Sir Arthur Conan Doyle has repeatedly told the Spiritualists that I will eventually see the light and embrace Spiritualism. If the memory of a loved one, gone to the protection of the hands of the Great Mystifier means Spiritualism, then truly I do believe in it. But if Spiritualism is to be founded on the tricks of exposed mediums, feats of magic, resort to trickery, then I say unflinchingly I do not believe, and more, I will not believe. (p. 270)

A Magician Among the Spirits received good reviews in the press and was well received by the public. It told many interesting and entertaining episodes from Houdini's own life and contained much firsthand information about famous mediums. It was here, for example, that Houdini revealed for the first time everything that Ira Davenport had told him about his methods.

However, this book cannot be placed on the same level with Podmore's *Modern Spiritualism*. As in a previous book by Houdini, *The Unmasking of Robert-Houdin*, there were various mistakes or, as Conan Doyle put it, Houdini "stuffed so many errors into his book." Walter Franklin Prince agreed, calling the book "strewn with blunders"; however, he also stated that "the errors which stare you in the face were not willful ones, since few of them were of any advantage to the argument"—something he could not say when he reviewed Conan Doyle's book *The History of Spiritualism*.

CONAN DOYLE'S BOOKS ON SPIRITUALISM

While Houdini was having his *A Magician Among the Spirits* published, a book which he considered to be "part of his monument," Conan Doyle had already published various books on the subject of Spiritualism. He had announced and discussed his conversion to the movement in *The New Revelation: or What Is Spiritualism*, published in 1918. The book did not receive good reviews outside Spiritualist circles and publications; the *London Times*, for example, had commented on Conan Doyle's "incredible naiveté," and the *Nation* had stated: "The book leaves one with a rather poor opinion of the doctor's critical abilities."

His next book, *The Vital Message*, published the following year, did not score better. The *Sunday Express*, in its book column, headlined: "Is Conan Doyle Mad?" In the review, the writer admitted a feeling of "benign contempt" in approaching Conan Doyle's psychic books. "One does not trouble to analyze the ravings of a madman. One shrugs one's shoulders, laughs, and forgets." However the *Express* did acknowledge Conan Doyle's gifts as a novelist and a historian, and admitted: "It is not easy to reconcile these facts with the hypothesis that he is stark, staring mad on the subject of the dead. He has established his right to be heard, and we may be wrong in refusing to hear him. There may be oceans of fraud and folly in spiritualism, but there may be a grain of truth in it." It is also interesting to note that in his movie *The Man from Beyond*, Houdini is seen reading from *The Vital Message*, a fact which certainly had pleased Conan Doyle who, at the time of its screening, was still friends with Houdini and had warmly praised the movie.

In 1921 Doyle published *The Wanderings of a Spiritualist*, a book detailing his lecture tour of Australia and New Zealand, along with the chronicle of his meetings with local mediums and psychics. "When we look back at the 30,000 miles which we have traversed," he wrote at the close of the book, "at the complete absence of illness which spared any one of seven a single day in bed, the excellence of our long voyages, the freedom from all accidents, the undisturbed and entirely successful series of lectures, the financial success won for the cause, the double escape from shipping strikes, and, finally, the several inexplicable instances of supernormal, personal happenings, together with the three-fold revelation of the name of our immediate guide, we should be stocks and stones if we did not realize that we have been the direct instruments of God in a cause upon which He has set His visible seal. There let it rest. If He be with us, who is against us?"

In 1922, there came the pamphlet devoted to the defense of the Crewe Circle, titled *The Case for Spirit Photography*, and the book which he considered the revelation of an "epoch-making" event, *The Coming of the Fairies*.

The following year it was time for another book chronicling his tours. *Our American Adventure* was devoted to his first American tour, the one in which his friendship with Houdini was still at its best. In it he had talked about his then-friend: "I may add that Houdini is not one of those shallow men who imagine they can explain away spiritual phenomena as parlour tricks, but that he retains an open—and ever, I think, a more receptive—mind towards mysteries which are beyond his art."

The book also contained Conan Doyle's version of the fateful Atlantic City séance:

> The reason, however, why I refer to my wife's remarkable power, which only came by slow development, is that my friend, Mr. Houdini, the greatest of magicians, sat with us one afternoon, and received a fifteen-page letter from his mother which made him very grave and thoughtful, though he is a most difficult man to convince. It was sudden inspiration of mine to ask him up to our room and see if we could get any evidence or consolation for him. It was a singular scene, my wife with her hand flying wildly, beating the table while she scribbled at a furious rate, I sitting opposite and tearing sheet after sheet from the block as it was filled up, and tossing each across to Houdini, while he sat silent, looking grimmer and paler every moment. We asked him to think a question in silence, and a correct name came instantly through my wife's hand. But then occurred the most marvelous thing of all. Houdini sat playing with the pencil when his hand was suddenly moved and he wrote the name "Powell." Now, Dr. Ellis Powell, my dear fighting partner in Spiritualism, had just died in England—worn out, I expect, by his own exertions, for he was a desperately hard worker in the cause. I was the man he was most likely to signal to, and here was his name coming through the hand of Houdini. "Truly Saul is among the Prophets," said I. . . . He muttered something about knowing a man named Powell, down in Texas, though he failed to invent any reason why that particular man should come back at that particular moment. Then, gathering up the papers, he hurried from the room. . . .

By 1924 their friendship had reached its breaking point, not secondarily because of their different opinions on the séance. In the book detailing his second lecture tour in the United States, *Our Second American Adventure*, Conan Doyle had dropped his admiration for Houdini's "receptiveness" towards psychic mysteries and, though he praised his skills as a magician, found him "most violent in his expressions of contempt and hostility" toward Spiritualism.

In a subsequent book, the two-volume *History of Spiritualism*, published in 1926, Conan Doyle's opinion on Houdini shifted even more toward the negative side. Regarding Houdini's statements on the Davenports not being real mediums, for example, Conan Doyle commented that

"Houdini has himself stuffed so many errors of fact into his book *A Magician Among the Spirits*, and has shown such extraordinary bias on the whole question, that his statement carries no weight." Also of interest are Conan Doyle's comments in relation to Margery, "the beautiful and gifted wife of one of the first surgeons of Boston." "This lady," wrote Doyle, "showed psychic powers some years ago, and the author was instrumental in calling the attention of the *Scientific American* Committee to her case. By doing so he most unwillingly exposed her to much trouble and worry which were borne with extraordinary patience by her husband and herself. It was difficult to say which was the more annoying: Houdini the conjurer, with his preposterous and ignorant theories of fraud, or such 'scientific' sitters as Professor McDougall, of Harvard, who, after fifty sittings and signing as many papers at the end of each sitting to endorse the wonders recorded, was still unable to give any definite judgement, and contented himself with vague innuendoes."

Conan Doyle published a few more books on the subject of Spiritualism, following Houdini's death in 1926 and before his own in 1930, and these will be covered in the following chapter.

Argamasilla: The Man with the X-ray Eyes

Shortly after the publication of his book, Houdini had the chance to conduct some tests with a young Spanish psychic, nineteen-year-old Joaquin Maria Argamasilla. The boy had been examined by Nobel Prize winner Charles Richet, by psychic researcher Gustave Geley, and by various Spanish scientists: all of them agreed on the fact that this young man had proved conclusively to their satisfaction that he could read through metal. However, his X-ray eyes could penetrate solid objects only "provided they were unpainted." His most popular test consisted in reading the time of day through a hunting-case watch furnished by any spectator. He also gave demonstrations of reading handwriting through closed metal boxes.

On April 22, 1924, Argamasilla, accompanied by his manager/interpreter and by a priest, met Houdini. The magician took a liking to the young, elegant, but comical-looking Spaniard. Argamasilla showed the box he was going to use: it was a long and narrow silver box, with a lid hinged to the back of the box and secured at the front by two hinged hasps, one of which was secured by a small padlock. As a further precaution, Argamasilla blindfolded himself with two wads of cotton and his own handkerchief. After this he was apparently ready to perform his miracles by reading the time on a watch closed in the box or words written on pieces of paper inserted in the box. Houdini immediately spotted the trick he used.

The bandage was not a problem: there are countless methods by which magicians can give the illusion of being perfectly blindfolded and still be able to see through it. Argamasilla was no exception, and Houdini had recognized a standard technique: "I have seen this man place his left hand to his forehead and by so doing almost imperceptibly raise the handkerchief to improve his downward line of vision." The box, in fact, was built in such a way as to make it possible to slightly raise one side of the lid: enough to allow a quick glance of the inside. Furthermore, Argamasilla used to stand with his back to a window, so that the light coming from it would make it easier to see inside the box.

That day Houdini said nothing of what he had discovered, but waited for a public demonstration that Argamasilla was going to give on May 6, at the Hotel Pennsylvania in New York City. In front of various journalists and scientists, the boy correctly guessed the time on the watches and the words written on slips of paper. His guesses, however, were not perfect but always contained some slight error: this helped in making him look all the more sincere. If it was a trick, it was frequently reasoned (and still is today by many psychic supporters), it would work perfectly every time!

When Houdini arrived at the hotel he brought with him two special boxes sealed with strands of copper wire and bolted shut: there was no possible way to raise the lids. He challenged Argamasilla to read through them, but the manager refused on behalf of his protégé and they left. Houdini duplicated, to the satisfaction of the reporters, all of Argamasilla's feats, after having been blindfolded and with five men holding their hands over his eyes.

Houdini met again with Argamasilla a few days later, during a second public demonstration. This time he agreed to use Argamasilla's box for the test, but asked that the psychic read a piece of paper that he had brought. That day, however, the sky was clouded and the piece of paper used by Houdini was a newspaper ad that could only be read close-up. After these experiences Argamasilla disappeared and nothing further was ever heard of him or, as the May 17, 1924, *Billboard* put it, "Battling Houdini went up against the Spanish kid . . . and knocked the X out of the latter's X-ray eye." As for Houdini, he kept the Argamasilla "watch trick" among his impromptu magic demonstrations, considering it "without a doubt, a wonderful trick in the hands of a conjurer."

HOUDINI'S PSYCHIC "MIRACLES"

In his book *A Magician Among the Spirits*, while discussing the fact that the most incredible and unexplainable feats accomplished by mediums are often the result of fortuitous coincidences, Houdini related an episode that happened to him:

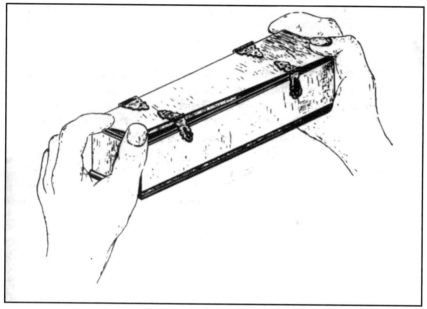

A drawing from Houdini's pamphlet on Margery
(a section of it was devoted to his investigation of Argamasilla's claims)
showing how the box could be opened to peek inside. (Harry Houdini,
Houdini Exposes the Tricks Used by the Boston Medium "Margery," 1924)

. . . [M]y greatest feat of mystery was performed in 1922 at Seacliffe, L.I., on the Fourth of July, at the home of Mr. B. M. L. Ernst. The children were waiting to set off their display of fireworks when it started to rain. The heavens fairly tore loose. Little Richard in his dismay turned to me and said:

"Can't you make the rain stop?"

"Why certainly," I replied and raising my hands said appealingly, "Rain and Storm, I command you to stop."

This I repeated three times and, as if by miracle, within the next two minutes the rain stopped and the skies became clear. Toward the end of the display of fireworks the little fellow turned to me and with a peculiar gleam in his eyes said:

"Why, Mr. Houdini, it would have stopped raining anyway."

I knew I was risking my whole life's reputation with the youngster but I said:

"Is that so? I will show you."

Walking out in front I raised my hands suppliantly toward the heavens and with all the command and force I had in me called:

"Listen to my voice, great Commander of the rain, and once more let the water flow to earth and allow the flowers and trees to bloom."

A chill came over me for as if in response to my command or the prayer of my words another downpour started, but despite the pleading of the children I refused to make it stop again. I was not taking any more chances. (pp. 245–46)

However, when demonstrating how he could duplicate impossible-looking psychic feats Houdini would never leave anything to chance. One example of this is the duplication of some experiments in thought transference made at that time in England by Professor Gilbert Murray (1866–?). Murray, a classicist at Oxford University and ex-president of the Society for Psychical Research (1915–1916), had passed from being a student of psychic claims to being the subject of such studies. He claimed, in fact, that he had discovered by accident the ability to guess words chosen at random while he was absent from the room.

Doyle had written to Houdini about the case: "telepathy is very simple —far more so than a code. I was able, with one good subject, an architect, to get figures reproduced. Prof. Gilbert Murray was great at it, and had an article upon his results in the *Journal* of the Society for Psychical Research."[4]

In view of the noise that the article made at the time, Houdini organized a meeting at his own house to which he invited a group of journalists, including Joseph Pulitzer Jr., editor of the *New York World,* and Walter Lippmann, probably the most authoritative reporter of the time. Houdini described what happened in a letter to his friend Joseph Rinn:

I was taken upstairs to a room, the door guarded, and the committee downstairs got into a corner near a window and mentioned certain things in a low tone (to Hardeen). Any subject selected was written, no carbon paper used, and this never left their hands. This was so that when the test was finished, things could be checked up. I was called into the room and was correct in the first two tests, and one test in particular was extraordinarily striking.

Dr. Edward J. Kempf, psychiatrist, thought of Buffalo Bill's tomb in Wyoming and the sculptor. That was selected for the test.

I was called down and slowly spoke what I visualized, and an extraordinary thing occurred. I told him of a scene that he thought of, but which he did not mention or write. I said: "I see a large plain. I see a great herd of black oxen. They appear to be stampeding. I see a man who is very hungry, that is, I get the impression that he is very hungry, and he is seated on a racing horse. He is chasing these oxen—no, they are not oxen, they are buffaloes; they have their heads down and are going like a whirlwind. He is shooting at them—no, I am wrong. I see a great many people who are hungry. They are thinking of food. This man is supplying them with food. You are not thinking of this man. This man has long hair and piercing eyes. You are thinking not of the man but of the monument. It is Buffalo Bill. You are thinking of his monument in Wyoming and the sculptor—is that right?"

Imagine, Rinn, what consternation there was when Dr. Kempf stated that it was correct, that he had visualized Buffalo Bill and the hungry men and the food, but he had not spoken or written same. It was the most startling thing that occurred there. I positively told the man what he was thinking of. You understand it was one of those hits. You know I do not claim any mental telepathy business.[5]

How did he do it? Probably with a different method than the one used by Murray (that is, if he didn't use telepathy, of course), but what counted to Houdini was the effect. Prior to the demonstration he had his friend, Italian magician Amedeo Vacca, wire the house with a "dictograph," a then-futuristic form of indoor transmission. In the guest room Hardeen would repeat audibly the choices of the guests, as if to fix them in the minds of those present, and, while in his study, Houdini would listen to them through a receiver.

ANNA EVA FAY: THE MENTALIST WHO BAFFLED CROOKES!

In his book *A Magician Among the Spirits*, Houdini had briefly written about a spectacular demonstration given by the medium Anna Eva Fay (Anna Eva Heathman, 1856–1927), who had convinced Sir William Crookes of the reality of her powers. Crookes, a famous and respected physicist of his time, had devoted a few years of his life, during the 1870s, to the investigation of Spiritualism, and had experimented with some of the best-known mediums of the time, among them Daniel Dunglas Home, Kate Fox, and Florence Cook. Cook, in particular, was famous for the materialization during her séances of a spirit form called "Katie King": an exact replica, in every respect, of the medium; the only difference between them was that the ghost wore white underwear. Notwithstanding the absurdity of the phenomenon (nobody had ever seen medium and "ghost" together in the same room), the mediumship of Florence was taken seriously thanks to Crookes's endorsement.[6]

Since Crookes was one of the scientists to whom Conan Doyle always referred to when insisting that the best minds in the world had been convinced of the reality of Spiritualism, Houdini was particularly interested in the case of Anna Eva Fay.

At the time of her involvement with Crookes, Fay performed as a vaudeville artist, presenting onstage a convincing demonstration of mind reading. Her tour of England had been under attack by magician John Nevil Maskelyne who accused her of fraud. She went to Crookes in an attempt to have him test her "powers" and, in the event of an endorsement, put to rest the accusations about her use of trickery.

Houdini poses with Anna Eva Fay in 1924. (McManus-Young Collection, Library of Congress, Rare Books and Special Collections Division, LC-USZ62-96050)

On February 1875, Crookes proposed an experiment that he had already used with Florence Cook. For these séances, Cromwell F. Varley, a fellow of the Royal Society like Crookes, had provided an electrical-control circuit, a slightly modified version of the one used by Crookes with Cook. To make sure that the medium, seated in a curtained cabinet, could not slip her bonds, Crookes asked her to clench both handles of a battery, so constructed as to interrupt the current if she let go of either handle, and send the meter to zero. Fay managed, somehow, to present her manifestations though the contact remained unbroken.

At a later séance, two of the guests appeared to be more skeptical than their host. When they inspected the electrical-control system, before the session began, they discovered that a damp handkerchief stretched between the handles would keep the circuit open. At the suggestion of one of these men, Crookes nailed the handles so far apart that a handkerchief could not span them. Apparently no one considered the possibility that a longer strip of cloth or some other type of resistor might be used. Success at these experiments fueled Annie's tour of the English counties.

In his book, Houdini had hinted at the method used by Fay to free herself from the bonds, but in July 1924, having learned that she was still alive and well in Boston, he decided to pay her a visit to get her version of the facts. Fay, in her late sixties, had white hair and walked with the aid of a cane; Houdini, however, still saw her as "one of the cleverest mediums in history" and noticed her "straw diamond white" hair and penetrating eyes from which "great big streaks of intelligence would flash in and out." "It is small wonder—he observed—that with her personality she could have mystified the great mental giants of the ages,—not our age, but of the ages."[7]

They talked for hours and she revealed to him all her secrets. "She spoke freely of her methods," Houdini noted. "Never at any time did she pretend to believe in spiritualism."[8] She told him how she had tricked Crookes at the electric test: she had simply gripped one handle of the battery beneath her knee joint, keeping the circuit unbroken but leaving one hand free.

Annie Eva Fay's revelation to Houdini of the way she had gulled Crookes was confirmed years later when psychical researcher Colin Brookes-Smith found at the Science Museum in London one of the galvanometers used by Crookes. The machine was repaired and brought to working order. Brookes-Smith reports that "there was no difficulty at all in sliding one wrist and forearm along over one handle and grasping the other handle, thereby keeping the circuit closed through the forearm, and then releasing the other hand without producing any large movement of the galvanometer spot." In a second test, he "tucked both electrodes successively right down into my socks and let go so that my hands were free without producing any large galvanometer spot excursions." In this way, not only did he confirm Eva's revelation but also "Houdini's 1924 footnote explanation that in 1874 Florence (Cook) could have detached one of the electrodes consisting of a gold sovereign and saline soaked blotting-paper pad from one wrist and held it under her knee."[9]

There is no longer any doubt that trickery actually took place during Crookes's tests, exactly as described by Annie Eva Fay; what still needs to be cleared up is whether he was a complete fool (unlikely), a willing accomplice (possible), or if he put too much faith in his electrical controls (likely).[10]

THE ANTI-SPIRITUALIST CRUSADE

In 1925, what had started as a search for true psychic powers became for Houdini a true anti-Spiritualist crusade. Houdini felt that Spiritualism could become a real menace to mankind: "The average man," he wrote in *A Magician Among the Spirits*, "does not seem to realize the suffering, losses, misfortunes, crimes and atrocities of which (Spiritualism) is the underlying cause and must bear the primary responsibility." He called these the "by-products of Spiritualism" and proceeded to give various examples in his book. "One of the saddest cases of modern times," he wrote, "is that of young Barnard College student, Miss Marie Bloomfield, who declared herself in love with a Spirit and finally was driven to suicide in order to join him. The young lady had been an ardent student of Spiritualism and very active in its cause."

A similar episode had also happened during Conan Doyle's first lecture tour in the United States. A few days after his arrival, the April 15, 1925, *New York Times* published the following:

> Mrs. Maud Fancher, of Newark, N.J., who took poison in the belief that she could act as spirit guide to her husband from beyond, died this morning. She killed her baby before she poisoned herself, in order that the child might not be left motherless.
>
> After taking the Lysol, Mrs. Fancher insisted that if she got well, she would make another attempt at suicide that she might reach another world and from there direct her husband out of business worries and other troubles into happiness. She became interested in Spiritualism when she and her husband attended a séance given by a distant relative. Before her death she reiterated her belief that from the beyond she could make her husband happy.

When confronted with the news, Conan Doyle had remarked: "The incident shows the great danger of the present want of knowledge concerning spiritual matters. We know from information from the beyond that suicide is a desperate and very grave offense, that the hand of Providence can not be forced and that the effect of a suicide is to separate the spirit of the offender from those whom he or she loves while they expiate the offense on the other side. If this poor woman had been better instructed she would never have ventured on such a deed."[11]

The statement had hardly sounded compassionate and had fueled further criticism. In an editorial, the April 17, 1925, *Times* had stated: "It is decidedly embarrassing, though rather unfairly so, for Sir Arthur Conan Doyle that the woman over in Newark . . . should have written out, in explanation of what she did, an elaborate statement of her beliefs and hopes to guide her husband, from the beyond, to prosperity that had not been theirs while she was alive. . . . Sir Arthur's defense from such accusations as may be made against him as a result of this pitiful occurrence will have to be that thousands of people have studied his views and have not thought of killing themselves or others."

In his battle, Houdini also attacked a popular game of the time, the Ouija board, whose name derived from the French and German words for "yes," and which it was claimed could put one in touch with the spirits. According to Houdini, the Ouija and the whole idea of Spiritualism could very well lead to insanity: "Spiritualism is nothing more or less than mental intoxication, the intoxication of any sort when it becomes a habit is injurious to the body but intoxication of the mind is always fatal to the mind." Thus, calling on the prohibitionist laws then in force, he asked for some law that could "prevent these human leeches from sucking every bit of reason and common sense from their victims."[12]

Houdini's war on fraudulent mediums took various forms. He tried to raise the level of awareness of the problem among judges and politicians; he wrote to President Calvin Coolidge asking for a government investigation of the phenomenon; through the newspapers he invited readers to denounce the mediums who had tricked them; he lectured for three months at New York's Police Academy, teaching the police the methods of swindlers and fraudulent mediums; he offered large sums of money to any medium who could demonstrate any kind of psychic power that he could not explain or duplicate.

Although the money challenges garnered large amounts of space in the newspapers, and though Houdini himself seemed to think of them as the final word on the reality or falsity of Spiritualism ("If they are genuine why they don't accept my challenge?" he always asked from the newspapers), they were quite devoid of logic. The fact that an apparent psychic phenomenon can be replicated by trickery does not necessarily mean that that specific phenomenon has been obtained by trickery or by that specific trick. The point is that it is not the critic who has the duty of showing the falsity of the medium's claims; but rather, it is he who claims to possess real psychic powers who must present reliable proof of his claims if he wants to be believed. That's why James Randi, today's foremost skeptic, promised in 1964, $10,000 to anyone who could demonstrate any psychic power "under controlled conditions": a very different thing.[13]

"The spiritualists claim that I am attacking their Religion," Houdini later wrote. "That is not true. I respect the real believers of the religion of Spiritualism. I am only exposing fraudulent mediums." In response to the accusation that should he finally witness some real demonstration he would never admit it, he stated the he "would feel it an honor if I could pronounce to the world that I had actually found a person who could communicate with the dead, but first I must be convinced. That should be easy if they are what they claim. But all who have accepted my challenges have failed. They all fall down."

MEDIUM HUNTING

Mediums did not accept Houdini's challenges. Well, if they would not come to him, he would go after them. He set up a sort of private investiga-

When Crime Poses as Spiritualism

Rose Mackenberg, one of Houdini's spies, models her different impersonations.
(*New York Herald Tribune*)

tion agency devoted to the debunking of frauds. One of the most active "agents" was a Toledo magician, Robert Gysel (1880–1938), whom Houdini considered "crazy." Gysel would vex the mediums in every possible way; he would harass them until, desperate, they would prosecute him. This was his objective: after having been sued he would countersue the medium for slander.

Houdini often employed the services of a Brooklyn private investigator, Rose Mackenberg. Young Rose would usually arrive in a city where Houdini was scheduled to perform or give a lecture, and infiltrate the rooms of the best-known local mediums. She was particularly adept at disguise, and would present herself as a jealous wife, a simpleminded maid, a neurotic schoolteacher, or a wealthy eccentric. At every séance she would receive assurances or news from dead children or husband, suggestions on how to invest money, or what to do about her job. When Houdini arrived in the city, Rose would pass him all the details about the mediums she had visited.

In a typical scenario, Houdini would invite the local mediums on stage (they frequently attended his shows), and when they refused he would call

Rose onstage. She revealed how the medium had produced messages for her from nonexistent departed husband and son. More than once, the medium had to run in humiliation from the theater.

Rose was also a great asset to Houdini when he wanted to show how easy it was to become "spiritualistic ministers." "To be a real minister," he explained to his audiences, "you have to spend eight to eighteen years, but to be a spiritualist minister you just have to say I hear voices." At that point Rose would show the long list of ministerial credentials that she had bought from Spiritualist churches; they were so many that she had been nicknamed "The Rev" by members of the Houdini troupe. "They asked me no questions as to whether I was sincere or not," she explained. "All they were interested in was the amount of money I could pay them."[14]

One of the most sordid aspects that Houdini's female investigators often had to face was sexual harassment by male mediums. More than once mediums, apparently in a trance state, tried to touch Rose. Houdini was so disgusted that he suggested she carry a gun, but she preferred not to.

Alberta Chapman, another one of Houdini's undercover investigators, recently revealed to Houdini historian Sidney Radner how mediums used to invite her to some very "peculiar" sittings in their bedrooms.

"Why are we in a room like this?" she would ask.

"Maybe I can bring the sensations back to you that Arthur gave you," came the reply. At that the medium tried to ease Alberta over to the bed. "And I would always have some excuse to get out of it," she explained. "I had to manufacture tears or hysterics and I would say, 'I'll come back the next day,' which of course I never did."[15]

Houdini sometimes employed his niece, Julia Sawyer, as a spy: "They think she is a little girl," he testified before the U.S. Congress in 1924, "but she is my private secretary, and you can question her about certain things, and I believe you will agree with me that she does possess some mentality."

"SHERLOCK HOUDINI"

Like his ex-friend's literary sleuth, Houdini also used disguises to enable him to enter unrecognized the houses of the mediums he wanted to unmask personally. One such case took place in Cleveland where Houdini, accompanied by County Prosecutor Edward C. Stanton and Louis B. Selzer, a reporter, went to the house of the medium George Renner. Houdini was disguised in old clothes and heavy glasses.

Renner, unaware of the trap into which he was falling, had the three men step inside his house. He took them to the séance room, where a table was ready with guitars, trumpets, tambourines, and spirit photographs. The conversation turned to Houdini, who Renner called a "four-flusher." "I once paid $2.50 to see him," said Renner. "He's a big frost and a faker. They chased him out of Massachusetts. When he says spiritualism is a fake, he lies, folks. Tonight we will prove that spiritualism is genuine and that Houdini is a faker."

The group was joined by three more people and all of them took their places around the table. The room was darkened and the guitar began to play. In a short while, Houdini informed Selzer that he was leaving his place. When he returned he whispered in his ear: "Be prepared." The trumpets seemed to rise and then they clanked back on the table. "Just as this sound was made," reported the journalist afterward, "a light blinded my eyes, and I saw, across the table, the medium with his hands all black, his face flushed, his eyes blinking."

"Mr. Renner, you are a fraud," said Houdini, holding a pocket flashlight. "Your hands are full of lamp black, Mr. Renner. The trumpets are also full of lamp black. That's where you got it on your hands." It was Houdini who, under cover of darkness, had smeared the trumpets with lampblack.

"I have been a medium for forty years," shouted Renner, "and I have never been exposed."

"Well, you are now," replied Houdini.

"Who are you?" asked the unmasked medium.

"My name," said the magician, removing his glasses, "is Houdini."

The man was later arrested, tried, and found guilty of obtaining money under false pretenses. He was fined twenty-five dollars and sentenced to serve six months in jail. However, his lawyer seems to have won a new trial on appeal.

The reactions to Houdini's crusade were of two kinds. The newspapers all over America supported him, and considered him the right man at the right moment. "It may be indeed," wrote Edmund Wilson in the *New Republic*, "that Houdini has appeared at a crucial moment in the history of spiritualism and that he is destined to play an important role. It is difficult to understand how a credulous disposition toward mediums can long survive such public exposures."

"The man is marvelous," wrote *Billboard* about his live exposés. "But that isn't all. His exposé of the means of fake mediums was as laughter-provoking as it was educational. The audience simply 'ate it up.' Seriously, the man, Houdini, aside from being a great magician and a scholar in the lines of psychic research, has personality. He breaths it. The audience feels it. He is a master of the science of illusion and has a vocabulary that any college professor might envy. By all means see Houdini. It is an inspiring, elevating and entertaining spectacle."

Variety as well praised his as "one of the best shows of the season at the Hippodrome" and added: "Houdini is the greatest showman in vaudeville today and a tremendous draw. His latest act surpasses anything he has ever attempted before on account of the world-wide interest in spiritualism. The humanitarian qualities of the turn can never be imagined by a layman unfamiliar with the hoaxes perpetrated by fake mediums on believers. Last wills and testaments have been changed through the trickery of mediums, where messages from the dead were used as the motivating power to induce some rich convert his or her fortune should be left to the scheming individuals who employed the fake mediums."

Of course not everybody was amused. The Spiritualists really hated him and tried in every way to stop him. "They are holding indignation meetings all over America against my exposé," he wrote to Harry Price.[16] Soon, however, the Spiritualists began to predict Houdini's death. Mediums in Boston had started to predict his demise within a year soon after the publication of his pamphlet detailing Margery's tricks, as a sort of punishment for his treatment of Mina Crandon. "Walter," noted Houdini in an interview, mentioning Margery's control, "has suggested the fact that I have about a year or less to live. In the last 10 years my death has been predicted dozens of times, and if the spiritualists (?) guess often enough sometime they will guess correctly."

Even Conan Doyle had received warnings at his home circle: "Houdini is doomed, doomed, doomed!" said one of the messages. "So seriously did I take this warning," remembered Conan Doyle, "that I would have written to him had I the least hope that my words could have any effect. I knew, however, by previous experience, that he always published my letters, even the most private of them, and that it would only give him a fresh pretext for ridiculing that which I regard as a sacred cause."[17]

MARGERY: THE SECOND HARVARD INVESTIGATION

Even if the publication of the *Scientific American* final report on Margery had ended the committee's investigation of the case, it certainly had not ended Houdini's personal investigation. Though he was refused entrance to any more séances with the medium, a journalist friend was able to infiltrate the group, Stewart Griscom of the *Boston Herald*, who kept him informed about the latest developments; this allowed the magician to continually update his stage exposé to the amazement of Margery's supporters.

"She is now ringing the bell box while it is being carried," Houdini wrote in a May 15, 1925, letter to Harry Price. "This is an imitation of the feat as I presented it during my lecture, so it proves that what one mystifier can do, can be duplicated by another. They have two bell boxes, one is a push button, they call it the boarding house bell and is something they said could not be done in the early stages. They have some ectoplasm ? In test tubes, but from the analysis given to me by two physicians, it is something entirely different. They cause a coin to jump from the table into the hand of one of the sitters. They have a round disk with a whole [sic] in the center. It is placed on the table and one of the sitters puts his nose in the center of it, and a hand pulls the back of his hair. They tell me (?) that the hand is entirely ectoplasmic but bones can be felt."[18]

"They certainly were greatly surprised to think I knew of their progress," commented Houdini. Actually, all these revelations not only surprised but greatly angered Dr. Crandon, who correctly assumed that Houdini had a spy in the circle, but he wrongly identified a man called Mansfield.

Houdini's attacks received support from an investigation conducted in the late spring of 1925 by a group of psychologists from Harvard University. Margery had already been the subject, in 1923, of an investigation by a group of Harvard psychologists, led by William McDougall (who would also later join the *Scientific American* commission). On that occasion, the investigators had remained very doubtful of the truth of what they had witnessed and had found evidence of cheating. The investigation, however, did not lead to the publication of a report.

This time, another group of researchers from Harvard, composed mainly of graduate students, had asked Margery's permission to conduct experiments on her powers, and she had accepted. "You want to know what it feels to be a witch?" she told a reporter when the news became public. "You know that's what they would have called me in Boston 150 years ago. And they would have hauled me before the General Court and executed me for consorting with the devil. But now they send committees of Professors from Harvard to study me. That represents progress doesn't it?"[19]

The results of the investigation, however, did not turn out to be what Mina would have hoped for. They were published in the November 1925 *Atlantic Monthly*, in an article titled "Science and the Medium: The Climax of a Famous Investigation." Its author, Hudson Hoagland, revealed that Margery had been observed performing various kinds of subterfuges.

She took off a luminous band that had been placed on her ankle to track her movements, and with her free foot managed to "float" a luminous disk; the Harvard group also established she had been able to use her right foot to ring a bell and to touch sitters. Finally, Margery fell into a trap. One experimenter, Grant H. Code, who had suggested that Mina's body cavities could act as a convenient storage warehouse for fake ectoplasm, set her up. Before one of the sittings, he offered to help her in the deceptions by freeing the hand he would be in charge of controlling: she immediately accepted and, during the séance, used it to take some fake ectoplasm out of her lap and put it on the table.

The group put forward a theory to explain all this. According to them, Dr. Crandon was sincere in his beliefs, as probably was Mina. The idea was that, based on a genuine belief in Spiritualism, on the powerful unconscious suggestion of Crandon, on the psychic literature she had been reading, and under the influence of their circle of friends, an artificial dramatic "Walter" personality had been created, into which Margery would lapse casually, unremembered by her normal consciousness, both in and out of séances, thus causing her not only innocently, so far as her normal consciousness was concerned, to produce the phenomena in the séances, but also to prepare beforehand the artificial accompaniments and apparatus generally.

When the report was published, Crandon reacted by circulating a booklet, *Margery, Harvard, Veritas,* purporting to reprint the full notes of the séances. This was supposed to show how Hoagland's version of the story differed from the "recorded facts." However, to the public the Harvard report seemed to be the final verdict on Margery.

To those who had doubted Houdini's attacks on the ground that he was merely an artist seeking publicity, the revelations of the Harvard group confirmed that Houdini had been right. "Just think how Houdini will shout," remarked Margery to her friends after the publication of the *Atlantic* article. And Houdini made sure that the news reached everybody. He talked about it from the stage and wrote letters to his friends and the other committee members. "A certain group of professors," he wrote to journalist Walter Lippmann, "after roundly abusing me, have accomplished in half a year what I did in one night. . . . This has been a wonderful vindication for me."[20]

The Margery case, however, was far from closed. Interesting new material would keep on piling up in the following years.

THE CRUSADE IN CHICAGO

In March 1926 the anti-Spiritualistic crusade reached its climax when Houdini's show arrived at the Princess Theater in Chicago. There he would stay for eight weeks and, during this period, he and his group of detectives unmasked the frauds of up to eighty local mediums! One of the highlights was the entrapment of medium Minnie Reichart, the description of which made the banner headline and most of the front page of the *Chicago American* of March 11. During the séance, which Houdini attended in disguise, a photographer took a flash photo that captured the medium holding a spirit trumpet with a handkerchief so as not to leave any traces.

Outside the theater in which Houdini performed was a long list, continually updated, of the local mediums being unmasked, with names and addresses. Three of them sued Houdini for slander; others, however, kept on predicting Houdini's death. (These cases never came to trial because Houdini died before they went to court.)

One day Houdini received, in his dressing room, an unexpected visit

Houdini poses with Anna Clark Benninghofen, a reformed spirit medium who had used a trumpet in her work. (McManus-Young Collection, Library of Congress, Rare Books and Special Collections Division, LC-USZ62-112379)

by a Mr. and Mrs. Benninghoefen, who complimented him on his crusade. Mrs. Benninghoefen, under the name of Anna Clark, had been a famous Chicago medium, also known as the "mother medium," because she had helped develop various young mediums.

"I will come any time or place to help you," she explained to Houdini, "as I now see the great good that is being done. You know, when I reformed I had no intention of going before the public and showing how the tricks were done; it was my desire to retire in private life, but when I saw the effect it had on the public I did think it advisable to show them just exactly how I did my work."

Houdini arranged for a press conference at the Sherman Hotel, where Mrs. Benninghoefen could present her complete repertoire and then reveal her tricks. The lights were lowered and phenomena started to manifest: trumpets rose and floated in the dark room, voices were heard coming from everywhere, ghostly hands appeared and disappeared. After a while, the lights were turned back on and the medium revealed her secrets: she could project her voice far because, in the dark, she had attached two trum-

On the stage of the New York Hippodrome, Houdini exposes techniques used by fraudulent mediums. (McManus-Young Collection, Library of Congress, Rare Books and Special Collections Division, LC-USZ62-66388)

pets, mouthpiece to mouthpiece; thus, whispering in the large end of one trumpet her voice could be heard from the far end of the other. She was also an accomplished ventriloquist and could speak with many voices. The ghostly hand was merely a glove coated with luminous paint and attached to black cardboard: by turning the cardboard she could make the hand appear and disappear.

"I really believed in spiritualism all the time I was practicing it," the medium explained, "but I thought I was justified in helping the spirits out. They couldn't float a trumpet around the room, I did it for them. They couldn't speak, so I spoke for them. I thought I was justified in trickery because through trickery I could get more converts to what I thought was a good and beautiful religion. When people asked me if the spirits really moved the trumpets, I told them to judge for themselves. So while I acted a lie, I didn't tell one."

At the end of the session, Houdini obliged the reporters by posing with Mrs. Benninghoefen and the trumpets.

On May 5, in Harrisburg, Pennsylvania, Houdini's tour closed its first season on the road. His anti-Spiritualistic crusade, however, would go on.

HOUDINI IN WASHINGTON

In February, Houdini, at U.S. Representative Sol Bloom's invitation, traveled to Washington to testify before a House committee in support of an anti-fortune-telling bill proposed by Bloom for the District of Columbia. Similar bills had already been enacted in various states, and were used to prosecute séance swindles. The hearing was open to the public and Spiritualists filled the room. In essence, Bloom proposed that "any person pretending to tell fortunes for reward or compensation . . . shall be considered a disorderly person. Any person violating the provisions of this law shall be punished by a fine not to exceed $250 or by imprisonment not to exceed six months."

"The thing that I object to," explained Bloom to the House of Representatives, "is that the District of Columbia to-day, the way I understand it, for the sum of $25 will give you a license to make a business of telling fortunes, etc., which is a fraud." Bloom then introduced Houdini, "who came in special and just got off the train," and asked him to make a statement about the bill. Houdini was asked to introduce himself: "I am an author; I am a psychic investigator for the scientific magazines of the world; and then I am a mysterious entertainer."

"This is positively no attack upon a religion," began Houdini's statement. "Please, understand that emphatically. I am not attacking a religion. . . . But this thing they call 'spiritualism,' wherein a medium intercommunicates with the dead, is a fraud from start to finish. There are only two kinds of mediums, those who are mental degenerates and who ought to be under observation, and those who are deliberate cheats and frauds. I would not believe a fraudulent medium under oath; perjury means nothing to them. . . . In 35 years I have never seen one genuine medium. Millions of dollars are stolen every year in America, and the Government have [sic] never paid any attention to it, because they look upon it as a religion."

The discussion, however, turned on the risks of personal liberty limitations, should such a law be approved; others thought that the bill was frivolous. "You believe the old adage of Solomon," asked a Mr. Gilbert, "which said 'A fool and his money are soon parted'?"

Interestingly, during the debate the name of Conan Doyle came out:

Mr. McLeod: I do not want to interfere with your statement, but you have made quite an extensive investigation, as has this gentleman. Why would it not be possible, if that is such an outrageous fake and fraud, that it would be discovered by such men as Conan Doyle, who is an outstanding authority?

Mr. Houdini: Conan Doyle is not an outstanding authority.

Mr. McLeod: He is accepted as one of the best.

Mr. Houdini: No; he is not accepted as one of the best. He is one of the greatest dupes, outside of Sir Oliver Lodge. Conan Doyle stated that I possess mediumistic powers, which I deny.

Mr. McLeod: How can you prove it?

Mr. Houdini: I admit that I do not possess mediumistic powers. They claim in a London psychic college I dematerialize my body, and that I ooze through and come out again and put myself together. That is Hewitt [sic] McKenzie.

Mr. McLeod: How do you do it?

Mr. Houdini: I do it like anybody else would do it. There is nothing secret about it. We are all humans. Nobody is supernormal. We are all born alike.

Various other witnesses were heard, among them Remigius Weiss, the man who had been able to obtain a written confession from the famous medium Henry Slade, and Rose Mackenberg, who detailed her visits under disguise to various mediums. The spiritualists began making noise so as to interrupt the hearings and have a chance to speak. The meeting was postponed until May 18.

On that date, some Spiritualists started to call Houdini a "brute," "vile," and "crazy." Houdini chose a peculiar line of defense. He called as a witness Mrs. Houdini:

Won't you step this way? I want the chairman to see you. . . . On June 22, 1926, is when we will celebrate our thirty-second anniversary. . . . Outside of my great mother, Mrs. Houdini has been my greatest friend. Have I shown traces of being crazy, unless it was about you? (Laughter)

No.

Am I brutal to you, or vile?

No.

Am I a good boy?

Yes.

Thank you Mrs. Houdini. (Applause)

A Spiritualist, Charles William Myers, was called among the witnesses, and declared: ". . . religion, organized religion outside of spiritualism is trying to down spiritualism." And to make himself clearer, he even addressed some racial remarks to Houdini and Bloom: "In the beginning, 3,000 years ago, or 2,000, Judas betrayed Christ. He was a Jew, and I want to say that this bill is being put through by two—well, you can use your opinion."

The bill was rejected; it appeared impossible to approve it without violating First Amendment guarantees. Houdini felt sorry about the outcome, but admitted that his handling of the case had not helped: "I think they were more interested in my manifestations," he wrote to a friend, "than they were in the mediums. I was sorry to see that as I really am sincere about the law."[21]

REESE UNMASKED

In July 1926, Houdini spoke from New York radio station WOR, denouncing all pretenders to supernatural powers. He further explained that all so-called pellet readers, that is, psychics claiming to be able to read messages written inside slips of paper, were swindlers even if they did not claim to use psychic powers. The reference to Bert Reese, the most famous champion of this specialty, who Houdini had trapped years before, was clear. After the transmission, Houdini received a frantic phone call at his home from an excited Reese.

Houdini, as usual, sent Reese the following day a letter by registered mail, with return receipt, "so that there can be no mistake of your attitude toward me." In it he detailed their first meeting: "In the séance you gave me," he wrote, "where you purported to read the five messages I had written, surmising that you must have some adroit method of opening the non-crinkling paper which you handed me, you will remember I purposely made peculiar shapes of the 'pellets' so that when you started to read my questions the astonished look on your face told me that you had been totally unprepared for this maneuver." He went on detailing Reese's accomplishments abroad, his performances in front of scientists, and then proceeded to propose a test: "I will write five questions or sentences. . . . Should you be successful in reading the five questions, I will pay you an extra $500. . . . We are both alive," was Houdini's conclusion, "you can reply."

Reese did not reply, but went personally to Houdini's home. He begged Houdini not to expose his work because he was an old man of eighty-three and made his living by giving people the impression that he possessed some psychic powers.

"If you don't claim to get messages from spirits," was Houdini's reply, "and if you admit that it is accomplished by natural means, I will close the argument."

"No," said Reese, "I don't claim to be a medium or a spiritualist, I don't get messages from disembodied spirits. Never claimed that."

"Well, you have fooled a lot of people."

"Oh, yes. . . . I can't keep their mouth shut. I am only an entertainer. . . . People have so much faith in me that I can cure them."

"What do you mean cure them?"

"Oh, I can do things for them, especially if they are hypochondriacs! I talk to them. Oh, I cure thousands. . . ."

Then returning to the subject of pellet-reading, Houdini said: "You have the best method in the world—that is, that I have ever seen."

"Yes, and I am going to keep it for myself!"

Typically, Houdini asked him to pose for a picture together, but Reese refused; then, Houdini made him promise not to claim mediumship or telepathic powers and let him out.

Soon after that, further proofs of Reese's deceptions came to the light. A few years earlier he had been investigated in Germany by a lawyer, Dr. Bruno Birnbaum, and by Professor Moll of the German Psychological Society. It appears that, while in Berlin, Reese had convinced a famous critic, Felix Hollaender, that some occult powers were working against him; however, since he found him such a nice person, he would help him.

"I will do something," said Reese, "that I have rarely done for anyone else. I shall defeat the machinations of the evil forces opposed to you. How many letters are in your Christian name?"

"Five," replied Hollaender.

"Good," remarked Reese. "Give me seventeen dollars for every letter in your name. I shall send this money to New York, where it will be used to combat the evil influences that conspire against you. I can say no more and explain no more. It is a matter of mutual trust. I warn you not to speak of this matter to any one else, not even your wife, or all my efforts will be frustrated."

It was a typical swindle, still used today by many self-claimed psychics, astrologers, and charlatans. By this means, Reese had been able to gather sums of money from gullible people who, more often than not, were also learned men of science and culture.[22]

THE BURIED FAKIR

In May 1926, soon after the hearings on the anti-fortune-telling bill in Washington, Houdini's attention shifted to a new wonder, imported to the United States by none other than Hereward Carrington, Houdini's old nemesis. Carrington had been the only member of the *Scientific American* committee who had declared from the start the genuineness of Margery's mediumship, and had worked as a sort of impresario in America for such mediums as Eusapia Palladino and Nino Pecoraro.

Carrington's new "attraction" was a self-styled Egyptian fakir, twenty-six-year-old Rahman Bey, who claimed to possess a supernormal power whereby he could suspend animation in his own body. He had opened at Selwyn Theater, in New York, performing various physical feats: he stopped his pulse, forced hatpins through his cheek, had a block of sandstone placed on his chest and pounded with a sledgehammer, and did various other tests. All the while, Carrington lectured the audience as a perfect master of ceremonies on yogis' and Hindus' powers of meditation and supreme control over their body functions. In his most astonishing test Bey permitted himself to be shut in an air-tight coffin for ten minutes or more, whereafter he would emerge alive and bowing. This, he explained, was possible thanks to his self-imposed "cataleptic trance."

Houdini, who went to the show and easily recognized many sideshow tricks which he had already explained in his *Miracle Mongers and Their Methods*, thought that Bey's scientific-sounding explanations were just a "lot of bunk." Furthermore, having noticed Houdini in the audience, Carrington had swiftly changed the tone of the presentation, claiming that Bey did not operate through supernatural, but only natural means. "That alone," noted Houdini afterward, "spiked my guns."

In July, Bey presented a new version of his coffin stunt: he announced that he would stay submerged in the Hudson River, sealed in a bronze casket, for an hour. As soon as the coffin touched the water, however, the emergency bell inside the casket started to ring. It took the workmen about fifteen minutes to open the lid, but Bey claimed he did not remember having touched the bell, since he was in a trance. Nonetheless, he could boast that he had survived for about twenty minutes in the sealed coffin.

At once Houdini determined to expose Bey for what he really was: a trickster. He issued his challenge and, through the *Evening World*, announced: "I guarantee to remain in any coffin that the fakir does for the same length of time he does, without going into any cataleptic trance." A few days later, as if to raise the bet, Bey again tried his stunt: this time, however, he was submerged in the water of the Hotel Dalton swimming pool where, unbelievably, he stayed for an hour.

HOUDINI'S LAST MIRACLE: SUBMERGED UNDER WATER

Houdini now had to keep his promise and duplicate the fakir's stunt. He had a bronze casket made by the Boyertown Burial Casket Company, the same firm which had supplied the bronze casket for Bey, and arranged with the Hotel Shelton, in New York, to use its swimming pool for the test. The challenge seemed lost from the start: Bey was twenty-six years old, Houdini was twice that age, having recently celebrated his fifty-second birthday; he was much heavier and more tired than a few years before, when he was accustomed to holding his breath even in icy waters. In any event, if there was someone in the world who could have a chance of staying inside a casket for more than an hour and then come out alive that was certainly the greatest escape artist that ever lived.

The casket could hold 26,428 cubic inches of air—less the space occupied by the body and by a telephone and batteries that Houdini had installed. Before the official test, and to avoid surprises, Houdini decided to secretly try the stunt at home. For the trial tests he used a glass top rather than the metal one, so that he could be observed by his doctor.

The first try took place on July 31, with Houdini's assistants and the doctor attending. Once the top had been shut, Houdini remained motionless. After forty-five minutes he started to perspire. He heard the doctor say: "I would not do that for $500." As time passed breathing became harder, each time he had to gasp for air he had to "pump with all my might for air." This convinced him that panic shortened the lives of those who were trapped for long periods in mine shafts or vaults. "With my years of training," he noted afterward, "I can remain apparently motionless without an effort. I kept my eyes open for fear I would go to sleep." When he could not take it any longer he signaled for the lid to be opened: an hour and ten minutes had passed. He was dripping wet from head to toe, but he had not felt too uncomfortable. This made him suspect that some air must have seeped inside.

For the next secret test, on August 4 at about noon, he had the lid made airtight. This time the casket was submerged in a large container filled with water. He felt the coffin moist and cold, the water seemed to chill the box; however, he felt more comfortable than at the first test. After fifty minutes he began taking longer breaths and started feeling very irritable: "I was annoyed by movements, annoyed by one of my assistants swaying over my head, even twisting of the key." Despite his nerves, he managed to stay sealed for an hour and ten minutes, as he had on the previous try. Now he felt ready for the real challenge.

The date chosen for the test was August 5. Houdini invited journalists from all over the United States and many of his friends, like Walter Lippmann and Adolph Ochs, publisher of the *Times*; Joe Rinn acted as timekeeper; Joe Dunninger, the up-and-coming greatest mentalist was there, as well as Carrington. The invitation read: "HOUDINI's experiment of attempting to remain submerged one hour in an airtight metal coffin."

Houdini had prepared himself by eating very light: "had a fruit salad and a half a cup of coffee." He felt somewhat nervous, "but that I attribute to the excitement of the test, not through any fear." In the three weeks of his training, he "reduced about twelve pounds."

Finally, stripped down to brown trunks and white shirt, Houdini made his entrance in the pool room. He noticed worriedly that the overcrowded pool area felt overly warm and thought that the air was rarified. Before entering the new galvanized iron box (a better-looking—and larger—model than the one used during his trials), Houdini was tested by physicians, who found him normal. However, they stated that a human being could survive inside a sealed box of that kind for only three to four minutes: soon, in fact, all the oxygen would be consumed and the casket would be filled with carbon dioxide. "If I die," remarked Houdini before the lid was soldered, "it will be the will of God and my own foolishness. I am going to prove that the copybook maxims are wrong when they say that a man can live but three minutes without air—and I shall not pretend to be in a cataleptic state either."

The coffin was finally sealed and lowered into the pool. It took about 700 pounds of iron and eight swimmers standing on top of the casket in order to keep it beneath the water line and level. Houdini felt disturbed by the strong heat he felt inside the box, and became more irritable than he had been during the tests. The men standing on the coffin seemed to be shaking it, and one even lost his balance and fell. The casket shot up above the surface and was quickly pushed down. "What's the big idea?" Houdini shouted through the phone to his assistant, Jim Collins. "What struck me?" He had visualized the box breaking in two and thought he was going to drown before he could be taken out of it. The effort of talking, however, left him gasping for air.

When the hour was reached, Collins phoned him with the news. Houdini, though breathing heavily now, wanted to try to stay a bit more. He reached for his handkerchief, which was wet, and pressed it to his lips, and feeling better he kept it there to lessen his strain.

"When Collins, my assistant phoned me that I had been in the coffin for one hour and twelve minutes," he noted later, "I was going to stay three more minutes, but watching my lungs rise and fall, thought I could stand the strain for another fifteen minutes."

He felt water trickling inside the box, and realized that the casket was slightly leaking.

"After one hour and twenty-eight minutes," he continued in his notes written after the experience, "I commenced to see yellow lights and carefully watched myself not to go to sleep. I kept my eyes wide open; moved on the broad of my back, so as to take all the weight off my lungs, my left arm being across my chest. I lay on my right side, my left buttock against the coffin, so that I could keep the telephone receiver to my ear without holding it, and told Collins to get me up at an hour and a half, thinking if I did go to sleep, he would get me up within that time."[23]

When the casket was finally taken out of water, Houdini felt a physical elation and a curious irritation. When the air-vent caps were unscrewed, he thrust up an arm. A doctor took his pulse: it had been eighty-four at the time of entry; now it was one hundred forty-two. The lid was ripped open enough to let Houdini climb out. He was again dripping wet and, according to Carrington, looked "deathly white."

Once at home he recorded all the details of his experiment and later sent them to Dr. W. J. McConnell, a physiologist with the U.S. Bureau of

Mines, feeling that his tests might be helpful to miners trapped in collapsed shafts. "When I was dictating this, I still had that metallic taste in my stomach and mouth; felt rather weak in the knees; had no headache, but just seemed listless." But he had beaten the fakir at his own game!

"There is no doubt in my mind," he added, "that had this test been where fresh air could have gotten into the galvanized iron coffin as I was put in same," and not in the hotel were the air was warm and foul, "I could have readily stayed fifteen or thirty minutes longer."

"Am having a coffin made with a glass top," he concluded his notes for Dr. McConnell, "and as soon as it is ready will let you know. I know you are doing a worthwhile work and as my body and brain are trained for this particular line, I am at your service. Don't be afraid to ask any question, I will be glad to let you know."[24]

Some magicians, and even Joseph Rinn, thought that Houdini must have used some hidden supply of oxygen. Houdini was annoyed at these suspicions: "There is a rumor going around," he wrote to a friend,[25] "that there is a gimmick to the thing. I pledge my word of honor there isn't a thing to it excepting to lie down and keep quiet. I trained for three weeks in water to get my lungs accustomed to battle without air, and after one hour, did have to struggle and believe only due to the training was I able to stay so long. Rest assured there is no gimmick, no trick at all—simply lying on your back and breathing shallow breaths is all you do. Did it twice in a coffin with a glass top to test myself. There is no doubt in my mind that anyone can do it."[26]

Carrington wrote a few years later: "Houdini remained submerged in a metal coffin for about an hour and a half; but when he emerged he was deathly white, running with perspiration and with a pulse of 142. I was present at this experimental burial, as at many others, and know whereof I speak. It is my opinion that Houdini appreciably shortened his life by this endurance burial."

Houdini was, in fact, getting tired. Nonetheless, he had very specific plans for his future years. He would start a new tour with his magic show in September 1926, a tour that would have taken him all over the United States and Canada. Once that was over, he would still do one final world tour with the show and then retire forever from the stage. However, he would never retire from show business; he felt that in the future he could devote more time to his literary ambitions and to his fights in "defense of the public." Spiritualism, however, was rapidly losing its appeal among the public—thanks also to his crusades—so, the new targets were going to be swindlers and con-men. Having already written a book on the subject in 1906, *The Right Way to Do Wrong*, he felt especially equipped to handle the subject.

HOUDINI BEATS FAKIR IN STAY UNDER WATER

Handcuff Wizard Remains in Sealed Tomb Half an Hour Longer Than Rahman Bey

Occidental science yesterday triumphed over oriental mystery when Harry Houdini, famous exploiter of the seemingly miraculous, duplicated the feat of Rahman Bey, Hindu mystic, in allowing himself to be buried alive.

Houdini remained for one hour and thirty-one minutes in the airtight galvanized-iron casket sunk beneath the swimming pool of the Hotel Shelton. Rahman Bey previously had remained an hour under water in a similar casket at the Dalton Swimming Pool.

Houdini admitted the occasion was the most important in his long and spectacular career. Before allowing himself to be encased in the casket he explained his reasons for doing the trick. He had no desire to "show up" Rahman Bey as a remarkably clever magician. The Egyptian youth who has amazed thousands all over the world by his feats, was, he said, gifted. But not in any supernatural way such as was being claimed for him by some of his backers. To prove that such a feat as Bey's could be done by anyone was his sole purpose in demonstrating it, said Houdini, adding:

"This event is the most important in my life. By keeping alive without air, except the little that remains in the casket, I hope to set a great example for miners who may be entombed and sailors who may find themselves upon a sunken submarine. I hope this demonstration will show men entombed anywhere how they may prolong their lives long enough for aid to reach them."

WEIGHTED DOWN.

Houdini wore a silk shirt and a pair of trunks when he stepped into the coffin. He did not put himself into the trance that Rahman Bey induced. His temperature was pronounced normal and his pulse 84 by Dr. W. J. McConnell, of Philadelphia. The casket was tested by Orson Munn, publisher of Science and Invention. The great box was lowered at 12:08.

Weights and six men were placed on it to make it sink. When after a half hour one man fell off and the casket almost turned over there was a gasp of fear from the hundreds of spectators. Had it not been for Houdini's ringing of a bell connected with a telephone in the hands of his assistant, James Collins, and which he pressed in-

What Answer, Rahman?

OUR MR. HOUDINI—He who carries a swell line of straitjacket openers and cell-busting novelties took on Rahman Bey's best trick yesterday and stayed under water in a coffin for ninety minutes. Dr. W. J. McConnell examined Harry before he stepped—

INTO CASKET!—In effort to prove no supernatural powers are necessary for this now popular trick, Harry applied American brand of Houdinism. They lowered him—

New York American article dated August 6, 1926, covers Houdini's underwater burial stunt at the Hotel Shelton. (Oscar Teale Houdini Scrapbook, Library of Congress, Rare Books and Special Collections Division)

..LG IT SIMPLE.

An hour passed, and it was supposed Houdini would rise, having duplicated Rayman Bey's feat. But another half hour went by, with staccato rings of the bell before the long peal for release.

Houdini's stocky figure was trembling and exhausted when he was pulled from the casket. This was ripped open with knives and pincers by the six workmen in frantic haste. Breathing in long gasps, Houdini said his only moment of fear was when his self-imposed tomb overturned. His temperature was 99, the same as the casket interior. His pulse had leaped to 142. Calling for a glass of water, he said:

"Fear causes more such deaths than lack of air. No human being can live without air, of course, and I am no block of marble. But by taking shallow breaths and conserving the small air supply it is possible to live,' you see, an hour and a half in a space with only enough oxygen to sustain life five minutes, according to physicians. But anyone claiming to do this feat by supernatural power lies. Anyone can do it."

Houdini added, however, that it was a pretty hard test for his mature years. He emphasized the fact that he had volunteered the demonstration and no offers of money were involved.

INTO WATER!—In Hotel Shelton pool in casket containing apparently only sufficient air for ten minute's submersion.

BLUB! BLUB!—With casket weighted by 2,000 pounds, Harry conversed with spectators by means of tiny signal bell until he had been—

UNDER 90 MINUTES!—Here's America's favorite illusionist, out of the casket, wondering if Rahman Bey has any other hard ones he'll have to try.

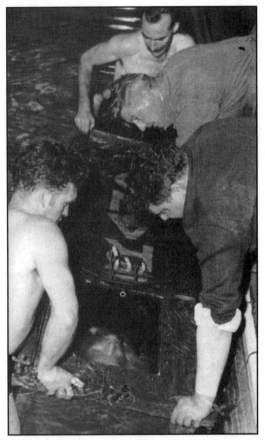

James Randi during the duplication of Houdini's stunt. (© James Randi Educational Foundation)

MARGERY FAILS AGAIN

Houdini's final tour of the United States officially opened on September 13 at the Majestic Theater in Boston. Being in Margery's territory once again, it was inevitable that he would look for news about her.

After the publication of the official verdict of the *Scientific American* committee, Walter Franklin Prince had resigned from the American Society for Psychical Research, the majority of whose members backed Margery's claims. He started a new association, the Boston Society for Psychic Research. His place as research officer inside the ASPR was taken by none other than Malcolm Bird. This news resulted in the immediate resignation from the society of various members, including Houdini, of course.

The recent Harvard investigation had badly stained Margery's reputation, and Malcolm Bird had planned a new investigation on behalf of the ASPR in order to clear her name. Another new member of the ASPR, Henry Clay McComas, a psychologist at Princeton University, who had openly admitted that he had accepted the post because he had been attracted by "more generous pay than any university dreamed of at that time," was going to join Bird in his investigation.

On his first visit to the Crandons, McComas expressed his surprise: "when Mrs. Crandon was presented she would completely upset all preconceptions of the famous medium. A very attractive blonde with a charming expression and excellent figure, the 'Witch of Lime Street' proved

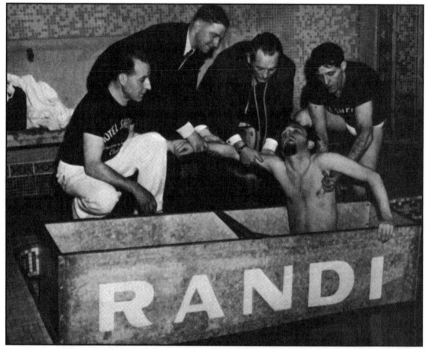

Randi is helped from the casket. (© James Randi Educational Foundation)

to be a thoroughly feminine lady with the best traits of a mother and housekeeper. Her vivacity, with the doctor's poise and dignity, made them a delightful pair for an enjoyable dinner. Both had a very diverting sense of humor and the conversation would never lag."

After a test séance, where phenomena abounded, though under no controls, McComas noted: "As you would leave late in the evening after saying goodbye to your new and interesting friends, you would probably find your thoughts taking one of two directions. If you had felt kindly toward the spiritistic interpretation of the things you had read about in psychic records you would probably say to yourself: 'This is the best argument for my belief that I have ever found'. If, on the other hand, your training and habits of thinking made spiritualism impossible you would say to yourself: 'What under the sun are these people up to? Are they planning to make a grand exposé of the spiritualists by presenting the greatest show of all and then explaining it? Maybe they are just having some fun, for the evening was full of amusing incidents,—could that be it?' "[27]

The official investigation included two other members chosen by Mc-Comas, Professor Knight Dunlap, a psychologist, and Robert W. Wood, "one of the greatest physicists in America,"[28] both from Johns Hopkins University.

During the investigation, which lasted about a year, Crandon was disturbed by the skepticism shown by Professor Wood. During one of the séances, the physicist had a "teleplasmic rod" put in the palm of his hand. "I squeezed it very hard," Wood reported later, "which produced no ill effect." A few minutes later he suggested that the cabinet and the medium be searched at once. "When Mrs. Crandon heard this," wrote McComas afterward, "she began to gag as though ill. She bent forward as though vomiting and hurried from the room. . . . An examination showed nothing upon the floor and the stomach performance seemed simulated." Dunlap concluded that the teleplasmic rod was just the intestine of an animal, filled with cotton and wired to make it rigid.

After a year of similar experiences the group presented to the research committee of the ASPR, on April 18, 1927, their final report, whose conclusion stated:

> In view of the above findings your Commission submits that the Margery mediumship is a clever and entertaining performance but is unworthy of any serious consideration by your Society.
>
> We submit further that the unwillingness of Dr. Crandon to allow the Commission to proceed with the investigation is a sufficient indication that no investigation by competent investigators employing the methods and checks required in all scientific research is likely to be permitted.[29]

When Houdini arrived in Boston, the commission's report had not yet been prepared, and McComas visited him backstage and urged him to attend a séance with Margery, to witness her latest feats. Apparently, Dr. Crandon had asked McComas to invite Houdini to a sitting the following Sunday, in order to challenge him to reproduce Margery's feats. Houdini, as usual, replied in a letter to McComas:

> Dear Dr. McComas:
>
> Confirming our conversation last night, so there is no misunderstanding, I will be delighted to sit in at a séance of 'Margery's' but have been repeatedly told that my absence was preferable to my presence.
>
> In view of the circumstances of which you told me—that the Crandons are willing for me to test the medium or sit in at a séance and are willing for me to test their so-called phenomena or illusions, will do so gladly. As you may not know the history of the case, I was bitterly attacked when I said that in my presence Mrs. Crandon presented nothing to prove she possessed any psychic power.
>
> At this time I would ask that I be permitted to take three or four college professors with me. To be fair to the medium, she can do her stuff in my presence and I will go right in and duplicate them, or if you wish, I will stop her from doing anything by having her controlled properly. Or I

will go into the séance room, make notes of the tests and the next day prevent her from doing anything (by keeping her properly under control) and promise faithfully not to injure her in any way.

If this is your desire and if you get me the same apparatus, wires and things she uses or has used, the exact lengths and measurements, I will guarantee to duplicate everything she does *under the same conditions*, not stricter conditions, but the *same*.

One thing I would like to call your attention to—mal-observation. You might think she does certain things in a certain way and describe it to me, whereas it will be entirely different before my eyes. So I ask that everything be measured. Every test carefully spoken over before I am secured so I can prove without a shadow of a doubt that her tests are performed this way, because the lady is subtle and changes her methods like any dexterous sleight-of-hand performer or any medium I have examined. Also give me ample time to make all arrangements during my stay in Boston.[30]

On hearing McComas detail the new phenomena presented by Margery during her séances, Houdini realized that he could not duplicate them on the spot only on the basis of an oral description. He needed first to witness the performance, and so he wrote to Crandon:

In view of the many rumors, some not so complimentary to me, have heard that you are perfectly willing for me to attend a number of séances during my stay here in Boston.

Am inquiring whether this is the truth as I hear a great many things that may be distorted. If you would permit me to come to the séances, I would be very glad to do so, after any of my performances this week.[31]

"In as much as the only value which could possibly be attached to your presence at Lime Street," wrote Crandon in reply, "would be because it would afford some amusement to watch your attempts to duplicate these phenomena, and since this you very wisely decline to do, there seems no other compelling reason for your coming again to Lime Street."[32]

Houdini still wanted to attend, and so he replied again to Crandon:

When Dr. McComas called on me, I distinctly said in front of witness, that knowing the Crandons' method of reporting for protective purposes I want to hand you, meaning Dr. McComas, an outline of my procedure. Instead of talking things over would write, so my statements could not be garbled.

The enclosed is a copy I gave Dr. McComas and which he said he would have you read, although it was not originally intended that you should have this letter. He informed me the next day that he had given you the letter. From same you can check up my statements. At no time was I willing to come to your house alone—always wanted a number of witnesses.

Please don't use the usual tactics of waiting until I leave and then grant me permission to come to a séance.[33]

The invitation, however, never came and Houdini's show left Boston and went to Worcester. The last chance for a confrontation between Houdini and Margery had been missed.

J. B. RHINE'S INVESTIGATION

One investigator after another remained unsatisfied by Margery's séances, and after Dingwall, the Harvard group, and the ASPR's commission it was time for Joseph Banks Rhine (1895–1980), professor at Duke University, North Carolina, who in 1935 would start the study of psychic phenomena (later termed by him "parapsychology") in a scientific laboratory. Invited by the ever enthusiastic Bird, Rhine arrived in Lime Street on July 1, 1926, and the Crandons greeted him with the usual hospitality. From the start Rhine and his wife, Louisa (1891–1983), knew that it would have been impossible to test the facts as they would have liked to. For example, they couldn't examine the substance with the lights turned on and Rhine was prevented by Crandon from examining the various instruments that filled the séance room that were supposed to document and measure this or that phenomenon. Still the professor was able to notice that the ropes of a device that was supposed to hold the medium had been removed, allowing complete freedom of movement. When Rhine saw Margery's foot kicking a megaphone during a séance to give the impression that it was levitating, the crudity of the deception was clear.

If he had been able to detect all these things in one séance, wondered Rhine, why didn't Bird with three years of experience have any suspicions? Could he be a confederate of the medium? Bird denied the accusations, saying that they were Rhine's "personal opinions," but the professor wondered what could have led men like Bird or Carrington to play the medium's game, and observed:

> It is evidently of very great advantage to a medium, especially if fraudulent, to be personally attractive; it aids in the "fly-catching business." Our report would be incomplete without mention of the fact that this "business" reached the point of actual kissing and embracing at our sitting, in the case of one of the medium's more ardent admirers. Could this man be expected to detect trickery in her?[34]

This could partially explain the motives of Bird and his colleagues, but what about Dr. Crandon? If he was a confederate, too, he certainly couldn't be motivated by the desire of a love affair with the medium, since she already was his wife. Rhine offered the following motive:

[Crandon] gradually found out she was deceiving him, but had already begun to enjoy the notoriety it gave him, the groups of admiring society it brought to his home to hear him lecture and to be entertained, the interest and fame aroused in this country and Europe, etc. This was especially appreciated by him in view of decided loss of position and prestige suffered in recent years.[35]

The publication of Rhine's report in the *Journal of Abnormal Social Psychology* (the ASPR had refused it because of its skeptical nature, just as it would later refuse to publish the McComas report) caused the inevitable protests by Margery, who reportedly said: "That's all poppycock. My husband attends all my séances and I would have to be very rash to go around kissing." Sir Arthur Conan Doyle, after reading the report, bought space in the Boston newspapers and inserted an ungentlemanly black-bordered notice stating simply: "J. B. Rhine is an Ass."

TRAGEDY!

When Houdini's tour reached Albany on October 11, Houdini was getting quite tired. Bess, his wife, had been ill and he had not slept for almost three days, in order to spend time close to her in New York. When he arrived in Albany, nonetheless, he went onstage and performed in the scheduled show. During the performance of the Water Torture Cell act, the apparatus that held him upside down suddenly snapped and he broke his left ankle. A physician ordered that he be taken immediately to the hospital, but Houdini refused since he wanted to finish the show.

Only after the curtains had been lowered on the closing act did Houdini agreed to go to the hospital, but again refused to get the needed rest; he had his foot put in plaster and went back on his scheduled tour. He continued to appear in his complete evening's entertainment of magic, escapes, and pseudo-Spiritualism, moving from Albany to Schenectady. On the eighteenth, he arrived in Montreal, Canada, where physicians strenuously advised him against continuing his public performances until his leg was healed. But Houdini was adamant. He went right on.

On October 22, Houdini was visited backstage by a few students. One of them began drawing a portrait of the magician, who was then lying on a couch and opening his mail. To the students Houdini looked like someone "much in need of a long, carefree vacation"; nonetheless, he was kind, affable, and made them feel comfortable. They talked for a while, and Houdini answered all of their questions. "Is it true, Mr. Houdini," asked a student named Wallace Whitehead, "that you can resist the hardest blows struck to the abdomen?"

The unexpected question took everybody aback. Houdini, who had never claimed such a thing, tried to change subject. But the student insisted, he wanted to know. Houdini replied that he had strong muscles in his arms and back.

"Would you mind if I delivered a few blows to your abdomen, Mr. Houdini?" was Whitehead's next surprising question.

Houdini agreed, but as he was trying to get up from the couch, the well-built young man began punching him in the stomach with terribly powerful punches.

"Hey there," cried out one of the students, "you must be crazy. What are you doing?"

Whitehead delivered a few more punches and, when Houdini murmured, "That will do," stopped his attack. The atmosphere slowly returned to normal as Houdini regained his breath. The portrait was finished and handed to Houdini. "You made me look a little tired in this picture," remarked the magician. "The truth is, I don't feel so well." He thanked the students and said good-bye.

That night he performed his show as expected, but between intermissions he rested on his couch in a cold sweat. After the performance he rushed to the station to catch a train for Detroit, where he was scheduled to open the next evening. On the train, however, the pain in his stomach became unbearable and a wire had to be sent ahead asking for a physician to meet them at the Detroit station.

The doctor found signs of appendicitis and urged him to enter a hospital. Houdini, instead, went to his hotel, where he shook with chills. He opened the show, although his temperature had reached 104 degrees, and he collapsed twice between intermissions. After the show was over, the magician was finally taken to Grace Hospital. He was operated on October 25 and his ruptured appendix was removed. However, the rupture had produced peritonitis, an infection that had already spread through Houdini's body. The situation was desperate, and the physicians issued a statement indicating that he was near death.

Houdini seemed to improve after the doctors gave him an experimental serum; but he had to be operated on again and his condition worsened. On October 29, he told Bess to "be prepared, if anything happens," meaning by this not only to expect the worst, but also to be ready should he try to come back from the other side. On the thirty-first Houdini said to his brother Theodore: "I'm tired of fighting, Dash. I guess this thing is going to get me."

At 1:26 P.M., October 31—Halloween—Harry Houdini died.

GOOD-BYE, HOUDINI

By some curious coincidence, Houdini's bronze casket, the one used for his buried-alive stunt, was left behind in Detroit while the rest of his equipment was packed up and returned to New York. It was then decided that Houdini's corpse would be shipped in it to New York and later used as his final coffin.

Newspapers all over the world detailed the tragic news, and almost all of them speculated about the causes. Some remembered the prophecies made by mediums of his death. Telegrams and messages arrived from all over the world. Sir Arthur Conan Doyle declared his shock: "I greatly admired him, and cannot understand how the end came for one so youthful. We were great friends. . . ."[36] And he added with characteristic generosity: "We agreed upon everything excepting spiritualism." Even Margery expressed her sorrow, and called Houdini a "verile [*sic*] personality of great determination."[37]

NOTES

1. Kenneth Silverman, *Houdini!!! The Career of Ehrich Weiss* (New York: HarperCollins, 1996).

2. Ibid.

3. Bernard M. L. Ernst and Hereward Carrington, *Houdini and Conan Doyle* (New York: Albert and Charles Boni, 1932).

4. Ibid.

5. Joseph F. Rinn, *Sixty Years of Psychical Research: Houdini and I Among the Spiritualists* (New York: Truth Seeker Company, 1950).

6. See also Trevor H. Hall, *The Medium and the Scientist: The Story of Florence Cook and William Crookes* (Amherst, N.Y.: Prometheus Books, 1984).

7. Silverman, *Houdini!!!*

8. Ibid.

9. *Journal of the Society for Psychical Research* 723, no. 43 (March 1965).

10. The case of Anna Eva Fay has been dealt with in Massimo Polidoro, "Anna Eva Fay: The Mentalist Who Baffled Sir William Crookes," *Skeptical Inquirer* (January/February 1998).

11. *New York Times*, April 15, 1925.

12. Harry Houdini, *A Magician Among the Spirits* (1926; reprint, New York: Arno Press, 1972).

13. It should be noted that James Randi's $10,000 prize was, a few years ago, raised to $1 million—however, nobody has been able to claim the prize.

14. Silverman, *Houdini!!!*

15. Transcript of Sidney Radner video interview, *They Came to See Him Die* (Coyote Run Pictures, 1996).

16. Gabriel Citron, *The Houdini-Price Correspondence* (London: Legerdemain, 1998).

17. Arthur Conan Doyle, *The Edge of the Unknown* (1930; reprint, New York: Barnes & Noble Books, 1992).

18. Citron, *The Houdini-Price Correspondence.*

19. *Collier's* 77 (May 8, 1925): 7–8.

20. Silverman, *Houdini!!!*

21. Ibid.

22. Samri Frikell (Fulton Oursler), *Spirit Medium Exposed* (New York: New Metropolitan Fiction, 1930).

23. Harry Houdini, letter to W. J. McConnell, August 5, 1925 (Library of Congress).

24. Ibid.

25. Silverman, *Houdini!!!*

26. The only person who did attempt the stunt, twenty years later, in 1955, was James Randi. He had a box built about the same size as Houdini's and was submerged in a pool in London for the TV show *Today*: he was able to stay submerged for one hour and three minutes. In 1958, he repeated the test in the same Hotel Shelton pool used by Houdini for his experiment. To commemorate the event, Randi was even able to find two of the assistants who, in 1925, had helped Houdini in his demonstration. This time, Randi stayed under water for an hour and forty-four minutes, beating Houdini's record by thirteen minutes.

27. Henry C. McComas, *Ghosts I Have Talked With* (Baltimore: Williams & Wilkins Company, 1935).

28. Wood, among other things, had been instrumental in 1904 in debunking the "N-rays" fiasco: a discovery that, at the time, had appeared to be on the same level as that of X rays. However, Wood had secretly manipulated the apparatus in such a way as to render impossible the observation of the N rays: when the experimenters insisted they were still seeing the rays, he was sure that they were only deluding themselves. See *Nature* 70 (1904): 530.

29. McComas, *Ghosts I Have Talked With.*

30. *Proceedings of the American Society for Psychical Research* 2, nos. 20–21 (1926/1927).

31. Ibid.

32. Ibid.

33. Ibid.

34. J. B. Rhine and Louisa E. Rhine, "One Evening's Observation on the Margery Mediumship," *Journal of Abnormal Social Psychology* 21, no. 4 (January–March 1927).

35. Ibid.

36. *New York Times*, November 2, 1926.

37. *New York Herald Tribune*, November 1, 1926.

THE FINAL YEARS 8

BESS AND SIR ARTHUR'S CORRESPONDENCE

Beatrice Houdini received about three thousand telegrams after her husband's death. It was small comfort, for she felt "crushed and broken." "The world will never know," she said, "what I have lost."[1] Some time later, while going through Houdini's personal documents, she found a last letter that he had written for her and hidden among the papers:

Theodore Hardeen and Bess Houdini visit Houdini's grave.
(McManus-Young Collection, Library of Congress,
Rare Books and Special Collections Division, LC-USZ62-112441)

Sweetheart, when you read this I shall be dead. Dear Heart, do not grieve;
I shall be at rest by the side of my beloved parents, and wait for you
always—remember! I loved only two women in my life: my mother and
my wife. Yours, in Life, Death, and Ever After.[2]

She also found various precious books dealing with Spiritualism and
allied topics, and she thought they could represent a nice gift to Sir Arthur
Conan Doyle, whom she still considered one of the best friends that Houdini had in life. Conan Doyle, however, felt averse to accepting them in
view of Houdini's anti-Spiritualistic crusade. He thus wrote to Bess on
December 3, 1926, to tell her so:

Dear Mrs. Houdini:

I thank you for your kind letter & your offer of books. I appreciate it much.
     At the same time it might place me in a delicate position if I were to
accept them. I shall probably sooner or later have to write about this
remarkable man, and I must do so freely and without any sense of oblig-
ation. I am sure you will understand.
     I have never concealed my belief that some of his "tricks" were of psy-
chic origin. On one occasion he told my wife that you yourself did not know
how he did *some* of them. The fact that he has not left his secret—a valuable
asset—would seem to point to the same thing. Now that he has gone, I don't
see that it can harm him in any way to discuss the idea,—as I may do, since
there is no reason why a man should not have psychic power—save that it
seems illogical to deny it to others if you have it yourself.
     I am sorry that shadows grew up between us. There was some story in
the papers here of his having shown up my wife's mediumship, so I had
to contradict as in the enclosed. We had (in our family circle) several
warnings as to his approaching end, but what could we do, for he would
have only mocked at them, and us, if we had sent them on.
     I am sure that, with his strength of character (and possibly his desire
to make reparation), he will come back. I shall be very glad, if you get a
message, if you will tell me. Zancig writes me that he has had a pre-
arranged test message from his first wife.
                         Your Sincerely,
                                   A. CONAN DOYLE.

A few days later, on December 16, Bess replied to Sir Arthur that
nothing he would write would damage Houdini's reputation:

My dear Sir Arthur:

Just read your letter and I am indeed sorry my offer of the books is refused.
I fully understand that whatever you do write about Houdini would just
be of your belief and his,—that surely would not be detrimental to Houdini the man, or yourself.

This same subject has been sadly abused by the press. Words were printed that Houdini never said or used. I, who have lived with him so many years, know what his beliefs were. If, as you believe, he had psychic power, I give you my word he never knew it. Often, in the night, I would waken and hear him say, "Mama, are you here?" and how sadly he would fall back on the pillow and sigh with disappointment. He did so pray to hear that sentence from his beloved mother, but as the world did not know of the secret buried in his heart (his Sainted Mother died before he reached her side) he hoped, and never, despite what was printed, gave up hope of hearing that one word—"forgive."

Two days before he went to his beloved Mother, he called me to his bedside (I had been very ill and forbidden to embrace him, as my illness was contagious), grasped my hand and prayed as only such a loving son could pray. He held my hand to his heart and repeated our solemn vow of our compact. "Mother has not reached me, dear. I never had that one precious word, but you, dear, must be prepared, if anything happens, dear, you must be prepared."

As my illness was so much more dangerous than his, at that time, and the doctors feared for my life, I naturally laughed at his fears—"Nothing, dear heart, will happen. We will soon be together on our vacation and forget all this illness." But this did not satisfy him. He again repeated the words in formation—"When you hear those words you will know it is Houdini speaking. The same message will go through to Sir Arthur, but in that formation only. Never, despite anything, will I come through otherwise; and with his dying kiss (although he did not know it then) I vowed to wait for that, and only that, message.

Dear Sir Arthur, Houdini was a level-headed man. He was deeply hurt whenever any journalistic arguments arose between you, and would have been the happiest man in the world had he been able to agree with your views on spiritism. He admired and respected you; therefore, as you say, you would be free to discuss this subject. Do so, surely it cannot harm him. Two remarkable men with different views.—It is usually the third party that distorts the word or meaning.

I will never be offended by anything you say for him or about him; but that he possessed psychic powers—he never knew it. As I told Lady Doyle often,—he would get a difficult lock, I stood by the cabinet and would hear him say, "this is beyond me," and after many minutes, when the audience became restless, I nervously would say, "Harry, if there is anything in this belief of Spiritism,—why don't you call on them to assist you?" and, before many minutes passed, Houdini had mastered the lock.

We never attributed this to psychic help. We just knew that that particular instrument was the one to open that lock, and so he did all his tricks. He buried no secrets. Every conjurer knows how his tricks were done—with the exception of just where or how the various traps or mechanisms were hidden. You, Sir Arthur, could do the same tricks. It was his stunts that were dangerous,—but it was Houdini himself that was the secret. His personality, his brilliant mind, that carried him through, and perhaps it will be this same Houdini who will come through to you or me.

Surely, our beloved God will let him bring me the message for which I wait, and not the silly messages I get from the various people who claim they hear from him.

Please believe me when I say that I have taken an oath to tell the world when I do hear from him,—also if a message directly to you, with our code comes through. The hour his soul went to his Maker (Sunday, at 1:26 P.M., October 31, 1926) and every Sunday at the same hour, I spend with him alone, in prayer.

Write, Dear Sir Arthur, just as your heart dictates. My beloved will understand, and no one else counts.

My love to you and yours,

B. H.

P.S. One exception to your article enclosed. Houdini's mother never spoke Yiddish, not even Hebrew,—German, French, Italian, Spanish and her own Hungarian only. Is there any objection to me presenting the sketchbook of your father or other books to your boys or Billy? Again lots of love to you all.

B. H.

Conan Doyle answered quite promptly, writing:

My dear Mrs. Houdini:

Your letter was a very beautiful one & I appreciated it much. Any man who wins the love and respect of a good woman must himself be a fine and honest man.

I think it is likely that the pressmen used to excite him and that he gradually got worked up upon this question. But you can understand that, to those of us who had personal experience, a hundred times over, in the matter, it was annoying to be placed in the position of either being a fool or a knave. So far as his work was confined to really fake mediums, we were all in sympathy. But he got far past that. It was a general wild attack upon all that we hold dear. But behind all that, I can see quite a different person,—a loving husband, a good friend, a man full of sweet impulses. I have never met anyone who left so mixed an impression upon my mind.

That he had psychic power—not himself understanding it—is surely borne out by your own experience when, faced by a lock which he could not force, he would make a mental appeal to what we should call his guide. He once said to my wife that even you did not know how he produced some of his effects, but I think he might have said "even I." I see no reason at all why he should not use such power if he had it. The Davenports had it, and I, knowing his early acquaintance with Ira Davenport, thought he might have got some power from him.

I will never say anything unkind of him, but I may discuss the general question of his powers when I have more leisure.

We should welcome your kind offer of my father's sketch book. It is most generous of you.

Yours very sincerely,

A. CONAN DOYLE

P.S. The only Houdini return utterance which seemed to me to have some sign of truth was from Mr. Burr, of Rochester, who has probably written to you. He said in it that there was no compact or test cypher as between me and Houdini. This is true & it was stated otherwise in the press, so that it read as if the message might be correct.

If your test sentence represents an idea you may get it. If it represents meaningless words or a collection of figures or letters you can hardly hope for it. They work by conveying ideas thro' the medium's brain, but it is much more difficult—nearly impossible—to get a mere symbol.

By the way Zancig, in Washington, had a Danish sentence which was to be a test with his first wife. He has now received that sentence which has quite converted him. I was wondering whether you could not get into [sic] touch with the same medium. It would be a great day for all of us, and, I believe, for him also, when you could say to the world "My doubts are gone. I have most undoubtedly had my message."

As a sort of postscript, Sir Arthur wrote in a subsequent letter:

Dear Mrs. Houdini,

I have just been re-reading your letter, and am much impressed by the beauty of it. He was fortunate to have such devotion.

If I have been rather restive under H's handling of the psychic question, you will understand, from the enclosed letter (typical of others), which I have had. Please burn it when read. It goes out of my memory.

I am going to see one or two mediums in the immediate future, and will let you know if I get results. If it is a sentiment you will get it. If it is a cypher, which means nothing, you will never get it.

With our affectionate regard.

A. CONAN DOYLE

(*over*):

We *do* meet in sleep, so it may have been that, when he woke as you describe, speaking of his mother, there was in his subconscious mind some reflection of the switched-off actual interview.

The "enclosed letter" referred to by Sir Arthur had been written by a James P. Clarke, and was dated October 21, 1926, just ten days prior to Houdini's death. In it, the author tells Doyle that he had just seen Houdini perform at the Princess Theatre in Montreal. During the question-and-answer part of his program, just after the unmasking of fraudulent mediums, someone asked him what he thought about Conan Doyle's work in psychic research. According to Clarke, "his reply was grossly insolent, insofar that he spoke of you as being just a 'writer of detective stories,' and eaten up with but one subject. Furthermore he said you were no different from the ordinary man—intellectually that you were not a scientist—and acted like a 'big school boy' at a conference in New York. He also stated you would believe anything—and the contemptuous manner in which he passed this remark was exceedingly unfair."

But what had prompted this Clarke to write to Conan Doyle was the "final retort" that Houdini was supposed to have made: "he said he wished you were there in front of him. He would 'tear you to ribbons'. Obviously he was taking advantage of the distance between London & Montreal."

When she read this, Bess hastened to reply:

January 12, 1927

My dear Sir Arthur:

I am indeed glad you read my letter as I wished you to. Again I want to tell you that, no matter what I read about my dear one, it could not cause me pain.

You know now that Houdini was a fine and good man; I have known it always. That his views were different, we knew. He did honestly try to get results, but failed. Referring to the letter from a Mr. Clarke, whenever Houdini spoke of you, it was with the greatest respect. The very worst thing he ever said against you was that you were credulous. He would tell the audience that you were angry with him—his words were "not for what I said, but for what Sir Arthur Conan Doyle was told I said."

How terribly distorted a phrase may become! Mr. Clarke's next "important part" (?) is that Houdini wished you were there, so he would tear you to ribbons! That is too ridiculous for words. What Houdini did say, not only at that performance, but all—"I can tear all books on Spiritualism to pieces," meaning he could (as he thought) refute them. Houdini's two secretaries took short-hand notes at every performance (in view of our many law suits), so I can give proof positive *re* his speeches.

I have heard Houdini tell a man, during the open forum, who asked "are all spiritualists crazy? Is Sir Arthur Conan Doyle crazy?"—"All spiritualists are not crazy. You do not have to be a spiritualist to be crazy, and I wish I were as sane as Sir Arthur Conan Doyle." No doubt you will hear many stories. The reporters are ever at my door. I know if I say "boo," they will print "boo boo," so I don't see them, but send them to my attorney, Mr. B. M. L. Ernst (whom you perhaps remember: he is now President of the Society of American Magicians and a wonderful man, also one of your greatest admirers and defenders. I will send you his address. I am sure you would be well repaid by sending him a line) and he tells the reporters just what he thinks of you.

My dear friends, if only you knew how my heart yearns to hear the precious message from my beloved,—it must be as he says, though. I have obeyed him all our life together. I will obey him in death. How strange it is, I have been reading his beautiful letters to me, and in all he signs himself, "yours in this life, in the next, and ever with you."

I have taken a liberty with your beautiful Christmas card (for which I thank you very much).

In Sing Sing prison, a man [Charles Chapin] (at one time a well-known Editor of a New York paper) had been sentenced for life. He committed a murder, some ten years ago. He killed the woman he loved devotedly, his wife, whom he wanted to spare all the ugliness of poverty; he tried to die himself, but failed. I knew his sad story, and Houdini was his very dear friend. I correspond with this man frequently, but as the subject of his wife is a most delicate one, I refrain to speak of her, but the message on the card seem to fit him. I sent him the card, with a note telling him from whom I received it, asking if he could read a message of forgiveness and condolence.

I am sure you will also forgive me sending it, as that poor lonesome soul will surely get from that message what his hungry heart looks for, and we, you two dear people and I, will be rewarded in the happiness it gives him.

I am sending you the book of Dr. Charles Doyle. It is beautiful, and Houdini always intended to present it to you, that was the one thing in his huge library that was sacred and marked "not to be sold at any price." I am doubly glad to send it, as the thought of having had it hawked about after my death was repulsive.

I find it is more a collection of letters, but the letters are so beautifully sketched and you will find, as Houdini did, many beautiful forms of angels. My great grief is that my dear one was called before he himself could give it. When next I go to my dear one's last resting place, I will place a flower there for you.

My love to all of you,

B. H.

To this, Sir Arthur replied:

Jan. 23, 1927

My dear Mrs. Houdini:

The book has arrived and filled me with surprise. It is beautiful and will mean much to the family, but it really seems like a series of miracles,— first that it should exist still, then that it should cross the Atlantic and finally that it should come back to me. I accept it as a peace-offering from your husband, and thank him as well as you.

There is, after death, a period of complete rest which varies in different cases. When H. has emerged from this, I am quite sure, knowing his determined character, that he will get back to you. I wish you would find out the medium from whom Zancig got the test from his wife. I wish also that you would get an interview with the gentleman whose name I enclose. Send him my card, but write as Mrs. H.—no name. Mediums always, if they are honest, get better results when they know nothing of their clients. When you go, tell him nothing save that you would be glad of any help you can get. He is an amateur and a nice fellow with good honest gifts. Please remember me to Mr. Ernst. I have not forgotten him.

Yours very cordially,

Arthur Conan Doyle

Conan Doyle in this letter gave Bess some suggestions on sitting with mediums, in the hope of getting a message or, possibly, the "code" which had been agreed upon before Houdini's death. Bess had not received any messages that she thought could be real, but had to some extent been apparently impressed by some episodes. She wrote about these to Conan Doyle, who wrote to her in reply:

March 8, 1927

My dear Mrs. Houdini:

I am most thankful that you have got so far. Now the more intimate test should come. How can we tell the difficulties & disabilities upon the other side? He may say afterwards "Why, you might as well have asked a man on a desert island to telegraph you."

Thank you for your bravery & frankness in admitting the facts. You have now earned the fulfillment. It *may* have been a test of you.

Conan Doyle thought it also correct to state clearly that no post-mortem test had been arranged between himself and Houdini: "There was a statement in the paper that you had said that I had some posthumous test with Houdini. I assure you this is not so. I had no such understanding. I have had a number of letters on the subject. One from a Miss or Mrs. ———, who asserts that Houdini had a presentiment that he would not return from this circuit. I wonder if this was true."

Again, Bess offered Conan Doyle some rare documents and letters from her husband's collection. Sir Arthur was quite pleased by the offer; however, he wrote her in July 1927: "It is very generous of you to offer me those letters, which of course would be appreciated, but I really think you should read my article about Houdini's powers before you make me presents. But you know that I (I should say "we") have every respect for you personally, and for him also, so long as he does not stand in the way of the most important thing upon earth, which is to prove immortality."

She decided to send the letters anyway, and on September 2, 1927, in writing to thank her Sir Arthur said: "I thank you heartily for the letters. I can see that they are of great interest, but have not had time to examine them closely. I hope to have some psychic news for you presently. Mr. McKenzie of the College got in touch, as he believes, with Houdini thro' a trance medium, Mrs. Garrett. I will have a sitting as soon as I can possibly arrange it. According to McKenzie's message, H. was still rather clouded in his mind, which is natural enough after the physical change. As he clears, the messages should clear."

A year had passed since Houdini's death, and Bess was going to unveil Houdini's monument at his burial site at the Machpelah Cemetery in Brooklyn. Sir Arthur wrote her on October 14, 1927: "Dear Mrs. Houdini, I should like to send a message of good will upon the occasion of the unveiling of your husband's monument. All differences must be suspended at such a time. He was a great master of his profession and, in some ways, the most remarkable man I have ever known."

In December 1927 Bess announced plans to take on the road a Houdini illusion never before presented on stage: "Freezing a Man in a Cake of Ice." At a press conference, an Indian in a rubber suit was lowered into a metal container. A ton-and-a-half block of ice was apparently frozen around him, using a carbon-dioxide and cold-water mixture. The ice was chopped so the man's face could be seen inside. The top was then chopped and the man lifted out of the icy prison.

Bess wrote to Sir Arthur telling him about her projects in show business; she also detailed a curious incident in which a glass broke at her house: could that be a sort of "manifestation" from Houdini?

February 12, 1928

Dear Mrs. Houdini:

I wish you every possible success with your new act. It sounds very marvelous—and a little dangerous—but that no doubt is just the attraction. May all go well. I shall be anxious.

   I think the mirror incident shows every sign of being a message. After all such things don't happen elsewhere. No mirror has ever broken in this house. Why should yours do so? And it is just the sort of energetic thing one could expect from him, if for some reason he could not get his message. Supposing our view of the future is true, is it not possible that the Powers might for a time forbid him to use those gifts which he was foremost in his lifetime in denying? But you will get your test. I feel convinced of that.

CONAN DOYLE'S LATER SPIRITUALISTIC EXPLOITS

Conan Doyle's life was completely ruled by his "mission," the Spiritualistic quest: "That is the work," he had written in *Memories and Adventures*, his autobiography, "which will occupy, either by voice and pen, the remainder of my life." It was also a very expensive work; by his own estimate he would invest some £250,000 over these years. He devoted all of the profits from his books and lectures to the cause, financing Spiritualistic literature, as in the case of *Light* magazine, and contributing to groups such as the Marylebone Spiritualist Association.

In 1925, he opened the Psychic Bookshop in London at 2 Victoria Street, near Westminster Abbey; it was part bookshop, part library, and part museum. "It has long seemed to me," he wrote in the January 24, 1925, *Light*, "that one of the weak points in our psychic movement is the complete disconnection between our splendid literature and the man in the street. He is as a rule absolutely unaware of its existence. . . . I would ask the support of all psychic students for this venture." Mary, Conan Doyle's elder daughter, was put in charge of the shop, although Sir Arthur and his wife as well would frequently take turns at the register.

"The venture," he wrote to Sir Oliver Lodge, "will cost me £1,500 a year but it may in time pay its own way. If not, I don't see how money can be better spent."[3] The venture, however, proved to be a considerable drain on Conan Doyle's resources. After four years, the loss was still too heavy (£5,000) and Conan Doyle declared the experiment over.

His money was also used to publish, through his own Psychic Press, his Spiritualistic literature. In 1927, for example, he put in print *Pheneas Speaks*, a collection of communications "from the other side," gathered from his wife's direct writing mediumship and through the intermission of "Pheneas," an entity who described himself as an Arab scribe of the city of Ur, the ancient Sumerian capital. "We would beg the most orthodox reader to bear in mind," he wrote in the preface, "that God is still in touch with mankind, and that there is as much reason that he should send messages and instructions to a suffering and distracted world as ever there was in days of old."

The book received harsh criticism, and helped alienate more of Conan Doyle's friends from him. Herbert George Wells, for example, thought that *Pheneas Speaks* was a "platitudinous bore," and went on: "This Pheneas, I venture to think, is an imposter, wrought of self-deception, as pathetic as a rag doll which some lonely child has made for its own comfort."

In the winter of 1928 Conan Doyle and his family embarked on a five-month lecture tour of southern Africa. The experience was not a happy one; the newspapers were hostile and the audience "listened with indulgence if not aquiescence." At his lectures he still talked about the Cottingley fairies, and still refused to consider the possibility of fraud: "I took the line in my lecture that I was prepared to consider any explanation of these results, save only one which attacked the character of the children. I am sure that when I had explained the facts there were few in the Hall who were not prepared to accept the photographs." The tour, which Conan Doyle considered a success, was detailed in his book *Our African Winter*.

Before the publication of *Our African Winter*, however, Conan Doyle privately printed a pamphlet, *A Warning*, in which he announced the coming end of the world. In the preceding five years he had collected so many warnings from mediums all over the world that he considered "impossible in my opinion not to take them seriously, for they represent in themselves a psychic phenomenon for which I know no parallel." His colleagues, however, were more perplexed than worried. Harry Price, for example, wrote in the *Journal of ASPR*: "The cataclysmic disaster of cosmic magnitude with which Doyle has been trying to make our flesh creep for the past two years still hangs fire and the dawn of 1927 finds us sleeping serenely in our beds, giving little heed to the devastating seismic catastrophe with which—says Sir Arthur—we are threatened by evil spirits on both sides of the veil. . . . We are now promised a new Armageddon for 1928!"

PECORARO TRIES AGAIN

"Can Houdini come back?": this was a question frequently asked after the magician's death. Sir Arthur was convinced that, after "a period of complete rest," he would return; Bess, on her part, was obviously skeptical, but probably wished to receive a sign. "I want so to believe in a communication with my husband," she told a reporter. "Every day I get letters from people who say they are able to feel his presence and catch his messages. But they have nothing to show me—no proof. Perhaps they are sincere, these mediums, but they are unconvincing."

One of the first mediums to claim contact with Houdini was Nino Pecoraro, the young Italian medium who had been securely tied by Houdini during the *Scientific American* tests.

When *Scientific American* launched its offer to mediums, another magazine devoted to the popularization of science, *Science and Invention*, took notice of the interest that soon had surrounded the *SA* investigation and quickly announced a prize of its own. The offer, however, appeared to be more a publicity stunt than a real quest of scientific interest, as it can be seen by the announcement in the June 1923 issue:

Science & Invention does not believe that there exists a proven scientific basis to vouch for the communication of the deceased with the living. *Science & Invention* believes that it can duplicate any avowed spiritistic phenomenon or manifestations effected by any medium, whether they be signals, table-rappings, spirit photographs, or other things. *Science & Invention* is willing to pay $1,000.00 to any company of sincere investigators, if we cannot duplicate such phenomena or manifestations to the satisfaction of a disinterested body of scientists.

The chairman of the investigating committee was the mentalist Joseph Dunninger. He was soon joined by Houdini's friend Joseph Rinn, who gave $10,000 of his own to increase the size of the award. The prize was later augmented when both Dunninger and Beatrice Houdini added $10,000 each to the challenge. The award, grossing $31,000, looked attractive enough to Nino Pecoraro who, on April 26, 1928, appeared at the offices of *Science and Invention*.

A preliminary séance, where nothing peculiar happened, had taken place at Bess's house. Now it was time for the official test. Nino, seated in a chair, was bound by the committee. His hands were covered by two leather gloves, which were sewn to his shirt. He was tied to the chair with ropes, their knots sealed. He was thus placed in a corner of the room and a curtain drawn in front of him. After ten minutes, a voice in falsetto claimed to be the spirit of Eusapia Palladino; soon after that, the voice claimed to be Houdini. "Both," commented Dunninger, "sounded as though uttered by Nino. Houdini's voice was far from natural." The voices kept promising remarkable phenomena: a wax hand impression, table raps, the materialization of Houdini's spirit . . . nothing occurred.

Arthur Ford's Message

A more convincing candidate to the claim of having received a real communication from Houdini soon appeared on the scene. The medium was Arthur Ford (1897–1971), a pastor of the First Spiritualist Church in New York City. He claimed that, on February 8, 1928, he went into a trance and, talking in the voice of "Fletcher," his spirit guide, had said that a woman identifying herself as the mother of Harry Houdini was anxious to speak. The spirit said that her son Harry had hoped for years to receive one particular word from her, the word "forgive," and added that: "His wife knew the word, and no one else in all the world knew it."

"Forgive" was, presumably, the last word uttered by Houdini's mother on her deathbed and did probably refer to one of Houdini's brothers, Leopold, who had been "guilty" of marrying Saide, the ex-wife of Nathan, another brother of Houdini. To the magician, this behavior had appeared morally inexcusable and led to the "removal" of Leopold from his life.[4] He could have not forgiven his brother unless his mother told him to; however, her death came before the matter could be resolved.

On learning of Ford's message, Bess promptly wrote the following letter to the medium:

My Dear Mr. Ford,

Today I received a special delivery letter signed by members of the First Spiritualist Church, who testify to a purported message from Houdini's mother, received through you.

Strange that the word "forgive" is the word Houdini awaited in vain all of his life. It was indeed the message for which he always secretly hoped, and if had been give to him while he was still alive, it would I know have changed the entire course of his life—but it came too late. Aside from this there are one or two trivial inaccuracies—Houdini's mother called him Ehrich—there was nothing in the message which could be contradicted. I might also say that this is the first message which I have received which has an appearance of truth.

Sincerely yours,
Beatrice Houdini[5]

Ford's supporters announced that Bess's letter confirmed the authenticity of the message, since the word "Forgive" could only be known by Houdini, his mother, and his wife. Sir Arthur, typically, considered the message genuine and "an outstanding case." The public, however, remained skeptical. The press, in fact, reported that the keyword had already appeared in print nearly a year before, on March 13, 1927, in the *Brooklyn Eagle*. In an interview she had given to the paper, in fact, Bess had specified that any authentic communication purporting to come from Houdini would have included the word "forgive." Furthermore, it was not true, as the "spirit" of Houdini's mother had said, that the word was known only to her, Houdini, and Bess, and "no one else in all the world knew it": at the time of her death, in fact, her magician son was touring Europe with his wife. The son at her deathbed was Theodore.

A few months later, on January 5, 1929, Ford announced that he had received the tenth and final code word of a message from Houdini. The following day, accompanied by members of his church, Ford went to Payson Avenue, where Bess had moved after Houdini's death. They found Bess lying on a couch, suffering from a fall down a flight of stairs—possibly caused by the drinking habit into which she had fallen. In an account written for the *New York Evening Graphic* before Ford's visit, Bess was described to be in a "semidelirium," calling for Houdini to return. She blacked out from time to time, and was "under constant care of physicians." It was in this state, then, that Ford's message was read to her: "Rosabelle, answer, tell, pray-answer, look, tell, answer-answer, tell."

A séance was fixed for January 8, shortly after noon. Ford went into a trance and began speaking in what he claimed to be Houdini's voice. The voice repeated the message and then said: "Thank you, sweetheart, now take off your wedding ring and tell them what 'Rosabelle' means." Bess, lying on a sofa, took off her ring and began to sing:

> Rosabelle, sweet Rosabelle,
> I love you more than I can tell.
> Over me you cast a spell.
> I love you, my sweet Rosabelle.

Ford, still speaking as Houdini, explained that "Rosabelle" was the song sung by his wife in their early days. The other code words in the message formed the word "B-E-L-I-E-V-E." Before leaving, the purported voice of Houdini said: "Spare no time or money to undo my attitude of doubt while on earth. Now that I have found my way back, I can come often sweetheart. Give yourself to placing the truth before all those who have lost the faith and want to take hold again. Believe me, life is continuous. Tell the world there is no death. I will be close to you. I expect to use this instrument (Ford) many times in the future. Tell the world, sweetheart, that Harry Houdini lives and will prove it a thousand times."

The secret code was the one used by Houdini and Bess when, in the early days of their career, they used to include a telepathy act in their show, similar to the one later made famous by the Zancigs. The code consisted of ten units, with each unit standing for a digit, and each digit, in turn, representing the position in the alphabet of a letter in the coded message:

> Pray = 1 = A
> Answer = 2 = B
> Say = 3 = C
> Now = 4 = D
> Tell = 5 = E
> Please = 6 = F
> Speak = 7 = G
> Quickly = 8 = H
> Look = 9 = I
> Be quick = 10 or 0 = J

Double-digit letters were indicated by combinations of the code words. For example, the fourteenth letter, N, would be signaled by the phrase "pray (1), now (4)." In Ford's message the nine words following "Rosabelle" formed the word "Believe" in this manner: Answer (B), tell (E), pray-answer (L), look (I), tell (E), answer-answer (V), tell (E).

Ford's group insisted that Bess issue another statement. It was written on Bess's personal stationery but by someone else, as the handwriting reveals. She was then asked to sign it. It read:

> Regardless of any statements made to the contrary, I wish to declare that the message in its entirety and in the agreed-upon sequence, given to me by Arthur Ford is the correct message pre-arranged between Mr. Houdini and myself.[6]

Margery, interviewed about the case, said: "Harry Houdini, in death, has furnished the world with evidence which conclusively refutes the theories which he so vigorously defended in life." As for Conan Doyle, he suggested that "this might become *the* classical case of after-death return."

Not everybody was convinced, however. Joseph Dunninger went to Bess's house and reminded her that the "secret code" had not been secret since its publication, the previous year, on page 105 of *Houdini: His Life Story*, the authorized biography written by Harold Kellock and based on Bess's "recollections and documents."

"I have seen it stated in the papers," Conan Doyle would later write to Kellock on this point, "that this accounts for Ford getting a posthumous message. This, however, I am sure you realize, is not correct. It was not the cipher that formed the test, but it was the message which was written in the cipher, and Ford could not have got that out of your book."

Bess, however, had stated to the *New York World*, on January 9: "I had no idea what combination of words Harry would use and when he sent 'believe' it was a surprise." Also, the fact that Houdini had had four lines of the song "Rosabelle" engraved inside Bess's wide gold wedding ring was hardly a secret.

"THE MESSAGE IS A HOAX!"

Two days after the séance, the notorious scandal sheet, the *New York Graphic*, headlined: "HOUDINI MESSAGE A BIG HOAX! 'Séance' Pre-arranged by 'Medium' and Widow." The allegation was that Bess herself had given Ford the code, in order to promote a lecture tour that the two were supposed to do together. The news caused an uproar, and Bess, still ill, wrote a moving letter to Walter Winchell, a columnist for the *Graphic*:

> This letter is not for publicity, I do not need publicity. I want to let Houdini's old friends know that I did not betray his trust. I am writing this per-

sonally because I wish to tell you emphatically that I was no party to any fraud.

Now regarding the séance: For two years I have been praying to receive the message from my husband; for two years every day I have received messages from all parts of the world. Had I wanted a publicity stunt I could no doubt have chosen any of these sensational messages. When I repudiated these messages no one said a word, excepting the writers who said I did not have the nerve to admit the truth.

When the real message, THE message that Houdini and I agreed upon, came to me and I accepted it as the truth, I was greeted with jeers. Why? Those who denounce the whole thing as a fraud claim that I had given Mr. Arthur Ford the message. If Mr. Ford said this I brand him a liar. Mr. Ford has stoutly denied saying this ugly thing, and knowing the reporter as well as I do I prefer to believe Mr. Ford. Others say the message has been common property and known to them for some time. Why do they tell me this now, when they know my heart was hungry for the true words from my husband? The many stories told about me I have no way to tell the world the truth of or the untruth, for I have no paper at my beck and call; everyone has a different opinion of how the message was obtained. With all these different tales I would not even argue. However, when anyone accuses me of GIVING the words that my husband and I labored so long to convince ourselves of the truth of communication, then I will fight and fight until the breath leaves my body.

If anyone claims I gave the code, I can only repeat they lie. Why should I want to cheat myself? I do not need publicity. I have no intention of going on the stage or, as some paper said, on a lecture tour. My husband made it possible for me to live in the greatest comfort. I do not need to earn money. I have gotten the message I have been waiting for from my husband, how, if not by spiritual aid, I do not know.

And now, after I told the world that I have received the true message, everyone seems to have known of the code, yet never told me. They left it to Mr. Ford to tell me, and I am accused of giving the words. It is all so confusing. In conclusion, may I say that God and Houdini and I know that I did not betray my trust. For the rest of the world I really ought not to care a hang, but somehow I do, therefore this letter. Forgive its length.

Sincerely yours,
Beatrice Houdini[7]

When it became known that Ford was using a copy of Bess's signed statement in some of his advertisements, Bernard M. L. Ernst, Houdini's and now Bess's lawyer, saw the possibility of a lawsuit against Ford. In reply, Bess wrote to him:

I wish to say that I did sign the letter. . . . I did not say that I believed that the message came through spiritual aid or that I believed in spiritualism.

I did say the words I heard were the words I expected to hear, etc. . . . I had a copy of the original letter I wrote to him somewhere but I am too ill to look for it and I really don't care. I never said I believed the letter came from Houdini. I never said I believed in spiritualism and I still say the same. I don't care what Sir Arthur Conan Doyle or Will Goldston say or do. I don't and never did believe the message genuine nor did I believe in spiritualism. I will write you clearly later if you will just give me a chance to get well. I don't care what you do to or about Mr. Ford.

Ernst didn't bring Ford to court, but the medium was, nonetheless, expelled from the United Spiritualist League of New York—at least for a while; shortly afterward he was reinstated "on the ground of insufficient proof" as to his possible fraud.

Bess disavowed Ford's message countless times. "There was a time," she told an interviewer later in her life, "when I wanted intensely to hear from Harry. I was ill, both physically and mentally, and such was my eagerness that spiritualists were able to prey upon my mind and make me believe that they had really heard from him."[8]

On March 19, 1930, she also asked Ernst to issue a statement: "For three years she had sought to penetrate beyond the grave and communicate with her husband, but had now renounced faith in such a possibility: she denied that any of the mediums presented the clew by which she was to recognize a legitimate message."

HOUDINI'S "PSYCHIC POWERS" . . . ACCORDING TO CONAN DOYLE

On June 20, 1928, Sir Arthur Conan Doyle wrote to Bess: "I have been writing a little monograph upon your wonderful husband (whatever view one takes of the origin of his powers, they are equally wonderful). . . . Every detail about him and his remarkable powers is of deep interest to me. . . ."

The monograph, *Houdini the Enigma*, had been published in July 1927 in the *Strand* magazine, the same journal that had become famous thanks to the publication of the original Sherlock Holmes stories. Retitled "The Riddle of Houdini," it was later included in Conan Doyle's book *The Edge of the Unknown* (1930) and opened with the following words:

Who was the greatest medium-baiter of modern times? Undoubtedly Houdini. Who was the greatest medium of modern times? There are some who would be inclined to give the same answer. I do not see how it can ever now be finally and definitely proved, but circumstantial evidence may be very strong, as Thoreau said when he found a trout in the milk jug. I foresee that the subject will be debated for many years to come, so perhaps my opinion, since I knew him well, and always entertained this possibility in my mind, may be of interest.

The monograph was composed of three parts. "I will first give some of my own personal impressions of Houdini," wrote Conan Doyle. These included his own version of the fateful Atlantic City séance:

> The method in which Houdini tried to explain away, minimize and contort our attempt at consolation, which, *was given entirely at his own urgent request and against my wife's desire*, has left a deplorable shadow in my mind which made some alteration in my feelings toward him. Conscious as I was of his many excellent and wonderful qualities, such incidents took the edge off my sympathies, and put a strain upon our friendship.

It should be noted that the séance had been the idea of Sir Arthur and Lady Doyle, for Houdini had been sunbathing on the beach when Conan Doyle contacted him to propose the séance. Sir Arthur himself had written so in his *Our American Adventure*: "It was a sudden inspiration of mine to ask him up to our room and see if we could get any evidence or consolation for him." Evidently, Conan Doyle's memory of the event had been somewhat blurred for, in a letter to Harold Kellock, written on September 19, 1929, he repeated the same erroneous version of the episode: "Of course we knew about the love he bore his mother, before the sitting. No doubt that was the reason why my wife, rather against her will, consented to give him a sitting at his own request."

"I will then dwell on some phases of his career," continued Conan Doyle in his introduction, "which show his singular character, and I will then endeavour to give the argument as to the source of his unique powers."

Conan Doyle, in fact, had in time become definitively convinced that Houdini's tricks were not tricks at all. Talking about his jail-cell escapes, for example, he wrote that he was "always searched to prove that he had no tools in his possession. Sometimes the grinning warders had hardly got out of the passage before their prisoner was at their heels. It takes some credulity, I think, to say that this was, in the ordinary sense of the word, a trick."

He did allow that Houdini did use trickery sometimes: "Of course, I am aware that Houdini really was a very skilful conjurer. All that could be known in that direction he knew." But this didn't mean much to him or, better, did mean that the trickery was just a smoke screen to hide his true powers: "Thus he confused the public mind by mixing up things which were dimly within their comprehension with things which were beyond anyone's comprehension."

Other conjurers, as well as Houdini's brother, did perform the same tricks. Not a problem: "I contend," he wrote, "that Houdini's performance was on an utterly different plane, and that it is an outrage against common sense to think otherwise." Although it may be true that there was only one Houdini, in reality his methods were, and are today, quite known among the experts.

Conan Doyle based much of his belief in Houdini's power on the observations of James Hewat McKenzie (1870–1929), the founder of the British College of Psychic Science, and "one of the most experienced psychical researchers in the world," at least according to Conan Doyle. In his book *Spirit Intercourse* (1916), he wrote:

> A small iron tank filled with water was deposited on the stage, and in it Houdini was placed, the water completely covering his body. Over this was placed an iron lid with three hasps and staples, and these were securely locked. The body was then completely dematerialized within the tank in one and a half minutes, while the author stood immediately over it. Without disturbing any of the locks Houdini was transferred from the tank direct to the back of the stage front, dripping with water and attired in the blue jersey-suit in which he entered the tank. From the time that he entered it to the time that he came to the front only one and a half minutes had elapsed.
>
> While the author stood near the tank during the dematerialization process a great loss of physical energy was felt by him, such as is usually felt by sitters in materializing séances who have a good stock of vital energy, as in such phenomena a large amount of energy is required. . . . This startling manifestation of one of Nature's profoundest miracles was probably regarded by most of the audience as a very clever trick.

"Can any reasonable man," added Conan Doyle, "read such an account as this and then dismiss the possibility which I suggest as fantastic? It seems to me that the fantasy lies in refusing its serious consideration." The fact that Houdini's milk can illusion, as this peculiar escape is known, is still performed today and that Houdini's original cans are open to inspection and give away their secret quite readily renders these considerations quite senseless.

Houdini had always denied possessing psychic powers, and Bess had confirmed this fact in one of her letters to Conan Doyle. These denials, however, looked to Conan Doyle as further proof of Houdini's powers: "Is it not perfectly evident that if he did not deny them his occupation would have been gone for ever? What would his brother-magicians have to say to a man who admitted that half his tricks were done by what they would regard as illicit powers? It would be 'exit Houdini.' "

Conan Doyle's monograph, *Houdini the Enigma*, ended with the following lines:

Be his mystery what it may, Houdini was one of the most remarkable men of whom we have any record, and he will live in history with such personalities as Cagliostro, the Chevalier D'Eon, and other strange characters. He had many outstanding qualities, and the world is the poorer for his loss. As matters stand, no one can say positively and finally that his powers were abnormal, but the reader will, I hope, agree with me that there is a case to be answered.[9]

Writing to Harold Kellock, he said concerning his biography on Houdini: "I think, however, that you may take the words 'An unsolved mystery' off your cover. It is I who have solved the mystery of Houdini and I have no more doubt that he used psychic powers than I have that I am dictating this letter. Surely you cannot in your own mind seriously believe that, when a man's two hands are padlocked four feet away from each other, he can use a picklock in order to free himself, or that there is any normal way in which a man can get out of a paper bag unbroken or out of a sealed glass tank?"

In Conan Doyle's last known letter to Bess, he talks about two mediums who claimed to have received messages from Houdini:

Dear Mrs. Houdini:

I can report two recent cases of interest. In the first, a friend of mine, Mrs. Stobart, had a message from a stranger. The message was that Houdini desired to send a message to Mrs. Stobart,—that she should go to a medium, and that a bunch of roses would be the sign that it really was Houdini who was speaking. She went accordingly to Mrs. Barkel (who had not been specially recommended). When Mrs. Barkel went into trance she said "There is a spirit here who desires to send a message, and carries a bunch of red flowers as a sign." No name was given, and then another power broke in and the first message was never given. But it struck me that the red flowers in themselves might possibly mean something.

In the other case, several messages came through to me, purporting to be from him, but nothing that convinced me. He finally was supposed to say, "I am not developed enough yet over here to get difficult tests through, but I have attracted my wife's attention by sounds & other signs of my presence, but there is an atmosphere of doubt & fear around her which is hard to penetrate." I give this for what it is worth.

CONAN DOYLE'S FINAL DAYS

In late 1929, Conan Doyle embarked on his last lecture tour. "I am off next week to do Holland, Denmark, Stockholm and Oslo," he wrote Harry Price. "My ambition is to speak in each European non-Catholic capital before I pass." In Copenhagen, he suffered a bout of agonizing chest pains but, as Houdini had done during his last days, refused to cancel his speaking schedule. He carried on, in near-constant pain, until the last lecture had been done. On his return to England he had to be carried ashore.

In one of his last letters, which he sent to B. L. M. Ernst, Houdini's lawyer, he wrote:

> I have been looking over my old Houdini bundle of letters, and I came on two or three very beautiful ones written by Mrs. Houdini after his death. I notice one allusion to you in which, after your name, she puts "President of the Society of Magicians and a wonderful man." . . . I write this in bed, as I have broken down badly, and have developed Angina Pectoris. So there is just a chance that I may talk it all over with Houdini himself before very long. I view the prospect with perfect equanimity. That is one thing that psychic knowledge does. It removes all fear of the future. . . . I have just read an article by Will Goldston, in which he declares Spiritualism to be a truth—and adds that Maskelyne was always of the same opinion. . . . I dislike Ford's advertisement very much. At the same time, when I remember Houdini's advertisements, there does seem a rough justice about it. . . . I send you a few notes which may help you. As to my own letters, use your own discretion. So long as they don't give pain to *third* parties, I have no objection to their publication. . . . Long experience has taught me that, if you don't play fair with the spirit-world, there is no more luck for you in this world. Poor H. was a conspicuous example; but I notice it continually. . . .

In January 1930 he fought one last battle. That month the Society for Psychical Research had published in its journal a review by Theodore Besterman of Gwendolyn Kelley Hack's book *Modern Psychic Mysteries*, which was based on articles by Ernesto Bozzano (1862–1943), a famous Italian psychic researcher. Bozzano was a naive investigator, ready to accept "miracles" without sufficient proof. He had participated in a series of séances at Millesimo Castle, near Savona, with the Marquis Carlo Centurione Scotto, a nobleman of Conan Doyle's acquaintance. The book described many startling episodes—including the Marquis's teleportation from one room to another—but failed to be convincing. The lack of controls and precautions against fraud and the total darkness in which the séances were held were sufficient elements for a critical review by Besterman, the SPR's librarian. "It must be already obvious," concluded Besterman, "that Signor Bozzano's claims are wholly unfounded, and that the Millesimo sittings have not the slightest vestige of scientific value. All groups of people have of course the unquestionable right to sit in circles for their own edification; but to put forward such a book as this as a serious contribution to psychical research, and to put it forward with such dogmatic claims of infallibility as Signor Bozzano's, is to bring our subject into contempt and disrepute."

Conan Doyle was furious. He first wrote a letter to the chairman of the council of the SPR:

> I have just read an article in the January number of the Journal by Mr. Besterman upon the Millesimo sittings. It is, in my judgment, such a series of misrepresentations and insulting innuendoes that it tends to lower the good name of the Society. The insolence by which the considered opinion of a man like Professor Bozzano, who was present, is set aside and treated with contempt by one who was not present, and who has had very little experience of psychical research, makes one ashamed that such stuff should be issued by an official of a Society which has any scientific standing. . . .
>
> I have long waited hoping that the Podmore, Dingwall, Besterman tradition of obtuse negation at any cost would die away. But as there is no sign of it, and the obsession seems rather to become more pronounced, my only resource is, after thirty-six years of patience, to resign my own membership and to make some sort of public protest against the essentially unscientific and biased work of a Society which has for a whole generation produced no constructive work of any kind, but has confined its energies to the misrepresentation and hindrance of those who have really worked at the most important problem ever presented to mankind.[10]

When the letter brought no reaction, Conan Doyle issued a public statement. He stated that for a generation "the Society has done no constructive work of any importance, and has employed its energies in hindering and belittling those who are engaged in real active psychical research. . . . It is necessary, as it seems to me, to call a halt, and to make inquiry as to how far the Society is to be forever in the hands of this small central body of reactionaries, or whether they really represent the opinion of the members. . . . I have waited long in the hope of some reform but I have now concluded that it is not to be expected, and that the influence of the Society is entirely for evil. I have, therefore, resigned my membership, and the protest would be more effective if those who agree with me would see their way to follow my example."[11] He then invited all to join the British College of Psychic Science, the one founded by Hewat McKenzie, who claimed that Houdini had possessed dematerializing powers. Only six members and one associate, however, resigned from the SPR in response to Conan Doyle's plea.

"Doyle," William Henry Salter (1880–1969), then honorary secretary of the SPR, commented in an unpublished manuscript, "was at this time the High Priest of Spiritualism which he himself described as a 'cult'. Most cults have their myths and legends which are valued by the faithful more for the emotional satisfaction they give than for their objective truth. His writings and speeches conformed to this type. In the triumphal progresses he made all over the world he satisfied the appetite of his followers with a hotchpotch of truth and a monstrous deal of slop; an outstanding example of how emotional bias can override intelligence, in Doyle's case intelligence of a rather high order."[12]

In his final days, however, Sir Arthur was not completely devoid of doubts, for in a letter to a friend, realizing that none of Pheneas's predictions had been fulfilled, he wrote that he had begun to wonder if he and his wife had been "victims of some extraordinary prank played upon the human race from the other side."

For a while his health seemed to improve. He even lobbied against an ancient law, the Witchcraft Act, dating to the reign of George II, which had been used to prosecute mediums. Back home, however, his health deteriorated badly, and on the morning of July 7, 1930, he was found lying on the floor, gasping for breath. Sensing his end, he asked to be sat in a chair where, surrounded by his family, he could look out at the Sussex countryside and die in peace. His last words were spoken to his wife. "You are wonderful," he said.

THE MARGERY CASE: HOUDINI VINDICATED

What had happened to Margery? After Houdini's death, the Margery case continued to attract the attention of investigators, but the revelations that piled up after 1926 would have made Houdini happy, since they all represented a full confirmation of what he had been saying for years.

Around 1926 Margery added a new effect to her repertoire; maybe one too many, as we shall see. Walter claimed that his ethereal body was such an exact replica of the one he had while alive that to prove his presence he could even create a fingerprint of his thumb in wax. Mina paid a visit to her dentist, Dr. Frederick Caldwell, to ask for a suggestion in carrying out the experiment. The doctor suggested the use of dental wax, which would make a detailed print. He softened a piece of wax in boiling water and pressed his thumbs into it to show the practicality of his proposal. Mina took Caldwell's sample and asked for a few pieces of wax. That evening at a séance she tried the experiment. She put some wax in a small basin and after the séance two prints were found. Margery claimed they were those of Walter.

Dr. Crandon insisted on having an expert of his acquaintance authenticate the prints. This shadowy figure, most probably a confederate, was named John Fife and claimed to be chief of police at Charlestown Navy Yard, and a recognized expert on fingerprints. W. F. Prince, who after the *Scientific American* investigations had continued to collect a file of private information regarding personal investigations on Margery's case, found out that the Boston Police Department had never heard of Fife. Crandon, however, claimed that the man had found thumbprints on Walter's razor that perfectly matched those left in the wax by the "spirit."

The success of this novelty led Dr. Crandon to employ at his own expense a Margery supporter, E. E. Dudley, to catalog every fingerprint left by Walter during the séances. Around 1931 Dudley began on his own initiative to collect the fingerprints of every person who attended a sitting with Margery. This way he could disprove the claims of those who said that the prints did not belong to Walter but to a live confederate.

Dudley was ending his weekly visits to collect the fingerprints of those who had participated in séances from 1923 to 1924 when he examined the prints of Dr. Caldwell, Crandon's dentist. While at home to compare the prints with those of Walter, he made a startling discovery. He carefully examined both sets of prints to be certain, but there was no mistake: the thumbprints that Margery claimed had belonged to Walter were identical in every respect to Dr. Caldwell's! Dudley counted no fewer than twenty-four absolute correspondences.

Clearly, the medium had used the wax samples on which Dr. Caldwell had pressed his thumbs to show Mina the procedure and had obtained imprint molds. It was easy in the dark to press the molds in the wax and obtain the effect that an entity foreign to the circle of sitters was the author.

Dudley informed the ASPR about his discovery but W. H. Button, then president of the ASPR, replied that he wasn't interested in publishing the evidence. The society was by then associated with Mina, since it had often defended her and had hidden unpleasant information about her. Prince, who had left the ASPR for this reason and had founded the Boston Society for Psychic Research (BSPR), had had enough. He accepted the Dudley revelation and an article was published in the society *Bulletin* in 1932. The scandal that followed had disastrous effects. It was no mere case of somebody claiming to see the medium use her foot to move a table; this time the proof of fraud was damning and definitive.

Further proof was made public with the results of a similar experiment. In December 1929 the Crandons had gone to London to sit in the SPR rooms. There, Margery had demonstrated the production of thumbprints in wax. At that time the phenomenon was still considered to be genuine in America. The SPR researchers, however, by carefully weighing the pieces of wax used in the experiment and those found in the séance room, were able to prove that the Crandons had surreptitiously introduced an extra piece. This destroyed the argument that the thumbprints could only have been made by Walter's spirit.

THE END OF MARGERY

Her supporters deserted Margery one after another, and the medium, older and heavier now, began to take consolation in alcohol. The séances continued and Crandon tried for some time to keep alive the interest in her "Psyche." At one of these sittings, for example, Margery tried to repeat the famous experiment of linking two wooden rings that had been attempted fifty years earlier by Professor Zöllner with medium Henry Slade. "Success!" rejoiced Dr. Crandon: Margery had been able to link two rings made of different woods. Here at last was a definitive proof, something solid that defied physics, matter through matter. Since it is not difficult to finish the wood along the split in such a way as to render it invisible to the eye, it was claimed that only X rays could establish the truth. The rings were sent to Sir Oliver Lodge in England for independent testing. When Lodge opened the parcel sent by the Crandons, however, he found that one of the rings had broken to pieces, probably during the trip. What could have been the only solid existing proof of the reality of the supernatural, the "Rosetta Stone" of Spiritualism, hadn't even been well packed. Dr. Crandon died in 1939 and Mina, an alcoholic, went into a state of deep depression. At one of her last séances she even tried to jump off the roof of the house.

What became of Malcolm Bird? After 1931 his name disappeared from the list of contributors to the ASPR. He vanished and nothing was ever heard of him. Hypotheses about his fate ranged from personal jealousy inside the society to his accepting a tempting work offer, but only recently with the discovery of some unpublished documents were some new facts about the relationship between Bird and Margery made public. Prince, in whose files the documents were found, hinted at it in a May 1933 article he wrote for *Scientific American*: "About two years ago . . . he [Bird] sent in to his employers a long paper claiming the discovery of an act of fraud and reconstructing his view of the case to admit a factor of fraud from the beginning. This paper has not been printed and very few of the believers in Europe or America know of its existence."

Here are some extracts from Bird's May 1930 report/confession to the board of trustees of the ASPR:

> [S]ince May 1924 when I first concluded that the case was one of valid mediumship, my observations have never been directed in any large sense toward the detection of fraud, and even less toward its demonstration. As I went along with my séances, here and there I made, as a matter of routine, observations that some particular episode was normal in its causation. . . .
>
> All that the present report aims to do is to acquaint the Board with the date upon which is based in my own mind, the statement which I have

made whenever occasion has arisen to make it: that the Margery phenomena are not one hundred per cent supernormal.

It is not now possible for me to state positively whether the episode occurred in July or in August, 1924. . . . The occasion was one of Houdini's visits to Boston for the purpose of sitting. . . . She sought a private interview with me and tried to get me to agree, in the event that phenomena did not occur, that I would ring the bell-box myself, or produce something else that might pass as activity by Walter. . . . This proposal was clearly the result of Margery's wrought-up state of mind. Nevertheless it seems to me of paramount importance, in that it shows her, fully conscious and fully normal, in a situation where she thought she might have to choose between fraud and a blank séance; and she was willing to choose fraud.

But the question remains: what had been the reason for Margery's deceptions? William Henry Salter, then honorary secretary of the SPR and subsequently president of the society from 1947 to 1948, explained in an unpublished manuscript preserved in the SPR's files:

I was present at one of the Crandon sittings in London [in 1929]. The psychology of the pair has always been a mystery. Crandon was a man of good family and good education, and prosperous in his profession of surgeon. Margery, his second wife, was not socially quite his equal. She was good looking, lively in manner, and attractive to men. On one of his visits to America Dingwall had thyroid trouble which Crandon successfully treated, and out of gratitude for that and even more because he had "fallen for" Margery, he defended her through thick and thin until the Dudley exposure, which he could not explain away. But until then she more than compensated for her social inferiority (not to be exaggerated) by the position she had won as a medium whose phenomena had been accepted by many learned men, and had baffled the sceptics.

. . . [W]hat was her husband's share in it? Was he taken in all along? Did he begin by believing, and continue in acquiescence, or collusion, what was his motive? I think it probable . . . that as to some of the phenomena at least he and she were in collusion. Was the motive simply to pull the legs of the learned? This would be more plausible if they had been able at some stage to turn around and say, see how we have gulled you. But ps. [psychical] Researchers of the more critical kind, whom there would have been some kudos in deceiving, were not deceived. From various Americans I heard vague talk that Crandon was not in good odour, socially and professionally, in Boston. I have tried both during his life, and after his death to get a plain statement as to this, but have always met with evasive shrugs of the shoulders. If, as has been hinted to me, he had brought himself within the law as an abortionist it is conceivable that Margery was able to blackmail him into colluding with her. I have no reason to believe this, except that it would account for conduct on his part that seems otherwise inexplicable.[13]

The most complete and convincing explanation for Margery's conduct, however, can be found in the W. F. Prince files at the ASPR, where there is a collection of unpublished documents and reports written by the Harvard scientists who tested Mina in 1925 and by various psychic researchers, from which emerges an interesting theory to explain the Margery phenomenon.

The séances, it emerges, were a sort of marital charade: Margery's intended audience was not Houdini, the *Scientific American* group, or the other investigators, but her husband, whom she hoped to delude in order to save their collapsing marriage. They were too different from each other, and Crandon quickly grew bored with her; he also had a strong fear of death. In trying to keep him at her side, Margery hit on the idea of manifesting spirits for him. It worked, and he now felt like a new Galileo for the half million followers of Margery. He demanded new phenomena, and forced his wife into new demonstrations with "downright brutality."

The opinion of the various experts was that Margery would have liked to give up séances and confess to fraud, except for knowing that it would end her marriage. Houdini's spy, Stewart Griscom, had even revealed to the magician that once, when he was alone with the medium, she disclosed to him her admiration for Houdini for not being taken in by her, and for not being afraid "to say where he stands."

"I respect Houdini," she said to Griscom, "more than any of the bunch. He has both feet on the ground all the time."[14]

It appears, furthermore, that, during the *Scientific American* séances, Margery had tried to use her sexual charms on him but had failed. "Her applesauce," wrote the magician, "meant nothing to me." However, it seems that it mattered to some other members of the committee. Carrington, in particular, revealed years later to an associate that he carried on a several months' affair with her. Margery confessed to Walter Prince's secretary that Carrington (whom she had nicknamed "Carrie") *was* good-looking," and while in the hot-weather sittings the other *Scientific American* investigators looked wilted, he looked "like a million dollar[s]." Bird also claimed to have had a romance with Margery. Although he would have liked it, this sounds improbable, at least judging from Margery's comments about him. She said that she found him "disgusting looking," the kind of man "you feel you want to sweep the house after."

Margery's story ends with a tale that sounds folkloric but duly suits the mysterious character that the medium had created for herself. Sitting beside Margery's bed in the last days of her life, psychic researcher Nandon Fodor suggested to her that she would depart happier should she dictate a confession to him and reveal the methods she had used to obtain her phenomena. Mina muttered something indiscernible. Fodor asked to repeat herself. "Sure," she said, "I said you could go to hell. All you 'psychic researchers' can go to hell." Then, with the old familiar twinkle of merri-

(From left) Edward Saint, Bess Houdini, and Theodore Hardeen.
(McManus-Young Collection, Library of Congress,
Rare Books and Special Collections Division, LC-USZ62-112409)

ment in her eyes she looked at him and chuckled softly: "Why don't you guess?" she said, and chuckled again. "You'll be guessing . . . for the rest of your lives."[15]

THE FINAL SÉANCE

Beatrice Houdini, now a white-haired little lady, had found a new companion, Edward Saint, an ex-carnival performer and magician. They both worked to keep Houdini's name alive and staged on October 31, 1936, the tenth anniversary of the magician's death, what was billed as "The Final Houdini Séance." Saint and Bess sent thousands of telegrams to friends, journalists, and magicians all over the world; the anticipation grew strong. On the thirty-first, a crowd of people gathered on the roof of the Knickerbocker Hotel under a starry sky. There were three hundred invited guests, forming "the outer circle," while thirteen scientists, journalists, and friends joined Bess and Saint in the "inner circle." The event was broadcast live via radio worldwide.

The sitting started with a recording of Edward Elgar's "Pomp and Circumstance," the march that Houdini used as his opening music for the shows he performed in the later years of his life.

Saint took charge of the proceedings: "Every facility," he noted, "has been provided tonight, that might aid in opening a pathway to the spirit world. Here in the Inner Circle reposes a 'Medium's Trumpet,' a pair of slates with chalk, a writing tablet and pencil, a small bell, and in the center reposes a huge pair of silver handcuffs on a silk cushion. Facing the Inner Circle stands the famous 'Houdini Shrine,' with its doors ajar."

Then the séance began. "Houdini!" cried Saint. "Are you here? Are you here, Houdini? Please manifest yourself in any way possible. . . . We have waited, Houdini, oh, so long! Never have you been able to present the evidence you promised. And now—this, the night of nights. The world is listening, Harry. . . . Levitate the table! Move it! Lift the table! Move it or rap it! Spell out a code, Harry! Please! Ring the bell! Let its tinkle be heard around the world!" Nothing happened.

"Mrs. Houdini," said Saint, "the zero hour has passed. The ten years are up. Have you reached your decision?"

"Yes," she replied. "Houdini did not come through. My last hope is gone. I do not believe that Houdini can come back to me—or to anyone. . . . The Houdini Shrine has burned for ten years. I now, reverently—turn out the light. It is finished. Good night, Harry!"

Bess died on February 11, 1943, making it clear before her departure that, in case of a life after death, she would never try to return: "When I go," she said, "I'll be gone for good. I won't even try to come back."

NOTES

1. The majority of quotes from letters exchanged between Conan Doyle and Houdini have been taken from Bernard M. L. Ernst and Hereward Carrington, *Houdini and Conan Doyle* (New York: Albert and Charles Boni, 1932). This is the source of quotes in this chapter unless otherwise noted.

2. Harold Kellock, *Houdini: His Life-Story, by Harold Kellock from the Recollections and Documents of Beatrice Houdini* (New York: Harcourt, Brace & Co., 1928).

3. Quoted in Daniel Stashower, *Teller of Tales: The Life of Arthur Conan Doyle* (New York: Henry Holt and Company, 1999).

4. He literally did so, as can be seen from a surviving photograph where Leopold's head has been scissored out by Houdini.

5. Milbourne Christopher, *Medium, Mystics, and the Occult* (New York: Thomas Y. Crowell Company, 1975).

6. Ibid.

7. Ibid.

8. Ibid.

9. Arthur Conan Doyle, "Houdini the Enigma," *Strand Magazine* 74 (July 1927): 134–43.

10. *Journal of the Society for Psychical Research* (March 1930).

11. Ibid.

12. W. H. Salter, *Reminiscences of the Society for Psychical Research* (Trinity College Library, Cambridge, Ref.O.15.75).

13. Ibid.

14. Kenneth Silverman, *Houdini!!! The Career of Ehrich Weiss* (New York: HarperCollins, 1996).

15. Thomas R. Tietze, *Margery* (New York: Harper & Row, 1973).

CONCLUSION

ARRY HOUDINI AND SIR ARTHUR Conan Doyle are undoubtedly two of the most intriguing and fascinating personalities of the twentieth century. What brought this odd couple together? It was an interest they shared: Spiritualism. Possibly they would have met anyway, sooner or later; however, it was Houdini who was the first to make a move.

He was always eager to make friends with important people and, by association, show the world that he was important too. In reality he was more famous than most actors or politicians of his time, but he certainly always had in mind the hard times he had passed through when he was a nobody, and when in his youth he had been so poor that he had had to beg on the streets to support his family. Thus, he probably needed continued reassurance that he was "great" and that he would never return to the dime museums and the beer halls that were his home during his debuting years. When he was already a star, and had met Theodore Roosevelt while crossing the ocean on the *Imperator*, he had a picture taken with the ex-president and sent it to his brother Bill, to show him, as he said, "that T. Roosevelt and your bro are Pals." But that was not enough. Since there were other men standing around the two, Houdini had the image airbrushed to take the group out of the picture. In the ensuing years, he distributed hundreds of copies to friends and journalists all over the world. Furthermore, he enjoyed the company of important people, and in particular, always seeking intellectual respectability, he liked to rub shoulders with men of letters.

Fascinated by Conan Doyle's literary ability, and by his authority as an artist and as an intellectual, Houdini sent him a copy of his book *The Unmasking of Robert-Houdin* while touring England with his magic show. Conan Doyle thanked him but expressed surprise at Houdini's statement that the Davenport brothers used trickery. The two men, he was convinced, were "probably the greatest mediums of their kind the world has ever seen." Houdini knew very well what the Davenport act was all about; however, he decided to keep quiet, happy at having started a correspondence with Conan Doyle and not wanting to spoil the start of a new friendship. "Regarding the Davenport Brothers, I am afraid that I cannot say that all their work was accomplished by the spirits": this is almost all he managed to say about them without committing himself in any way.

Conan Doyle had very strong convictions about Spiritualism, to him it was the New Revelation: not so much a belief, but rather a certainty: "I *know* spirit communication is a fact."[1]

"People ask me," he wrote in his *Memories and Adventures* in 1924, "what it is which makes me so perfectly certain that this thing is true. That I am perfectly certain is surely demonstrated by the mere fact that I have abandoned my congenial and lucrative work, left my home for long periods at a time, and subjected myself to all sorts of inconveniences, losses, and even insults, in order to get the facts home to the people. To give all my reasons would be to write a book rather than a chapter; but I may say briefly that there is no physical sense which I possess which has not been separately assured, and that there is no conceivable method by which a spirit could show its presence which I have not on many occasions experienced."

"If a man can see, hear and feel all this," he concluded after a long list of experiences he had had in Spiritualism, "and yet remain unconvinced of unseen intelligent forces around him, he would have good cause to doubt his own sanity. Why should he heed the chatter of irresponsible journalists, or the headshaking of inexperienced men of science, when he has himself had so many proofs? They are babies in this matter, and should be sitting at his feet. . . ."

He was in fact convinced of being a great psychic investigator, possibly the greatest: "With all modesty," he wrote, "I am inclined to ask, is there any man on this globe who is doing as much psychic research as I?" However, he had never actually conducted *one* real psychic investigation, safe from a visit to a supposed haunted house. All he did was visit mediums, do exactly all they asked him to do, and he would accept as evidential all they would say or do during the séances. This could hardly be called "psychic research."[2]

Houdini's approach to Spiritualism was more cautious, to say the least. Although he tried to present himself to Conan Doyle as a longtime expert in the field, Houdini had never conducted an in-depth study of the subject until then. Also, it is not true, as popular belief would have it, that Houdini was drawn to Spiritualism following the death of his mother, seeking a medium who could put him in touch with her. She died in 1913 and it was not until 1920, when Houdini met Conan Doyle, that his interest in Spiritualism would become central for the remaining years of his life.

He knew all the tricks of the trade, but, at least in the beginning, was probably willing to believe that there was something to Spiritualism. Certainly, there may have been a small hope at the back of his mind as to the possibility of talking again with his beloved mother. His open mind, however, quickly closed as soon as one medium after another turned out to be just a trickster. Some were very clever, and Houdini always acknowledged a good performance when he saw one. "I'll put it in writing that he was the slickest I have ever seen," he wrote about Bert Reese; "He is a powerfully built fellow, has great curved shoulders and an enormous amount of endurance" was Houdini's appreciation of Nino Pecoraro. But the spirit-fakir he most admired was Margery: "There is no doubt in my mind, what-soever, that this lady who has been 'fooling' the scientists (?) for months resorted to some of the slickest methods I have ever known and honestly it has taken my thirty years of experience to detect her in her various moves."[3]

However, their "professional" ability was not enough to convince Houdini of the reality of their professed psychic powers, as it had so completely convinced Sir Arthur. However, he preferred to hide his real feelings from his friend, as long as it was possible.

Conan Doyle, on his part, had great esteem for his own critical facul-ties: "I am a cool observer and don't make mistakes," he was fond of declaring. He was perfectly sure that he could detect trickery at any time: "I am sure," he stated publicly, "no medium has ever deceived me." Probably no one could say that, not even Houdini. When the magician said that he doubted that Conan Doyle could really detect trickery when faced with it, Sir Arthur looked amazed at him. "Why, Sir Arthur," was Houdini's admis-sion, "I have been trained in mystery all my life and every once in a while I see something I cannot account for."

Anything that Conan Doyle could not explain became, in his mind, automatically psychic. Since he could not fathom how Houdini performed his miraculous escapes, and notwithstanding Houdini's constant reassur-ances to the contrary, Conan Doyle became convinced that even the magi-cian was actually a powerful medium who could dematerialize his body!

One of the most striking examples of Conan Doyle's credulity can be found when Houdini showed him a simple children's trick, in which one apparently removes the first joint of his thumb, shows it separate from the rest of the hand, then replaces it. On that occasion Lady Doyle "nearly fainted" and Sir Arthur stated: "I think what interested me most was the little 'trick' which you showed us in the cab. You certainly have very won-derful powers, whether inborn or acquired." Houdini could not believe how easy it was to fool Sir Arthur Conan Doyle.

"With all his brilliancy and child-like faith," was Houdini's estimation, "it is almost incredible that he has been so thoroughly convinced, and nothing can shake his faith."

Conan Doyle's extreme confidence in his own powers of observation made him the victim of countless frauds and hoaxes. His own kind nature turned out in the end to be his worst enemy. He was so honest, so frank, so generous, so sympathetic that it appeared unthinkable to him that anyone should be out to trick him. Unfortunately, such was the case.

When speaking in public he would frequently toss in the names of famous scientists like Crookes, Lombroso, and Wallace to show that even they, with all their intelligence and ability, had been forced by the evidence to embrace Spiritualism. How could these great minds have been tricked? "They cannot continue to think I am a credulous fool," was his reasoning, "so long as my observations are corroborated by such [men]."

Houdini, however, knew very well why scientists were not the best persons to investigate Spiritualism: "As a rule," he said, "I have found that the greater brain a man has, and the better he is educated, the easier it has been to mystify him." He knew that if you want to "catch a thief" you go to a thief, and if you want to catch a trickster you need a trickster. He was at first annoyed and then enraged by the mediums who used the same tricks that he used in his shows but, unlike him, claimed supernatural means. He was honestly outraged by the cynical ripping off of poor and bereaved people who would pay failed magicians to get in touch with someone they deeply loved and mourned for.

Also, it cannot be denied that, when Houdini saw that his involvement in Spiritualism brought him huge amounts of publicity from the newspapers, he realized that he could turn his private interests and concerns into a profession. He was becoming too old for his strenuous escapes, and Spiritualism offered him a chance to take on a new professional role: the defender of truth. If Conan Doyle could tour the world proclaiming that Spiritualism was a reality, he could certainly become the leading skeptic on the subject.

He remained, however, a showman even in psychic research. He would rather go for some easy stunt that would look great in the newspapers or onstage rather than for patient, but sometimes dull, experimentation and testing. An example of this is the use of the huge cabinet in the Margery séances. Undoubtedly the box looked impressive and dramatic; however, it was not the best way to conduct that kind of experiment. The idea was that ectoplasm protruding from the body of the medium was responsible for ringing bells and moving objects: by encircling Margery in a box Houdini could only demonstrate that his cabinet had prevented "anything" from coming out of it. When testing psychics, however, it is of capital importance to devise fraud-proof controls that match the most favorable conditions for a successful outcome of the test. The risk, as in the case of the "Margie box," is to provide a fake psychic with a perfectly logical excuse in case of failure to manifest.

During séances Houdini's first reaction when he thought he had detected trickery was to dramatically jump up, point a flashlight in the face of the medium, and publicly denounce him or her. When he participated in investigations along with other researchers, as with the *Scientific American* committee, Houdini knew that he could not do as he liked; however, sometimes he had to be held to prevent him from interrupting the séance. And on a few occasions he would even escape from this restraint. In the case of Valiantine, for example, after participating in the sitting that unmasked him, he rushed to tell the story to a journalist: it made the front page but brought him many reproaches from fellow members of the committee and even from journalist friends. "This is a regrettable consequence of Mr. Houdini's hurry to convince his friends that he was not such a 'simpleton,'" wrote the May 30, 1923, *New York Times*. "Except for that, probably half a dozen Valentines [*sic*] could have been exposed, and the impressiveness of the disclosures would have been greater."

What kept together for nearly four years two people like Houdini and Conan Doyle, holding such drastically different opinions and approaches to life? It was Houdini who had started their relationship, and it was frequently he who would write the other, telling about some news or sending a news clipping or a recommendation for a book. It is particularly amusing to read between the lines of their correspondence the continuing competitiveness that characterized their friendship. Once, Conan Doyle remarked about the books he had on his desk while working. Houdini promptly wrote him: "When you say there are ninety-six volumes on your desk, it may interest you to know that I travel with a book-case containing over one hundred volumes, and recently, in Leeds, I bought two libraries on Spiritualism." Not to be outdone, Conan Doyle replied: "I have 200 now—and have read them too!"

We have already seen what were Houdini's probable "motives" for his friendship with the writer. What about Conan Doyle's interest in the magician?

Sir Arthur was certainly fascinated by what he considered to be "the most curious and intriguing character whom I have ever encountered." Furthermore, he was probably sure that he could convince Houdini about the reality of Spiritualism: in so doing, he would have gained to his side a most powerful ally. "I can see you sometime," he wrote Houdini, "as your true experiences accumulate, giving a wonderful lecture, 'Phenomenal Spiritualism—True and False,' in which, after giving an account of your adventures with fakes, you will also give an account of those which bear inspection. It would be a very great draw. Fake photos and true ones."

As time passed, however, Houdini did not appear to become more convinced than he was when they first met: "The more I investigate the subject," he wrote, "the less I can make myself believe." What finally induced Conan Doyle to realize that Houdini would never abandon his skepticism was his reaction to the fateful Atlantic City séance.

Possibly wanting to ease his friend's grief over his mother's death, Sir Arthur had invited the magician to a very special séance, with his wife as the medium. Houdini was possibly more than ever ready to believe, for he knew that, for once, he was not facing a fraud but only sincere people. His hopes of real contact, however, were dashed when he realized from many details that the message purporting to come from his dead mother was actually coming from Lady Doyle's willingness to please. He had not expressed his real beliefs to his friends, for fear of hurting the Doyles' feelings: "I did not have the nerve to tell him." However, he later wrote an article about his experiences in Spiritualism in which he clearly declared: "I have never seen or heard anything that could convince me that there is a possibility of communication with the loved ones who have gone beyond."

When Doyle read that he became furious: this meant that the séance his wife had given Houdini didn't mean a thing to him. He considered this a personal affront and an insult, and wrote so to him. He even stated that he didn't want to discuss the subject any more with him, "for I consider that you have had your proofs and that the responsibility of accepting or rejecting is with you. . . . I leave it at that, for I have done my best to give you truth."

Houdini explained his views on the séance and added: "I trust my clearing up the séance from my point of view is satisfactory, and that you do not harbor any ill feeling, because I hold both Lady Doyle and yourself in the highest esteem. I know you treat this as a religion, but personally I cannot do so for, up to the present time, and with all my experiences, I have never seen or heard anything that could really convert me."

But the rift had come and their relations rapidly deteriorated. Conan Doyle became more rigid and intolerant regarding Houdini's pronouncements on Spiritualism: "Our relations are certainly curious and are likely to become more so, for so long as you attack what I *know* from experience to be true, I have no alternative but to attack you in return." Houdini, on his part, tried for a while to ease things. He apologized to Conan Doyle for a few misunderstandings and wrote letters to the newspapers asking that words that had been attributed to him, and that had indisposed Conan Doyle, be changed. However, when he realized that *anything* he did or said on Spiritualism annoyed Sir Arthur he decided he could no longer bear the situation and started to speak openly on all aspects of Spiritualism.

A few months after the Atlantic City séance they stopped corresponding by letter (it was Conan Doyle who would not answer Houdini's last letter) and started exchanging sharp words in the newspapers. Conan Doyle accused Houdini of being biased, a publicity-seeker, and would refer to him as a victim of a syndrome he called "Houdinitis," meaning the belief "that manual dexterity bears some relation to brain capacity." Houdini, on his part, said that "there is nothing that Sir Arthur will believe that surprises me," and called his ex-friend "a bit senile . . . and therefore easily bamboozled."

What had started as a fascinating and promising meeting of minds ended in reciprocal accusations and insults. Personally, Houdini and Conan Doyle had liked each other from the start and could have been great friends until the end of their days; however, the subject that had brought them together, Spiritualism, in the end turned out to be so crucial in their own lives that it became the reason for their breakup.

NOTES

1. The majority of quotes from letters exchanged between Conan Doyle and Houdini have been taken from Bernard M. L. Ernst and Hereward Carrington, *Houdini and Conan Doyle* (New York: Albert and Charles Boni, 1932). This is the source of quotes in this section unless otherwise noted.

2. Arthur Conan Doyle, *Memories and Adventures* (Boston: Little, Brown & Co., 1924).

3. Gabriel Citron, *The Houdini-Price Correspondence* (London: Legerdemain, 1998).

BIBLIOGRAPHY

WORKS BY HARRY HOUDINI

1906. *The Adventurous Life of a Versatile Artist.* Privately printed.

[1906] 1975. *The Right Way to Do Wrong: An Exposé of Successful Criminals.* Boston: privately printed. Reprint, Las Vegas: Gambler's Club.

1908. *The Unmasking of Robert-Houdin.* Boston: Privately printed (the British edition, published in 1909 by George Routledge and Sons, Ltd., contains as a supplement: *A Treatise on Handcuff Secrets*).

1920. *Magical Rope-Ties and Escapes.* London: Will Goldston.

1920. "Why I Am a Skeptic." *Variety*, September 24, 1920, pp. 33ff.

[1920] 1981. *Miracle Mongers and Their Methods.* New York: E. P. Dutton & Co. Reprint, Amherst, N.Y.: Prometheus Books.

1922. *Houdini's Paper Magic.* New York: E. P. Dutton.

1924. *Houdini Exposes the Tricks Used by the Boston Medium "Margery."* New York: Adams Press.

[1926] 1972. *A Magician Among the Spirits.* New York: Harper & Row. Reprint, Arno Press.

No date. *Life, History and Handcuff Secrets.* Privately printed.

ON HOUDINI

Anonymous. 1907. *Secret of the Great Handcuff Trick.* Boston: Mutual Book Company.

Arcuri, Lawrence. Ca. 1973. *The Houdini Birth Research Committee's Report.* New York.

Brandon, Ruth. 1993. *The Life and Many Deaths of Harry Houdini.* London: Martin Secker & Warburg Ltd.

Cannell, J. C. 1932. *The Secrets of Houdini.* London: Hutchinson & Co.

Christopher, Milbourne. [1969] 1970. *Houdini: The Untold Story.* New York: Thomas Y. Crowell. Reprint, New York: Pocket Books.

———. 1976. *Houdini: A Pictorial Life.* New York: Thomas Y. Crowell.

Citron, Gabriel. 1998. *The Houdini-Price Correspondence.* London: Legerdemain.

Culliton, Patrick. 1997. *Houdini Unlocked,* 2 vols. Hollywood, Calif.: Kieran Press.

Doerr, H. R. No date. *The Secrets of Houdini's Feats Explained*. Philadelphia: Privately printed.

Dunninger, Joseph. 1928. *Houdini's Spirit Exposés*. New York: Experimenter Publishing Co.

Ernst, Bernard M. L., and Hereward Carrington. 1932. *Houdini and Conan Doyle*. New York: Albert and Charles Boni.

Fast, Francis R. 1929. *The Houdini Messages*. New York: Privately printed.

Fitzsimons, Raimund. 1980. *Death and the Magician: The Mystery of Houdini*. London: Atheneum.

Gibson, Walter B. 1930. *Houdini's Escapes*. New York: Harcourt, Brace & Company.

———. 1932. *Houdini's Magic*. New York: Harcourt, Brace & Company.

———. 1976. *The Original Houdini Scrapbook*. New York: Crown Sterling.

———. 1976. *Houdini's Escapes* and Magic. New York: Blue Ribbon Books.

Gibson, Walter B., and Morris N. Young. 1953. *Houdini on Magic*. New York: Dover Publications.

———. 1961. *Houdini's Fabulous Magic*. Philadelphia and New York: Chilton Company.

Gresham, William Lindsay. [1959] 1968. *Houdini: The Man Who Walked Through Walls*. New York: Henry Holt & Company. Reprint, New York: MacFadden Books.

Hammond, William Elliott. Ca. 1926. *Houdini Unmasked*. Privately printed.

Hardeen, Theodore. 1926. *Life and History of Hardeen*. California: Privately printed.

———. 1927. *Houdini, His Life and Work in Prose and Picture*. Privately printed.

Henning, Doug, and Charles Raynolds. 1977. *Houdini: His Legend and His Magic*. New York: Times Books.

Hugard, Jean. [1957] 1989. *Houdini's "Unmasking"; Fact vs Fiction*. Brooklyn: *Hugard's Magic Monthly*, June 1957–January 1959. Reprint.

Hull, Burling. 1916. *The Challenge Handcuff Act*. New York: Privately printed.

Kellock, Harold. 1928. *Houdini: His Life-Story, by Harold Kellock from the Recollections and Documents of Beatrice Houdini*. New York: Harcourt, Brace & Co.

Kendall, Lace. 1960. *Houdini, Master of Escape*. Philadelphia: Macrae Smith Co.

Lund, Robert. 1956. "Afterword on Houdini." *Abracadabra* (October–December): 561–67.

Meyer, Bernard C. 1976. *Houdini: A Mind in Chains: A Psychoanalytic Portrait*. New York: E. P. Dutton.

Polidoro, Massimo. 1997. "Houdini v. The Blond Witch of Lime Street: A Historical Lesson in Skepticism." *Skeptic* 5, no. 3: 90–97.

———. 1998. "Houdini and Conan Doyle: The Story of a Strange Friendship." *Skeptical Inquirer* 22, no. 2 (March/April): 40–46.

———. 2001. *Il grande Houdini* (The Great Houdini). Milan: Piemme.

Pressing, R. G. 1947. *Houdini Unmasked*. Lily Dale, N.Y.: Dale News.

Randi, James, and Bert Randolph Sugar. 1976. *Houdini: His Life and Art*. New York: Grosset & Dunlap.

Rinn, Joseph F. 1950. *Sixty Years of Psychical Research: Houdini and I Among the Spiritualists*. New York: Truth Seeker Company.

Sardina, Maurice. 1950. *Where Houdini Was Wrong*. London: George Armstrong.

Shavelson, Mel. 1977. *The Great Houdinis*. London: W. H. Allen.

Silverman, Kenneth. 1996. *Houdini!!! The Career of Ehrich Weiss*. New York: Harper-Collins.

———. 1996. *Notes to Houdini!!!* Washington, D.C.: Kaufman and Greenberg.

Weltman, Manny. 1993. *Houdini: Escape Into Legend*. Van Nuys, Calif.: Finders/Seekers Enterprises.

Williams, Beryl, and Samuel Epstein. 1950. *The Great Houdini*. New York: Julian Messner.

Wilson, Edmund. 1925. "Houdini." *New Republic* (June 24).

———. 1928. "A Great Magician." *New Republic* (October 17).

Zolotow, Maurice. 1946. *The Great Balsamo, World Renowned Magician and King of Escape Artists*. New York: Random House.

———. 1969. Book Review of *Houdini, The Untold Story*, by Milbourne Christopher. *New York Times*, March 23, 1969.

Selected Works by Arthur Conan Doyle

1887. Letter, *Light*, August 27, 1887, p. 404.

1916. "A New Revelation. Spiritualism in Religion." *Light* (November 4): 357–58.

1918. *The New Revelation*. London: Hodder & Stoughton.

1921. *The Wanderings of a Spiritualist*. New York: George H. Doran.

1921. *The Coming of the Fairies*. London: Hodder & Stoughton.

1923. *Our American Adventure*. London: Hodder & Stoughton.

1924. "Early Psychic Experiences." *Pearson's* (March).

1924. "What Comes After Death." *Pearson's* (April).

1924. *Our Second American Adventure*. London: Hodder & Stoughton.

1924. *Memories and Adventures*. Boston: Little, Brown & Co.

1926. *The History of Spiritualism*. London: Constable.

1927. *Pheneas Speaks: Direct Spirit Communications in the Family Circle*. London: Psychic Press and Bookshop.

1927. "Houdini the Enigma." *Strand* 74 (July): 134–43.

1927. Letter, *Strand* 74 (September): 266.

1928. *A Word of Warning*. London: Joseph Wones.

1929. *Our African Winter*. London: John Murray.

[1930] 1992. *The Edge of the Unknown*. New York: G. P. Putnam's Sons. Reprint, New York: Barnes & Noble Books.

On Conan Doyle

Baker, Michael. 1978. *The Doyle Diary*. London: Paddington Press.

Carr, John Dickson. 1949. *The Life of Sir Arthur Conan Doyle*. New York: Harper & Brothers.

Cooper, Joe. 1990. *The Case of the Cottingley Fairies*. London: Robert Hale.

Coren, Michael. 1995. *Conan Doyle*. London: Bloomsbury.

Doyle, Adrian Conan. 1945. *The True Conan Doyle*. London: John Murray.

Frankfort-Moore, Frank. 1930. "The 'Fads' of Sir Arthur Conan Doyle." In *A Mixed Grill*. London: Hutchinson & Co.

Gibson, John Michael, and Richard Lancelyn Green, eds. 1986. *Letters to the Press*. Iowa City: University of Iowa Press.

Hall, Trevor H. 1978. *Sherlock Holmes and His Creator*. London: Duckworth.

Harris, Melvin. 1978. "The Man Who *Wasn't* Sherlock Holmes." In *Strange to Relate*, pp. 96–109. London: Granada-Dragon Books.

Higham, Charles. 1976. *The Adventures of Conan Doyle*. London: Hamish Hamilton.

Jones, Kelvin. 1989. *Conan Doyle and the Spirits: The Spiritualist Career of Sir Arthur Conan Doyle*. Wellingborough, U.K.: Aquarian Press.

Nordon, Pierre. 1964. *Conan Doyle, A Biography*. New York: Holt, Rinehart and Winston.

Orel, Harold, ed. 1991. *Sir Arthur Conan Doyle: Interviews and Recollections*. New York: St. Martin's Press.

Pearsall, Ronald. 1977. *Conan Doyle, A Biographical Solution*. New York: St. Martin's Press.

Pearson, Hesketh. 1943. *Conan Doyle, His Life and Art*. London: Methuen & Co.

Polidoro, Massimo. 1998. "Houdini and Conan Doyle: The Story of a Strange Friendship." *Skeptical Inquirer* 22, no. 2 (March/April): 40–46.

Prince, Walter Franklin. 1930. "Houdini and Doyle." In *The Enchanted Boundary, Being a Survey of Negative Reactions to Claims of Psychic Phenomena, 1820–1930*, pp. 144–62. Boston: Boston Society for Psychical Research.

Randi, James. 1982. "Fairies at the Foot of the Garden." In *Flim-Flam! Psychics, ESP, Unicorns and Other Delusions*, pp. 12–41. Amherst, N.Y.: Prometheus Books.

Stashower, Daniel. 1999. *Teller of Tales: The Life of Arthur Conan Doyle*. New York: Henry Holt and Company.

Willis, Chris. N. d. "Sherlock and the Spiritualists." *Skeptic* 9, no. 4: 6–8.

ON SPIRITUALISM

AA.VV. 1925. "The Psychic Investigation: Claims of 'Margery' to Produce Supernormal Phenomena Are Rejected by the Committee." *Scientific American* (April).

Abbott, David P. 1907. *Behind the Scenes with the Mediums*. Chicago: Open Court Publishing Co.

Anonymous. 1869. *The Davenport Brothers, the World-Renowned Spiritual Mediums*. Boston: William White and Company.

Barrett, William. 1918. *On the Threshold of the Unseen*. New York: E. P. Dutton.

Besterman, Theodore. 1930. *Some Modern Mediums*. London: Methuen and Company.

Bird, J. Malcolm. 1923. "Our Psychic Investigation." *Scientific American* (January): 6–7.

———. 1923. "Our Psychic Investigation in Europe." *Scientific American* (May–October.)

———. 1923. "Our First Test Séances." *Scientific American* (July).

———. 1923. "Another Mediumistic Failure." *Scientific American* (December).

———. 1923. *My Psychic Adventures*. London: George Allen and Unwin.

———. 1924. "Psychic Adventures at Home." *Scientific American* (January).

———. 1924. "Our Psychic Investigation Advances: We Find a Medium Whom We Cannot Characterize as a Conscious Fraud." *Scientific American* (February).

———. 1924. "Our Next Psychic." *Scientific American* (July).

———. 1924. "The 'Margery' Mediumship." *Scientific American* (August).

———. 1925. *"Margery" the Medium*. Boston: Small, Maynard & Co.

———. 1928. "The Margery Mediumship I." *Proceedings of the American Society for Psychical Research* 20.

Brandon, Ruth. 1984. *The Spiritualists*. Amherst, N.Y.: Prometheus Books.

Carrington, Hereward. 1908. *The Physical Phenomena of Spiritualism*. Boston: Small, Maynard & Co.

———. 1909. *Eusapia Palladino and Her Phenomena*. New York: B. W. Dodge & Co.

———. 1919. *Modern Psychical Phenomena*. New York: Dodd, Mead & Co.

———. 1930. *The Story of Psychic Science*. London: Rider & Co.

———. 1937. *The Psychic World*. New York: G. P. Putnam's Sons.

———. 1946. *The Invisible World*. New York: Beechurst Press, Bernard Ackerman, Inc.

Christopher, Milbourne. 1975. *Mediums, Mystics and the Occult*. New York: Thomas Y. Crowell Company.

Code, Grant, Hudson Hoagland, and Everard Feilding. 1928. "Concerning Mr. Feilding's Review of Mr. Hudson Hoagland's 'Report on Sittings with Margery.' " *Proceedings of the Society for Psychical Research* 36: 414–32.

Crandon, LeRoy Goddard. 1925. "The Psychic Investigation: 'Report of Progress' from 'Margery's' Point of View." *Scientific American* (January).

———. 1930. *The Margery Mediumship: Unofficial Sittings at the Laboratory of the Society for Psychical Research, London, December 6, 7 and 8, 1929*. Boston: Privately printed.

Crawford, W. J. 1921. *The Psychic Structures at the Goligher Circle*. London: John M. Watkins.

Dingwall, Eric J. 1928. "Report on a Series of Sittings with the Medium Margery." *Proceedings of the Society for Psychical Research* 36: 79–158.

———. 1962. *Very Peculiar People*. New Hyde Park: University Books.

———. 1966. *The Critic's Dilemma*. Crowhurst: Privately printed.

———. 1973. "Gilbert Murray's Experiments: Telepathy or Hyperaesthesia?" *Proceedings of the Society for Psychical Research* 56, no. 208: 21–39.

Dudley, E. E. 1933. "The Margery Mediumship II." *Proceedings of the American Society for Psychical Research* 21.

Dudley, E. E., Arthur Goadby, and Hereward Carrington. 1932. "Finger Print Demonstrations." *Bulletin of the Boston Society for Psychic Research* 18.

Dunninger, Joseph. 1935. *Inside the Medium's Cabinet*. New York: David Kemp and Co.

Evans, Henry Ridgley. 1897. *Hours with the Ghosts*. Chicago: Laird & Lee.

———. 1906. *The Old and the New Magic*. Chicago: Open Court Publ. Co.

Farrington, Elijah. 1922. *Revelations of a Spirit Medium*. Facsimile reprint: London, Kegan Paul; introduction and notes by Harry Price and Eric J. Dingwall.

Feilding, Everard. 1926. "Review: Mr. Hudson Hoagland's 'Report on Sittings with Margery.' " *Proceedings of the Society for Psychical Research* 36: 159–70.

Flynn, John T. 1926. "The Witch of Beacon Hill: An Interview with 'Margery.' " *Collier's* 77 (May 8): 7–8.

Fodor, Nandor. 1966. *Encyclopedia of Psychic Science*. Secaucus, N.J.: Citadel Press.

Ford, Arthur. 1968. *Unknown but Known*. New York: Harper & Row.

Ford, Arthur, and Marguerite Harmon Bro. 1958. *Nothing So Strange*. New York: Harper & Brothers.

Free, E. E. 1924. "Our Psychic Investigation: Preliminary Committee Opinions on the 'Margery' Case." *Scientific American* (October).

Frikell, Samri (Fulton Oursler). 1930. *Spirit Medium Exposed*. New York: New Metropolitan Fiction.

Geley, Gustave. 1923. "Materialized Hands: The Franek Kluski Wax Molds, and the Conclusions that May Be Drawn from Them." *Scientific American* (November): 316–74.

Hall, Trevor H. [1962] 1984. *The Spiritualists*. London: Duckworth. Reprint, *The Medium and the Scientist*. Amherst, N.Y.: Prometheus Books.

Hoagland, Hudson. 1925. "Science and the Medium: The Climax of a Famous Investigation." *Atlantic Monthly* 136 (November): 666–81.

Lodge, Oliver. 1909. *Survival of Man*. London: Methuen & Co.

Maskelyne, J. N. 1876. *Modern Spiritualism*. London: Frederick Warne.

McComas, Henry C. 1935. *Ghosts I Have Talked With*. Baltimore: Williams & Wilkins Company.

McKenzie, J. Hewat. 1916. *Spirit Intercourse, Its Theory and Practice*. London: Simpkin, Marshall, Hamilton Kent & Co., Ltd.

Podmore, Frank. [1902] 1963. *Modern Spiritualism: A History and a Criticism*. 2 vols. London: Methuen & Co. Reprint, *Mediums of the Nineteenth Century*. 2 vols. New Hyde Park: University Books.

———. [1910] 1975. *The Newer Spiritualism*. London. Reprint, New York: Arno Press.

Polidoro, Massimo. 1995. *Viaggio tra gli spiriti: indagine sui "fenomeni" dello spiritismo* (Journey Among the Spirits: An Investigation on the Phenomena of Spiritualism). Carnago (VA): Sugarco edizioni.

———. [1999] 2000. *Nel mondo degli spiriti* (Into the World of the Spirits). Padova: CICAP. Reprint, Roma: Avverbi.

Price, Harry. 1933. *Leaves from a Psychist's Case Book*. London: Putnam & Co.

———. 1936. *Confessions of a Ghost-Hunter*. London: Putnam & Co.

———. 1939. *Fifty Years of Psychical Research*. London: Longmans, Green and Co.

Prince, Walter Franklin. 1924. "Experiments by the Scientific American." *Journal of the American Society for Psychical Research* 18, no. 6 (June): 389–422.

———. 1926. "A Review of the Margery Case." *American Journal of Psychology* 37 (July): 431–41.

———. 1930. *The Enchanted Boundary*. Boston: Boston Society for Psychic Research.

———. 1933. "The Case Against Margery." *Scientific American* (May): 261–63.

Rhine, J. B., and L. E. Rhine. 1927. "One Evening's Observation on the Margery Mediumship." *Journal of Abnormal and Social Psychology* 21: 401–21.

Richardson, M., and L. R. G. Crandon. 1925. *Margery, Harvard, Veritas: A Study in Psychics*. Boston: Blanchard Printing.

Rinn, Joseph. 1954. *Searchlight on Psychical Research*. New York: Rider & Co.

Salter, W. H. 1931–1932. "The History of George Valiantine." *Proceedings of the Society for Psychical Research* 40: 389–410.

———. *Reminiscences of the Society for Psychical Research*. Unpublished manuscript, Trinity College Library, Cambridge, Ref. O.15.75.

Spraggett, Allen. 1967. *The Unexplained*. New York: New American Library.

———. 1973. *Arthur Ford: The Man Who Talked with the Dead*. New York: New American Library.

Tabori, Paul. 1950. *Harry Price: The Biography of a Ghost Hunter*. London: Athenaeum Press.

———. 1972. *Pioneers of the Unseen*. New York: Taplinger Publishing Co.

Thorogood, Brackett K. 1933. "The Margery Mediumship III." *Proceedings of the American Society for Psychical Research* 22.

Tietze, Thomas R. 1973. *Margery*. New York: Harper & Row.

Wallace, Alfred Russel. 1874. *A Defense of Modern Spiritualism*. Boston: Colby and Rich.

OTHER SOURCES

Booth, John. 1988. *Dramatic Magic*. Los Alamitos: Ridgeway Press.

———. 1990. *Creative World of Conjuring*. Los Alamitos: Ridgeway Press.

Boston, George L., and Robert Parrish. 1947. *Inside Magic*. New York: 1947.

Christopher, Milbourne. [1962] 1991. *Panorama of Magic*. Reprint, New York: Dover Publications.

———. [1973] 1996. *The Illustrated History of Magic*. New York: Thomas Y. Crowell. Reprint, Portsmouth, N.H.: Heinemann.

Dunninger, Joseph. 1954. *100 Houdini Tricks You Can Do*. New York: Arco Publishing Company, Inc.

Evans, Henry Ridgley. 1932. *A Master of Modern Magic: The Life and Adventures of Robert-Houdin*. New York: Macoy.

Free, E. E. 1924. "Our Psychic Investigation: Preliminary Committee Opinions on the 'Margery' Case." *Scientific American* (October).

Frost, Thomas. 1876. *The Lives of the Conjurors*. London: Tinsley Brothers.

Gibson, Walter B. 1974. *Dunninger's Secrets*. Secaucus, N.J.: Lyle Stuart.

Goldston, Will. 1903. *Secrets of Magic*. Liverpool: Mahatma Magical Company.

———. 1929. *Sensational Tales of Mystery Men*. London: Will Goldston, Ltd.

Hopkins, Albert A. [1898] 1976. *Magic: Stage Illusions, Special Effects and Trick Photography*. Reprint, New York: Dover Publications.

Hull, Burling. 1916. *The Challenge Handcuff Act*. New York: Privately printed.

Mulholland, John. 1932. *Quicker Than the Eye*. Indianapolis: Bobbs-Merrill Company.

———. [1938] 1979. *Beware Familiar Spirits*. Reprint, New York: Charles Scribner's Sons; with an introduction by Martin Gardner.

Polidoro, Massimo. 1995. *L'illusionismo dall'A alla Z* (Magic A to Z). Carnago (VA): Sugarco edizioni.

Polidoro, Massimo. 1997. *Dizionario del paranormale* (Dictionary of the Paranormal). Milan: Esedra.

———. 1998. *L'illusione del paranormale* (The Paranormal Illusion). Padova: Franco Muzzio Editore.

———. 2000. *Il sesto senso* (The Sixth Sense). Casale Monferrato: Piemme.

Randi, James. 1992. *Conjuring*. New York: St. Martin's Press.

Reynolds, Charles, and Regina Reynolds. 1976. *100 Years of Magic Posters*. New York: Grosset & Dunlap.

Robert-Houdin, Jean Eugène. [1859] 1964. *Memoirs of Robert-Houdin, King of Conjurers*. Reprint, New York: Dover Publications; with introduction and notes by Milbourne Christopher.

Silvan (Aldo Savoldello). 1977. *Arte Magica* (Art of Magic). Milan: Rusconi

U.S. Congress. (1924). *Fortune Telling, Hearings before the Subcommittee on Judiciary of the Committee on the District of Columbia House of Representatives. 69th Cong., 1st sess., on H. R. 8989, February 26, May 18, 20 and 21, 1924.* Washington, D.C.: Government Printing Office.

JOURNALS, MAGAZINES, AND NEWSPAPERS CONSULTED

Only the major periodical and newspaper articles have been included in the lists; other useful articles were found in the following publications.

Atlantic Monthly
Billboard
Boston Herald
Boston Journal
Brooklyn Daily Eagle
British Journal of Photography
Bulletin of the Boston Society for Psychic Research
Chicago American
Denver Express
Denver Post
Evening Graphic
Genii
International Psychic Gazette
Journal of Abnormal and Social Psychology
Journal of the American Society for Psychical Research
Journal of the Society for Psychical Research
Light
London Times
Magic
Medium and Daybreak
Morning Post
Nation

Nature
New Republic
New York American
New York Herald
New York Sun
New York Times
New York Tribune
New York World
Oakland Tribune
Pearson's
Proceedings of the ASPR
Proceedings of the SPR
Science and Invention
Scientific American
Scienza & Paranormale
Skeptic
Skeptical Inquirer
Sphinx
Spiritualist
Strand
Sunday Express
Toledo News-Bee
Variety

INDEX